Ama-Deus, the love of God, is one of the ... *rs at the physical, mental, emotional and spiriti* ... *nuch needed healing technique into the modern* ...

Norm Shealy, M.D., Ph.D.
Energy Medicine: The Future of Health

"*Inspires your sense of love and the experience of your soul. It's not just a remarkable read; it teaches you a new perspective on healing modalities.*"

Lynn Andrews, NY Times Bestselling author of
The Medicine Woman Series

In trying modern times, this book gives us an important look at the sacredness of the culture of the Guaraní, who love only love, the people and the land. We would do well to learn from them.

Molly Larkin – Author
The Wind is My Mother

Ama-Deus is not only the remarkable story of hidden treasures found deep in the Amazon and the chambers of the Heart; it is also the story of a remarkable woman, and her quest to bring Love to Light. Beth's account and telling of Ama-Deus is a great adventure, a deep mystery, and a wise discovery of Self.

Denise Iwaniw, Sacred Pipe Carrier - Author
Embracing the Mystic Within

Ama-Deus, a wonderful spiritual book, chronicles the journey of an energy healing method from the South American Guaraní tribe and around the globe to its use as an intervention in a medical setting. The energy and the tools within the book open your mind and heart to a greater understanding of Love as a soul's final destination, but also as part of your daily practice. The book inspires your heart and infuses your spirit with the greatest desire to feel and know Love in the deepest sense. Highly recommended for your entertainment and enjoyment.

Dra. Caron Goode, NCC Author
Kids Who See Ghosts, guide them through fear

Love and the commitment to know and follow God's desire for us is the common bond that brought Beth and Gerod together. Gerod regards the energy of Ama-Deus as high-level and loving and is honored to support its on-going availability to each person seeking knowledge and awareness, healing and love. This book is a wonderful compilation of history, story, and the possibilities that exist for all.

Katharine Mackey - Author
Soul Awareness: A Guide's Message

AMA-DEUS

Healing with the Sacred Energy of the Universe

Elizabeth Cosmos, PhD

Ama Deus Energy Press
Lowell, MI

Ama Deus Energy Press
P.O. Box 93
Lowell, MI 49331
ama-deus-international.com

ISBN: 978-0-9962780-0-3 printed book
ISBN: 978-0-9962780-1-0 ebook

Cover art by Beatrice Multhaupt
Cover Design by Katie McCabe

Library of Congress Control Number: 2012912919

Publisher's Cataloging-In-Publication Data
(Prepared by The Donohue Group, Inc.)

Cosmos, Elizabeth.
    Ama-Deus : healing with the sacred energy of the Universe / Elizabeth Cosmos, PhD.

    pages ; cm

    Issued also as an ebook.
    Includes bibliographical references and index.
    ISBN: 978-0-9962780-0-3

    1. Aguas, Alberto Costa. 2. Spiritual healing. 3. Energy medicine. 4. Alternative medicine--Brazil. 5. Energy--Therapeutic use. 6. Vital force--Therapeutic use. 7. Guarani Indians--Social life and customs. 8. Guarani Indians--Medicine. I. Title.

RZ421 .C67 2015
615.8/51

Ama-Deus® is a registered trademark licensed by
The International Association of Ama-Deus, LLC

CONTENTS

To the Uncreated Light and Love and
To all who dance in its image and likeness.

ACKNOWLEDGMENTS

You can give without loving,
but you cannot love without giving.
—Amy Carmichael

Indebtedness and deep gratitude seem not to fully encompass my expression of thankfulness for all those who stood near in the creation of this book—please know that you are all etched in my heart.

To my parents, John and Margaret Cosmos; stepfather, Alan Ryan; and my children, Michael and Christopher, I am so thankful for all their patience, support, and understanding.

To those who helped so patiently with my writing—Christopher Cosmos, from start to finish; David Stuursma, the first great push; Patricia Duncan, seeing so clearly the message and helping shape the manuscript; Stephen Buhner, Jean DeBruyn, Maricel Gaines, Margery Guest, Amber Guetebier, Bethany Rose Prosseda, and Linda Sechrist for support along the way; Caron Goode, in masterfully bringing me so eloquently through the detailed and lengthy homestretch. To all those who so graciously offered to endorse this work; Lynn Andrews, Caron Goode, Denise Iwaniw, Molly Larkin, Katherine Mackey, and Norm Shealy, all of whom are extremely busy in their own work.

To those who stood near, Alberto Aguas's family, Lynn Afendoulis, Rachel Attard, Lori Bruno, Gaiana Cherpes, Nancy Fox, Catherine Frerichs, Bruce Gregory, Mary Hanson, Amy Hass, Penny Hawkin, Diane Herbruck, Denise Iwaniw, Devra Ann Jacobs, Mary Jervis, Beatrice Multhaupt, John Murphy, Bob Nunley, Nancy O'Donahue, Sharon Pisacreta, Julie Ridenour, Karen Rosasco, Kyle Rozema, Ellen Satterlee, Stephen Schmidt, Sprague Family, Linda Stansberry, Tom and Malley, Mary Elizabeth Wakefield, and Berney Williams. For Stokey, who never left my side, many days without his normal walks and dinner late into the nights, he is a true companion.

For the researched pieces, thank you to the staff at *Psychic News*, London, Trevor Stockill, Ellen Fassio, the Paul family, Richard Reed, Marilyn Rossner, Rachel Salley, CeCe Stevens, and Christian Vianna. To Beatrice Multhaupt, Diogenes Ramires and Alvaro Tomaz, your translations were invaluable as well as David Fix and Michael Lechner for technical assistance.

Thank you Anita Jones and Sharon Castlen for taking me to the next level of publishing.

To Elder Arcimandrite Ephraim, for expanding my understanding of the Uncreated Light.

To all the instructors and practitioners of Ama-Deus, your passion and heart for sharing this beautiful method around the world is inspiring; and your excitement for this book as well as Ama-Deus keeps me going. To all my friends who helped by sending healing energy, Geshe Rinchen Choygal, Nancy Fox, Denise Iwaniw, Pilar Fernandez-Santos, Cai Bristol; and to Alberto, for continuing to whisper in my ear and all the angels and celestial guides. I am eternally grateful for those people in my life who have loved me, as all these experiences have brought me to a point in strength of spirit to complete this project.

Finally, but not in the least, to the Guaraní and all indigenous peoples who have felt generational misplacement, I am so grateful for the exemplary knowledge in caring, and living in harmony with the environment, and humbled by the sacrifices made to maintain sacred ways.

INTRODUCTION

Ama-Deus® is a method of energy healing that was preserved for thousands of years by a tribe of Guaraní in South America. Alberto Costas Aguas, a world-renowned energy healer from Brazil, who after several years in exile, returned to his native land and found himself working with this tribe of Guaraní. The Guaraní recognized him as a great healer and the one they were expecting, and initiated him into their sacred ways and transferred to him their ancient wisdom.

This is a story of the Guaraní, who for thousands of years held on to this knowledge until the time came to share with the world how to heal with Love. Both the Guaraní and Alberto believe that Love is in all healing. Alberto Aguas, who risked his life to preserve this knowledge, brought it to North America, where my story with this ancient wisdom begins.

This is a story of Love, and a story of my personal healing that led me to a greater understanding of Love. In 1989 I met Alberto and was first introduced to this spiritual healing method that he called Ama-Deus. Over the course of the subsequent twenty-three years I became an instructor and practitioner of Ama-Deus, researched the life of Alberto, studied the history of the Guaraní, practiced Ama-Deus in a clinical setting, and obtained a doctorate degree using Ama-Deus as the intervention. This direct experience with Ama-Deus has shown me how Love can offer liberation from our fears and fill our being with peace, balance, and harmony—the real and true treasure for any human being living in the world today.

Interwoven in four parts is a fictional story of the Guaraní forest people as life was at the time of Christ, tracing their journey of keeping sacred ways until the world cycled forward to reclaim the meaning. I dreamed these vignette's of life in past times, and each introductory vignette gives an account in the life of a young shaman, Arapotiyu, as he makes his journey to maintain harmony for the forest people.

This story of Arapotiyu's journey is repeated in Alberto's journey thousands of years later with the same purpose, to maintain harmony in the world and bring Love to all seekers willing to be finders.

You will feel the passion of Alberto's and Arapotiyu's lives as they strove so diligently to preserve this knowledge. The Guaraní had protected this sacred wisdom as they passed this knowledge down orally from generation to generation until it was time to share with the world.

This story is equal parts an exploration of the spirit and the universe through *Ama-Deus* as well as a journey to understand Love. It invites the mind to breathe deeply from the heart and dares each of us to look within and touch our souls.

Beth Cosmos

PART I

A YOUNG HEALER IS DYING

♦ ♦ ♦ ♦ ♦

In the land of the forest people, in the village of Takuaty, the place of bamboo, the Great Light of the day was descending. Mbaracambri stirred in his hammock. He felt his body quiver; his heart heard the first tones and words of a song. He looked over to his wife Yyvkuaraua and caught her eyes smiling at him.

Moving in silence, Yyvkuaraua knew to put away the herbs she was preserving and prepared herself for the nightly gathering of prayer with her husband. Mbaracambri stood up and reached for his akangua'a hanging from a cross pole above his hammock. The akangua'a created a beautiful crown of feathers on his head. This ceremonial headdress was part of a sacred way, but also indicated his status of pajé, one with the wisdom of many songs. Reaching into the hammock and retrieving his mbaraká, his revered rattle, he quietly stepped from the thatched roof dwelling.

As darkness was quickly descending in the forest, Mbaracambri walked toward the Hill of Birds. Yyvkuaraua lifted a long section of bamboo adorned with feathers, her takuá, for pounding out the rhythm of song, and walked with her husband as she had done many times before. The presence of the moon and bright stars through the forest canopy allowed Mbaracambri to see others gathering. This was the way of the forest people.

The song he felt stirring in his heart while walking brought deep feelings of gratitude for the good life that the great celestial father, Ñande Ru, provided his uncorrupted village. He felt the goodness in the gathering of the community, of his wife Yyvkuaraua, his son Veraju, who was showing signs of manhood, and of his daughter Kitu, who recently concluded a ceremony for joining the women's moon cycle. Mbaracambri smiled as he thought of the prophetic dream announcing the birth of his youngest son, Arapotiyu. In the dream, celestial beings surrounded a beautiful village ancestor, who had great healing abilities, and announced the coming of this pajé, who would continue to lead the forest people.

Through his song during this particular prayer gathering, Mbaracambri was seeking guidance for the village. The mother-father creation was their guidance, and the communication with the great celestial beings was a source of life to this village of forest people. Standing in a place at the Hill of Birds, where he stood for many seasons of maize, Mbaracambri closed his eyes and hummed, as Yyvkuaraua created the rhythm by pounding her takuá on the ground. Yyvkuaraua created an earthy vibration that rose from the earth and embraced his whole body. He could not hold back the song in his heart and raised his arms and face to the star-dappled sky. Shaking his mbaraká, the sacred rattle, he sang an ancient prayer.

In unison, the women joined Yyvkuaraua in pounding their takuás, and the men chanted with Mbaracambri. Within minutes, the forest was filled with song and reverberation from the pounding of takuás. As Mbaracambri went deeper and deeper into his song of praise and gratitude, the village's elder pajé, who was dressed in a feathered cloak, stepped forward and tilted his head back, raising his face to the night sky. His enraptured face turned toward the pulsating star people in the sky, directing his chanting above to Ñande Ru, the one Great Being, and then to the four sacred directions. The men chanted in a louder voice and with a faster rhythm, as the elder pajé prayed in each of the four directions, facing first to "Ñanderovai" in the direction of the rising light.

This chanting of many prayers to the celestial world continued all through the darkness. As the elder pajé continued to lead the chanting, Mbaracambri slipped into ecstatic trance. Through visions, he would see and feel word souls, the ayvú, or the voice of the Great Father, swell in his heart. The singing and chanting continued through the darkness while Mbaracambri held his trance state.

The ceremony continued all through the darkness following with the nightly pathway of Jesyju, the moon, through the pulsating star people until Jesyju's clear light descended to meet the rising of Kuarahy's many streaming golden rays of light. When the first rays of gold light appeared, in unison, the forest people stopped chanting; and with outstretched arms and faces raised upward, they felt powerful energetic surges flow through their bodies.

In the charged silence, Mbaracambri and the elder pajé stood together in front of the community, facing the rising golden light, and carried out their ritual for claiming this powerful energy. Maintaining their outstretched arms, the community moved in flowing beauty with the ceremony of jirojy. Lowering their heads and flexing their knees, they gracefully moved their arms to solemnly gather the golden rays to their bodies. Many had tears of joy streaming down their gold-lit faces from the ecstatic feelings.

When the chanting and graceful communal movement of jirojy was complete, frequently, a small brown bird, Irapuru, pierced the silence. This song was an omen that the Great One heard and received the morning prayers and ceremony. However, today there was no song.

As it was in every prayerful communication at the Hill of Birds of Mbaracambri's life, the forest people gathered at the base of the hill. Mbaracambri shared the visions and the ayvú, the word souls that came to him. The elder pajé carefully listened to Mbaracambri's visions before giving directions to the daily activity of the village. As the men dispersed from the Hill of Birds, they engaged in greetings and friendly conversations, each off to complete with a glad heart the sacred messages and guidance from the celestial world.

Mbaracambri went to the side of the elder pajé and, as was the custom, took him by the arm to help him down the hill. A neighbor, Tangara, greeted the elder pajé and Mbaracambri and took the opposite arm.

Tangara then spoke to Mbaracambri, "We are all happy to celebrate your son Veraju moving into manhood."

Gently squeezing the elder pajé's arm, Mbaracambri replied, "Yes, it warms my heart to see the women preparing the food and drinks, while we all wait to hear Grandfather Pajé's word souls to start the celebration. How is your pregnant wife, Tangara?"

"You move my heart to a place of concern for her. Because of the poor harvest of last year and the very poor condition of the maize this year, the additional child would be a burden upon the village. How are we going to feed another child with our meager reserves and prospects of a poor harvest? I feel especially fearful in not hearing the Irapuru's song this morning."

Mbaracambri responded calmly to Tangara, "Do not worry. The celestial beings, as they have in the past, will provide a good way of life."

"But, Mbaracambri, I am very worried that we might all starve."

With calm reassurance, Mbaracambri replied, "Fear not, my friend, for the community and, certainly, my family will share our reserves, as this is the good way of life of our people." Still holding the elder's arm, he stopped walking and turned to Tangara. "More importantly, our early morning word souls and visions for the day ask us to continue the meager harvesting. In addition, I received a sign to hunt the small pig and seek out honey in the area of the beautiful flowers. Do not give into these feelings, my friend, instead pray harder to the gods. We are guided and our good true father, Ñande Ru, will not abandon us."

The elder pajé patiently listening, said in a rich, compassionate voice, "Tangara," pausing for a breath, "I am very pleased that you have shared your feelings, which I am sure have touched others in the village, and so we will speak to all of the signs of weakening harmony, the lack of mbiroy. We stand in this beautiful place as directed through our word songs, this aromatic and light-filled space bountiful in communication with Ñande Ru. Prayers to the gods must be constant this day, to beseech the Light for clear understanding for all the forest people."

As he said these last words, he turned, looking to Mbaracambri, who replied, "I hear you, Grandfather. In glad heart, Yvvkuaraua and I will continue to sing and dance on this day given to us by the gods, as you are suggesting. Tangara, will you join us?"

"No, my friend, I will gather those who hunt and make the dance to pray for the pig that you saw in your dream. My empty stomach will enhance my hunting skills. I will meet you at the Opy, the house of prayer, when the last light of the great Kuarahy is resting."

The elder pajé smiled as he listened to the two younger men. He then spoke in gentle kindness, "These are all good actions, my sons. I will go now to share the beautiful words with all our people."

Tangara smiled and, raising his arms in the air, walked away, his words trailing behind him. "I am ready, Grandfather, for a good hunt!"

Smiling and watching Tangara as he broke into a quick trot, the elder pajé turned and slowly shuffled off to his hammock, where he looked forward to giving directions to the village.

Mbaracambri found his wife already preparing maize as their son Arapotiyu watched. Seeing his father, Arapotiyu rose from his squatting position. "Father, I will leave now to stand at the side of Grandfather Pajé."

"This is good, Arapotiyu, listen and observe well." Mbaracambri turned to his wife, "Yvvkuaraua, let us eat little as Grandfather Pajé has instructed dance and song this day, and I will need your help."

Starting at a young age, Mbaracambri had received several sacred songs in his dreams. As he grew so did the beautiful songs and clarity of vision in his dreams. Mbaracambri worked alongside the aging Grandfather Pajé to support the village with visions he received while praying. Grandfather Pajé was a great healer; together with Mbaracambri's visions, they provided the forest people a good harmonious life. He knew why the elder pajé had asked for him to sing and dance this day. Mbaracambri had an earlier vision in his dream of the death of the elder. Grandfather Pajé was not sad; more so he was filled with joy in preparing for his move to the Land with No Evil, a place of perfect balance.

Arapotiyu came and stood by Grandfather Pajé as he lay in his hammock. The elder pajé was to instruct the village in activities that would maintain harmony within their forest. Arapotiyu watched and listened as the elder pajé assigned activities. Some young men and women were sent to gather wood; others fetched the honey; men gathered to dance before the hunt; grandmothers were teaching how to weave hammocks; younger women tended the gardens. In return, the village supported the pajé so that he could continue the sacred work to maintain the forest people's way of life.

The elder pajé then turned to advise the young apprentice. Arapotiyu received songs at a young age in his dream that indicated his path of becoming a great pajé like his father and grandfather. This was not new to Grandfather Pajé or to the parents, as they had seen the signs in dreams of the coming of this great soul. The community of forest people celebrated the goodness of having strong mediators to the celestial worlds.

Meanwhile, near his thatched lodge, Mbaracambri finished his meager ration of manioc and maize. He washed his face from a large gourd of water. Then, in a flash, he sensed the sudden quiet of the forest. He tensed and, instantly, his ears heard an unusual whistling sound. A volley of arrows rained down and sickening human howling rent the air. Mbaracambri's whole body shook as he realized an attack on the village was occurring, and he sprang to protect Yyvkuaraua when several men blocked him.

He fell forward, and on bended knee, he cried out to the great warrior chief standing just beyond his fierce guards. In the moments waiting for the warrior chief to react, Mbaracambri heard cries from his people who were struck with arrows. He quickly assessed the area surrounding him. He saw the elder pajé wounded in his hammock.

In a commanding voice for all to hear, the chief warrior proclaimed, "I am Tupanchichù, leader of the coastal Tupinambas." Riveting his eyes on Mbaracambri, Tupanchichù gestured for him to stand.

Upon rising, Mbaracambri asked the richly decorated leader, "What is the purpose of your attack since you come in surprise and not in the open as brave warriors?"

Tupanchichù made a menacing move with his arms for quiet and, holding his position, explained, "The coastal peoples have been meeting for several moons to discuss the sickness that takes the life breath and is spreading through our villages. A great vision was shared at these meetings that the people have failed to properly honor Jesyju, the moon god. Therefore, the counsel of many chief warriors declared that in three moons, a great ceremony to honor and praise Jesyju will be held. This ceremony will include singing, dancing, and making sacrifices. Most important, to appease the great Jesyju, we will offer a human sacrifice, as this is the way of the coastal people."

Mbaracambri's eyes grew wide, as it was not the normal tradition of his village of forest people to take a soul's life. Only Ñande Rú calls back a celestial soul. He responded to the warrior chief, "Tupanchichù, how much of our small community reserve of manioc or small store of ducks might be offered to this great ceremony?"

Tupanchichù smiled menacingly and responded to Mbaracambri's offer, "Understand the animals you hunt and the maize that you grow are within Tupinamba territory. All this is rightfully ours. Several seasons ago, you moved into the edges of our domain, and we are carefully watching your moves. At this time, we are not interested in your meager store of food. We are here to give your village a great honor." Tupanchichù spread his arms wide and spoke to the whole village, "Throughout our villages, the coastal people heard of a special pajé born to this village of forest people." Turning to face the elder and young apprentice, he continued, "This village will be honored with the sacrifice of this young apprentice of your elder pajé."

Mbaracambri quickly scanned the area by the wounded elder pajé and saw warrior guards holding Arapotiyu by the arms.

Tupanchichù turned to Mbaracambri and said, "We will now take your honored son to our village and commence the process in order to make him a worthy sacrifice to the great goddess Jesyju. We will also take some women and men as slaves. If you try to stop us, we will slay all of you. As you have heard, Tupanchichù's people are the most feared coastal warriors, and we will keep this status. It is because you have not slain nor eaten our ancestors that you are spared this day. Do not give us reason to show our strength." Tupanchichù immediately turned away, and Mbaracambri watched the warrior chief depart with the guards who took Arapotiyu.

Yvkuaraua and the others taken as slaves had already disappeared into the forest. Mbaracambri held his breath, feeling terrible despair as Arapotiyu turned and looked into his eyes. Rather than feeling great honor as portrayed in the coastal Tupinambas' village customs, Mbaracambri had great pain in his heart and deep sorrow filled his being in reading his son's pleading eyes. Mbaracambri fell to both knees as he listened to the moans of the injured. He could only watch as Arapotiyu was taken from the village to begin his journey to the village of coastal people.

CHAPTER 1

Help From an Unlikely Source

No one has a copyright on God's Love.
—Alberto Aguas

The season was late autumn, and the weather was cold in Michigan. Most of the leaves had fallen, and the scent of winter penetrated the ground. On this sunny Saturday morning of 1989, I left early to drive to a weekend spiritual workshop. The directions indicated a home in a country setting, which felt cozier and preferable to the typical stale rented hall or hotel room. At this time, spiritual workshops were a comforting thought, and seeking knowledge of this kind was not new. As far back as I can recall, my consistent pattern included actively asking questions and seeking answers to the meaning of life.

Right now, my all-out quest for spiritual understanding was of prime importance. Within a three-month period, I had experienced a hurtful divorce, given birth to my second son, buried my father, left a management position of more than ten years, packed up a household in Bloomfield, New Mexico, and then drove across the country. Returning to my family roots in Michigan and settling into an old farmhouse not far from my newly widowed mother, I slowly pieced my life back together, driven to find spiritual answers about this extreme time of emotional upset.

Over a four-year period prior to this workshop, the needs of my newborn, my three-year-old son, and my grieving mother motivated me to get up each day and put one foot in front of the other. Reflecting on all these recent events—frequent flashes of ugly divorce, my father's quick and untimely death, and birthing my second son—a fierce determination arose to create a way of not attracting similar situations into my life. The heavy feeling in my heart from the discord continued to remind me of being unbalanced. In that moment of understanding, on my knees praying aloud, I made a direct and solemn vow to God: "I will heal this burdened feeling. I will heal before accepting any type of personal relationship and find a way to raise myself out of this despondent feeling. I will lovingly care for my children. Please show me the way."

I hold a strong desire to raise my children with as much unconditional love as possible. They are the bright lights in my life. Standing and feeling the potency of making a verbal commitment, a willful determination took hold of my mind to find a way to heal, to be responsible to myself as well as my children.

I arrived at the address and turned into a long sweeping driveway lined with tall pine trees. I saw a steep-roofed house with vaulted windows tucked into the peaceful ambience of a wooded lot. Not the first to arrive, I parked, stepped from the car, and strong earthy pine scent filled my nose.

At the entryway to the house, the door opened into a kitchen area, where several people were engaged in friendly conversation, and a woman bent over a small registration table. A stranger, I merely moved through the line until it was my turn to register. As I signed in, a feeling of uneasiness crept over me.

For the first time, I stepped out from under the guidance of a good friend to follow my own intuition to attend this workshop. She was much more experienced with these kinds of workshops. While hurriedly scanning the room, not seeing a familiar face, my unshakable certainty was quickly fading. How could this be? I thought I knew all the "new agers" in town. Perhaps this workshop was not in my best interest. I should have attended the Friday night free lecture to get a preview of the weekend events.

The uneasiness engulfed my whole body. Seriously doubting my intuition, I questioned my motives: *What was I doing here? I could be home playing with my children. Who were these people? Everyone seemed to know each other. I did not know anyone.*

I scanned the living room at the different chairs and pillows positioned in a semicircle that looked out the vaulted windows and strategically chose a high-back chair close to the window. This afforded me a location that was not in the middle of the seating, but off to the side. The speaker was easy to pick out, as he was the only male in the room. I crossed the room to the chair, and our eyes met briefly; he acknowledged me with a quick warm smile. I settled into my seat and observed everyone as the program started.

The speaker, dressed in an oriental-styled dark blue silk shirt and black trousers, stood before the tall windows, which framed a grove of pines. A round wooden dining table held his personal notes, a single lit white taper candle, a small tape player, and cassette tapes. As people took their seats, another woman taped a large piece of white plastic to one of the windows to serve as a writing board. Fourteen other participants gathered in chairs or cushions in the half circle facing the table and speaker. After a short gracious introduction by our host, "We are very pleased to bring you a very gifted Alberto Aguas from Brazil," the program began.

Alberto Aguas wasted no time getting started. "Thank you, Cindy and JB, for having me here," Alberto said. "I am honored to be here with you." Turning to the plastic sheet taped to the window, he wrote and carefully announced, "*A-MA—DE-US* is Latin for '*To Love God.*' This is the name of the healing system. And please excuse my English." I do not believe anyone cared about his Brazilian accent and broken English for his voice was pleasingly rich. I relaxed.

Alberto spoke with uninhibited passion and displayed an authority that only a man living a purposeful life possesses. To hear him was to hear a vocalized concert honed from years in professional theater. His voice rang with bright, rich tones of variety and color, and his striking green eyes connected to each of ours, as the touch of a gentle hand. He was magnetic—aesthetically, intellectually, and spiritually attractive.

On notepaper, I wrote the words *Ama-Deus* and the meaning *To Love God* as he lectured briefly about his work with the Guaraní, an indigenous tribe in South America. He described the initiation into their sacred healing tradition on the banks of the Amazon. I paused in my note taking, listening intently, as he stood tall and explained, slowly, and carefully pronouncing each word in a loud tone, "I will describe now how you will be for the initiation. Each one of you will individually come to the table and receive the initiation. If there is anyone uncomfortable, now is the time to leave." He paused looking around the room.

Again, the uneasy feeling crept back into my body and mind, blocking out his voice. *What had I gotten myself into now? I should have gone to the free lecture the night before. I would have a better understanding of what to expect.* I quickly reminded myself that nothing happened when I received the Reiki initiation. That initiation was painless and really made me giggle, not that I wanted to be irreverent. Why did I feel like I needed to run from this place? Quickly glancing around the room to view other faces, no one spoke or moved to leave. I looked in the direction of the door. To leave would mean to cross in front of everyone and make a disturbing exit.

The full force chatter continued in my head as the first person on the other side of the room approached the table. *How could I have gotten myself into such a predicament? Oh well, everyone seems to be coming out okay. I am in this now.* Hot and panicky, I closed my eyes and took a deep breath to squelch the fluttering fear in my stomach. To this day, I am not sure where the strength came from when Alberto's eyes motioned for me to step up to the table and receive the initiation.

After respectfully standing before the table to receive the initiation, a ritual of prayer from Alberto, and returning to my safe chair, a great peace unfolded. Was this tranquility a result of relief from the ritual being over, or did something actually happen? The sudden calmness allowed my body, my emotions, and especially my mind to relax. Again, I closed my eyes and encountered a serene peaceful state until the music for the initiation ceremony stopped, and then Alberto said, "This initiation can give you new views, new experience, and new life." Opening my eyes as he drew out the word *life* in his rich Brazilian accent, a light turned on for me at that moment. In a renewed vigor for being part of the class, I became fully immersed and focused for the rest of the day.

After the initiation within the first hour of the class, a journey unfolded with Alberto as our guide. A new perspective to energy healing opened with Alberto, the mentor, escorting the class through this ancient wisdom. As Alberto guided everyone on how to connect to Ama-Deus, a comfortable feeling was established—something very familiar. Ama-Deus is a heart-based, hands-on healing method using sacred symbols preserved in the Guaraní oral tradition. This heart-based method of accessing Divine Love was something I sought for a long time.

I gained new knowledge and great awareness of self-healing through the experiential journey during the class. Through his gifted understanding of the spiritual world, Alberto used key phrases and quotes to urge us to heal ourselves, while we learned the different applications of sacred symbols. He would say such phrases as, "No one has a copyright on God's love," or "Nothing is too hard for me, it is too hard for my ego," and "You cannot heal until you first love," and still another, "Never withhold your love, that is what keeps you coming back."

I was ecstatic to hear him referencing the heart and love for healing. Needless to say, I did not wish for the class to end. My intuition had not been too far off after all! The discomfort at the start of class was only fear of change. Experiencing the transformation from discomfort to peace offered opportunity for grasping and appreciating how Love is a powerful agent for healing, for bringing on change.

I had been attempting to understand love for as long as I could remember. I am not alone. Love means so many things to so many people. Some see it as an action; others feel love. Alberto saw love as his connection to the Source of all things. The name he gave to this connection was *Ama-Deus* meaning *"To Love God."* The word *God* is humankind's best meager attempt to give a name to a reality that words cannot express and the mind cannot know. In the same breath, it must be said that Love and God cannot be separated. It is a mistake to ask, "What is Love?" Love is not a *what*; more correctly, Love is *who*. Love is a living-forever-without-end Being. Love is a force experienced within the heart. Alberto's gift of Ama-Deus opened my heart and led me on a pathway to healing.

The class was all of Saturday, extending into Sunday, and finishing with a nice meal of vegetarian lasagna in the early evening. As everyone merrily engaged in conversation while eating, I sat in quiet amazement, laughing at the initial idea of trying to escape, and overjoyed for following through with the initiation. The anticipated excitement driving to the workshop was spot on. The entire two days were staggering.

Within this short space of time, so much had occurred. I was in awe of the awakening of knowledge, sensing an expanded awareness. Several times throughout the workshop, Alberto would catch my eye to see if I was paying attention. When he caught my eye in this swift and direct manner, there was such intensity. He would catch me off guard, and I was not sure why he was singling me out. Later, I learned this was not a reprimand, but rather his way of teaching and placing emphasis on what had just transpired. In subsequent classes, I learned he could easily read one's thoughts.

For instance, on the second day of class, he passed around a picture of himself for each person to view. He continued to lecture while the picture was being passed. I do not recall his reason for this act. I do recall vividly the moment when the small black and white photo passed into my hands. My eyes and hands froze in looking at and holding the photo. Instantly becoming self-conscious and wondering if others were watching, my inner voice declared, *Relax! People here are used to such oddities.* As quickly as this magnetic feeling from holding the picture had come, another feeling set in motion my being pulled into the photo of a small no-more-than-five year old boy in bib overalls standing near a tree. Deeply focused on the photo, experiences of Alberto's childhood flashed through my thoughts, hearing again my inner mind reveal, *He is very sick.* I tried to tear my eyes away from the picture, which felt like two magnets being pulled apart. Finally succeeding, I hurriedly passed the photo to the person on my right, simultaneously looking up at Alberto, who never broke with his lecture and managed to swiftly shoot a piercing glance that made me shrink back in my seat.

With downcast eyes and pushing back surprised thoughts of Alberto possibly being ill, I had questioning thoughts. *How could this great healer, who was so full of life, be sick? And why did he pass this picture around? Why was I so acutely aware of it?* I abruptly interrupted the flow of thoughts, turned back to the lecture, and dismissed this episode with the photo. What was I to do with this premonition? I brought my attention back to listening and turned my thoughts to hearing about this wonderful sacred wisdom. The substantial information pulled together and synched bits and pieces of other energetic studies and provided spiritual clarity to many experiences in my life. The class definitely held reward for spiritual truth.

◊　◊　◊　◊　◊

In reflecting on this entire experience in the first class, I often asked people whether they have seen the movie *Close Encounters of the Third Kind* by Steven Spielberg. Richard Dreyfuss plays the role of a cable worker who investigates a power outage and encounters a mysterious white light from above. Like Dreyfuss's character, who became obsessed with finding the answer to his experience, I could not get enough and felt obsessed with Ama-Deus. In the practice of Ama-Deus, something so exhilarating pulled on every sense of my body, emotions, and mind. This extended to every detail. For instance, I immediately had to find the music Alberto used in class and stuck it in my children's Mickey

Mouse cassette player, listening to it continually and taking it everywhere with us—room to room, in the car, or during showers. You need only ask my two sons. They will say that, in waking and sleeping, they were subjected to the music. Alberto's words after the initiation, "This can give you new views, new experiences and, new life," were vibrantly true for me. Little did I consciously know at this time how many abundant new life experiences and views were forthcoming.

In practicing other healing methods prior to Ama-Deus, there were no tangible feelings of warmth in my hands or sense of connection like observing and hearing from other practitioners. I did, however, have powerful experiences with Ama-Deus. Some of the first effects that came about were physical.

For example, in the practice of Reiki, a close mentor suggested to place your hands on yourself as you go to sleep in order to receive healing energy in the sleep state. Taking this advice very seriously, I was used to falling asleep with my hands gently cupped around my throat. After receiving the Ama-Deus initiation, this habitual pattern of the hand position relentlessly woke me. What could only be described as an intense surge of electrical charge flowed through my body. My hands felt as if they were stuck in a socket. In a lucid state, I made continual attempts to remove my hands, break the flow of electricity, and return to sleep. Many times through the night for several months, I worked to remove my hands from this position.

This strong feeling of energy flow also occurred in working energy healing with others. As soon as the steps that Alberto taught were taken to connect with this healing system, a feeling of a strong surge of energy entered the top of my head, accompanied with a sound like that of rushing wind. This flowing surge of energy moved down through my throat into the chest area, sometimes so strongly that I gasped for breath. This flow continued to move from the chest to my arms and, ultimately, out through my hands.

Whenever I had a caring thought to help others—whether an image of nature, an animal, or a person—the energy would flow of its own accord. In tapping into Ama-Deus, clearly, something else was in control of the energy flow. After embracing a tree or a dog or placing my hands on a person, this gushing flow began and then ended of its own accord. This ending was the signal to retract my hands.

Alberto offered a week of healing sessions after the weekend Ama-Deus class. The class and his brilliant ability to work with healing energy quickly spread. The Ama-Deus workshop booked up quickly for his return visit and stories trailed for several weeks after he left. With this news traveling around town, people were curious and wanted to experience this healing technique. Ecstatic to share this new spiritual tool with others, several people from a circle of like-minded friends came to my home to experience Ama-Deus.

Friends and friends of friends came to experience Ama-Deus sessions. Most knew me as a skeptical questioning Reiki practitioner. Following session after healing session, people left with the keen desire to attend his next class. A healing session started by having the person lie on a massage table, and then I asked, just like Alberto instructed, "What would you like this healing for?"

The friend responded, "I have this nagging headache that will not go away."

"Okay, to begin, I will lay one hand on your forehead and one on your solar plexus. There might be the movement of my hands from this position during the healing session to work with the other energy points or chakras."

After they shared why they wanted healing, I asked them to close their eyes, relax, and listen to the music, while turning on the cassette player. The music would begin—the same music Alberto used in class, the soundtrack from *The Mission*. The spiritual routine to invoke the energy started after taking a deep relaxing centering breath, followed by positioning my hands on the forehead and the solar plexus. This hand position was used simply because that is what I had observed Alberto doing. Once the flow of energy started, the hand position would change, following to places where the flow continued. The energy gave direction for the hands; and the tears flowed down my face. Using Ama-Deus was such a glorious feeling. Time after time, the energy would teach me.

With this particular healing session, even though the person requested help for headaches, my hands did not move to the head. After the initial position and connecting to healing energy, a scanning over the body with my hands would locate, and then move to follow the flow of energy. When the flow dramatically increased, the hands settled in this area until the flow stopped. I was not in control, but rather an instrument, not the musician. My hands came to rest in the abdominal area where the flow of energy was the strongest. With complete trust in the All-Knowing presence of energy and knowing in my heart that all was perfect, I held this position until there was no flow or sound of energy. Gently lifting my hands from her body and turning down the music, a response came immediately forth.

"Wow, how did you know to do that?" the person softly responded.

"I do not know, I am being directed."

"My headache is gone!" She then proceeded to share about the complicated issues in the abdominal area.

I raised my hands high in the air in the arrested position and said, "It is the energy, not me. You can do this too. Just sign up for the class. The teacher is coming back." Then I walked to and huddled over a furnace vent.

"What are you doing?" She asked with a puzzled facial expression while sitting on the side of the healing table.

"I am trying to warm up!"

Immediately following a session, cold invaded my body. Usually, after the person left, I would crank up the thermostat and huddle over a warm furnace vent with a blanket, capturing every bit of heat to surround my body.

This was not the only physical experience. My neck would visibly pulsate after invoking and connecting to the energy. The pulse was so strong that my neck in the beginning was very sore to touch. Wearing a turtleneck concealed this pronounced movement. In time, I learned that this physical discomfort was my body attempting to adjust to this higher frequency of energy. Eventually, after three months of giving healing sessions every day, I adjusted to the incoming invoked energy.

For six months, every day people came for sessions. Sometimes there would be one person; on other days, three would show up at my doorstep. The gratitude for Ama-Deus coming into my life and being able to share with others overrode the physical side effects. A great amount of experience was gained from the numerous sessions; however, after multiple daily sessions with no break, I needed a rest. Packing up the old van in early spring, the children and I headed to Florida to stay with family. The rest and single focus of my children also allowed reflection and integration around this dramatic turn of events. No longer was my neck sore to the touch after sessions, and sleeping with my hands on myself was no longer disturbing. Gratitude filled my being in thinking of the commitment and vow to heal, and peace claimed my heart in finding this new spiritual tool.

In reflection during this mini respite, I no longer questioned whether Ama-Deus was real or how it worked. I so resonated with Ama-Deus, feeling as if I had come home. The strong peaceful presence moving through my body gave me courage. Witnessing the outcomes over and over was continual verification. Listening and feeling where to place my hands stopped the questioning and curious observation took over. Observing the beautiful outcomes that happened rather then questioning if energy healing worked became the mode of operation. Faith and belief were the first steps with Reiki. Experiences were the next steps with Ama-Deus, giving way to a direct knowing that energy healing was real no matter which technique was used. The beautiful feelings experienced as a practitioner were beyond description, and I found myself often saying, "I could do this all day!"

My good friend Kathy watched some of the healing sessions and said, "Beth, you need to stay in your body, you need to get grounded."

I joyfully responded, "Oh, but this feels so good." The feelings of energy flowing through my body were sensory experiences, and I knew this as well as I knew my own face, so familiar, so loving, and so incredibly comfortable.

◊ ◊ ◊ ◊ ◊

The real question all my life was not just *why are we here on Earth*, but what part does *Love* have to do with this earthly journey. Searching all my life for the meaning of unconditional compassionate Love, I now stood at a threshold. Ama-Deus was a tool to begin a new journey to help answer that question. In the first sessions of using this heart-based healing method, I moved out of *belief* in unconditional Love to a *knowing* of this compassionate Love from direct experience. Alberto was right; new potentials awaited anyone game enough to develop a relationship with this heart-based healing method—new experiences, new views, and certainly, new life.

The period of time that brought intense life situations with a divorce and death, tangled with the birth of my second son, although most certainly brought sadness, more importantly drove me in greater concentration of purpose to find the meaning of Love. Four years later, after this tumultuous crossroad in my life, I was introduced to Ama-Deus.

This is not to say that, during the four years prior to Ama-Deus, I sat idle. The other classes and therapies I encountered during the four years of seeking spiritual knowledge were preparation for this vital moment with Ama-Deus. Key people who entered this transitional phase of personal searching indeed equipped me with a broader spiritual understanding and significantly aided my first steps of healing. Those first steps held dramatic outcomes.

Most of my life was overshadowed with great trepidation in being with people. Before the commitment to heal and before Ama-Deus, there was not the ability to look someone in the eye. Now, I hold a steady gaze. Before, I could not leave a message on an answering machine. Now, I am able to speak with even the most intimidating people in growing confidence. Much of the fear that once possessed me has lost its power. My steadfast intention to heal, focused searching, and active engagement during the four-year healing phase brought me to a point to be able to receive Ama-Deus, to step up and receive the initiation. My heart had been touched, and that opening of heart brought newness to life and willingness to heal in a new way.

Alberto and his message of Love opened my heart to receive. The complete trust with this new adventure and willingness to immerse myself in all life had to offer is best summed up in T. S. Eliot's words from *Four Quartets: Little Gidding*.

> We shall not cease from exploration
> And the end of all our exploring will be
> To arrive where we started
> And know the place for the first time.[1]

Ama-Deus is so simple to use, so peaceful and gentle, so loving. When someone loves us, even negative things become positive. When we are surrounded by love, we see the world from a different perspective. Being so enamored with the knowledge and the escalating experiences learned in the first level, I could hardly believe a year had passed when finding myself delightedly sitting in the second level. My assured enthusiasm to attend the second level and learn more brought a group of friends together filling Alberto's class to capacity.

People even flew in for the class as far away as Arizona to honor my newfound treasure. None were disappointed with either the class or the healings offered by Alberto. The weekend was filled with joy and laughter. In spite of the infectious joy in the air, however, one thing nagged at my heart. Something very strong was amiss for him, and a concerned feeling for his health rose while observing him teach the first level at the YWCA.

Not being encumbered with note taking, I could absorb information at a deeper level as well as watch at closer proximity his teaching methods. This uneasy feeling for his health lingered through class.

During the breaks, he strategically moved away from any opportunity to call concern on himself. Instead, before the class and during the breaks, there were fun and playful conversations.

"Hellooo, Betty!" he said in a loud voice when we first caught sight of each other and shared a great bear hug. All through the weekend, he called me Betty. At first, I thought he did not know better, and I tried to correct him. Locking eyes with me and raising his deep voice, he said, "I *know* your name, Bet! There is a more intimate way of calling friends, right?" My cheeks gave away my embarrassment at correcting him. Then in a shy way, he shared that all his close friends call him "Alby." My heart warmed with his endearing approach, and he became "Alby" to me in private conversations.

Alberto slightly changed the format from the previous year to accommodate teaching two levels in one weekend. The first level was taught all in one day, and I noted how the instructions were organized as compared to my two-day first level workshop. The next day, the entire second level class was taught and held at the private residence where the first level was first presented the year before. This second level class held a completely different atmosphere for me from the first time, as most of the people attending were my friends, and Alberto loved showering special attention on them. Alberto was energized about not only the large attendance but also because all attending were so immersed in the class.

As a teacher, Alberto conducted the classroom like a maestro. Everyone enthusiastically followed his lead. If he wanted to sing, everyone burst into song. When he would bring the class into meditation, its depth and purity were astonishing. Everyone was engaged, and laughter erupted spontaneously. At the end of the weekend, all of the students chatted brightly, took turns hugging each other, and smiled for photographs. At one point, Alberto grabbed my shoulder, spun me around, and hugged me tight just as the camera shutter closed. I treasure this photo and keep it close at hand on my desk. Then he removed from my hair a small clip and pinched it between his fingers. With wide eyes and chuckling in a deep voice, he exclaimed inches from my face, "Piranha!" Gifted with wisdom, he still had the sweetness and heart of a child.

Following the weekend, Alberto had a booked week of private healings. Being a certified massage therapist, arrangements were made for me to massage him in the evening. This helped my concerned feelings for his well-being, seeing past his outside appearance and knowing he was very ill. My concern slackened in learning that, after this week of teaching, he would be returning to Brazil for several months' rest and a visit with the Guaraní.

Alberto did not refer much to the Guaraní during an Ama-Deus class. Any details in the class given about the Guaraní were mostly in reference to the first steps as it pertained to his experience of the initiation. Alberto was reluctant to talk further about the Guaraní during the class. If people asked, he simply brought them back to the present moment in gratitude for what they were receiving. He did reveal that *The Amazon the Kingdom of the Healing* was a separate presentation that he gave on occasion. He strictly protected any details of the Guaraní's exact location and discouraged outsiders from thinking of exploring this very fragile and endangered culture.

One does not become more spiritual by being around the Guaraní or any indigenous culture for a time. Spiritual growth occurs from within the heart. People became charmed with the idea of a tribe of Indians in the Amazon, rather than realizing the importance of staying focused with the gift they were receiving at that moment, the message that Alberto risked his life to preserve and bring to the Western world. The opportunity to heal during the workshop was vital and fundamental to his mission in life, and Alberto took this task very seriously.

Later, in listening to his taped lectures and in remembering our private conversations, I learned more about the profound experiences Alberto had with the Guaraní. This information clearly indicated that all his life experiences culminated in his fifties in meeting and working with this indigenous group of people.

For many years, Alberto had traveled the world giving lectures about the spiritual world and spiritual healings. He had seen and been with some of the great healers and mediums of our time. However, when he met the Guaraní, he went home and knew their ways well.

For over ten years, Alberto worked and lived among the Guaraní. As kindred spirits will, the Guaraní recognized his gifted healing ability. More importantly, they felt his capacity for love. As a result, the tribe openly shared their spiritual approach to healing with him. While he worked side by side with the shaman or pajé, Alberto learned how the Guaraní used herbs. He watched their massage techniques and observed auricular acupuncture that used bamboo shoots. The insight that became most important to him was their practice of a sacred ancient oral tradition for healing from a soul awareness. The Guaraní chose to initiate Alberto into their sacred tradition after he demonstrated sensitivity to their perspective on life and shared their views on the principles of healing.

Alberto never dreamed he would show others how to work with healing energy, which came naturally to him since he was a small child. On several occasions, I caught him saying that he never imagined himself as a teacher. Certainly, there was a time he would have never thought he would be thrown in prison either. Such was his concern and love for the Guaraní, as he protested on several occasions to the Brazilian government the neglect of the people and the disrespectful encroachment of outside land development agencies on Guaraní land and surrounding forest areas. Alberto risked his freedom without fear, and he paid dearly. When you are in open communication with your heart, your soul leads you to places that the mind cannot foresee. This is how Alberto chose to live.

Aside from the classes, Alberto spoke of his love for the Guaraní in passionate lectures. He talked of the sacred ways of these people, who have carried their oral tradition intact for over six thousand years; and how they unconditionally shared with him all their knowledge; and how, without reserve, he fought for their rights and their land. He traveled during the last ten years of his life to share what he was learning from these spiritual people. Love and healing were the dominant themes in his lectures. The Guaraní and Alberto shared the same view that without Love, there is no healing. Alberto understood, without a doubt, how his life had been shaped and prepared to work with the Guaraní and is best summarized in his lecture notes.

> We are the reflection of what we are thinking, so let us carefully program our minds for this new world. In doing so, together, always together, we can radiate this energy that is pure cosmic Love and each one of us will be channels for the healing energy. More and more I see myself not as a healer full of techniques and different theories but as a love giver. More and more I am discovering that my old prayers in healing today are nothing more than love statements. More and more I can clearly see and capture that I am not a miracle man, that you and I together are miracle people we are all the same in our humanity, with this cosmic love we will all have the same possibilities and consequently we are all healers in potential [sic].

As the third year rolled around and Alberto arrived to teach, I found a very frail man. When he walked into the classroom and saw the alarmed look on my face, he simply smiled. Not the smile of unfettered joy, but one that acknowledged my distress. He knew what was in my mind and heart. He looked exhausted. He approached and wrapped his arms around me and spoke in a soft voice. "Will you sit there?" he asked and pointed to the chair in the middle of the front row. Little did we know that this would be his last session instructing his much-loved Ama-Deus.

Again, most of the forty-two people attending the class were friends. My mind was so entrenched with aiding him; I took little notice of their presence. An assistant manner took over; I remained in an alert receptive state for any possible need he might have for teaching. Sitting front and center, a definite rush of energy began. In his weakened state, Alberto did not have the strength to fully enter into the energy without a source of help. As he started the class, a river of energy flowed through me to him. He had me come up and lay on a massage table as he demonstrated the different sacred symbols. During the breaks, we would quietly sit off to the side together as he nursed some broth made earlier at home. People were unusually quiet. The room felt gloomy to me. He was cold. Never did I question why he pushed himself or what he could do for himself. My heart was simply in a holding pattern for whatever needs he might have. I loved helping him, and in turn, he sought out my participation.

In this class and others, Alberto consistently brought me forward to demonstrate the healing method. In my mind, then as a student and friend, I looked no further into the future than to the wonderful opportunity at the moment. Later, I realized beautiful stepping-stones were being lovingly placed on my life's path.

He did not make the complete week of private healings; he was too weak. I continued to bring him food at his request and would sit quietly while he ate. Our conversation wound around simple mundane things like the latest advancements for autism and casual conversations around the need of visiting with his mother. "You know, someday they will find the root cause of autism!" My mind was half listening to him and wondering if I should bring up what he was going to do to help himself.

Then he quickly interjected, "I need to see my mother. She was talking with me [telepathically], and I am concerned for her health. I would like to see her before she passes."

"Are you sensing her time is near?"

"Yes."

"Will you go home from here?"

"I will go to the East Coast and finish my tour with one more class before I go to visit with my mother."

Alberto did not teach another class after that weekend. Alberto flew to the East Coast and stayed in the home of a trusted friend where he took time to heal and gain strength. Our friendship was such that we spoke on the phone every single day, sometimes several times a day, for nearly nine months. I also sent care packages of cookies and wrote fun notes.

During this period, a natural progression of my study in energy healing expanded. Alberto was in tune with this expansion phase and acknowledged key evolvements. One of the side effects was a strong telepathic ability to communicate with him. This was strengthened after he had me practice Ama-Deus using a specific sacred symbol that aids in traveling to visit another person. To perceive telepathically was natural to him; however, for me, it was exciting and the latest adventure in using Ama-Deus.

One evening, while preparing a family meal, I could hear him in my mind, strongly requesting for me to practice that very minute. We sort of bantered back and forth in our minds.

"I am cooking now and will be distracted and not present for this experience."

"Please, *gooo* and *dooo* now," he strongly responded.

I finally gave in and lay on the living room floor and proceeded through the steps. A magnificent experience transpired. Immediately there was a sensation as if going through a tunnel of light, accompanied with a very fast funneling sound lasting for several minutes before abruptly ending in a space of feeling close to Alberto. I could hear him breathing.

"Very good," he responded. I relaxed into the moment.

"Thank you."

He loved to teach people about spiritual ways, and he cherished the opportunity to help people heal.

Joy radiated from Alberto when he gave healing sessions. He had a giving soul. Everyone recognized this beautiful trait. To summarize the last few months of his life, I would say that Alberto Aguas, in all his physical discomfort, never lost sight of helping others. Even though he was tired, he accepted calls from friends who requested healings. I distinctly remember one of our conversations on the subject of offering healing during a time that he himself needed to rest. His beautifully rich voice was tired, and he talked quietly and slowly, "You know, [he gave the name] called, and he asked me to do a healing. I told him, yes, I would do this. But you know, Betty, he never asked about my health." He paused, and I was waiting for his next words.

I finally broke the silence and carefully asked, "Are you okay?"

He exhaled a long breath saying, "People are exhausting, but this is okay."

In our relationship, my goal was to stay back and not take anything from him. He gave so much already to others; I did not want to be an added burden. But there was no stopping him from giving.

Alberto was known to the world as a profound healer, and many times, this is all they could see. People simply would forget his human needs. I watched as people surrounded him with their needs—taking from him with a deep hunger for what he possessed. Some sought healing, others clamored just to be near his energy, and many were drawn to his celebrity status and refined looks. No matter the inconvenience, he accommodated everyone he could. This was his nature, and it was beautiful. Alberto always looked for opportunities to help people heal, and he never had to look far.

Alberto did not see himself as a miracle worker. He did not look for miracles, but that is not to say he did not marvel at the outcome and mystery of his work. Being with Alberto, I never felt like he was putting on a show or false front. More often, he would steer clear of scenes that drew attention to him. He had tremendous respect for spiritual and energetic properties; he did not aggrandize or exaggerate. He did not have to. In his perspective and in his life, the spiritual world was not supernatural or miraculous; it was as natural and normal as breathing. Yet I did witness, several times, his extraordinary gifts in healing and playfulness, which seemed to definitely be in the paranormal category.

Of all the fond memories and many extraordinary stories that could be told of my experiences with Alberto, the story of the cardinal is the most fun. This story happened during his convalescing stay on the East Coast. In one of his calls, he asked in the opening line, "How are you today?"

I responded, "Wonderful!"

"How are you wonderful? Every time I call, you are always wonderful. Only pigs are wonderful *ALLLL* the time!"

We both laughed very hard. Even if I had something happening in my life, I purposely shied away from asking for his help while he was so depleted. I only wished to be accommodating and in a giving mode for him.

"What time are you waking up tomorrow?"

"I am not sure." This was true, for the children kept me on different schedules.

"Well, pick a time," he said.

"Okay, 6:30 a.m."

He then proceeded to talk about mundane things, never giving me a clue as to why he wanted to know my waking schedule. He never had a set time to call during the day; it was always at different times, but always sometime in the evening and sporadically during the day. Thinking he was looking to see how early he could call, I never gave this request another thought.

The very next morning, a loud scratching at my bedroom window woke me. I lived in an old farmhouse, and the head of my bed was pushed up to a window in the second-story bedroom. A small wooden headboard covered the lower portion of the window. Lifting my head from the pillow to look out over the headboard, I gasped in response to being almost nose-to-nose with a bright red cardinal clutched to the screen. I held my breath and did not move. He was chattering away. I was beginning to shake from controlling my physical body and taking small breaths. Now, the time was going on for this character to be on the screen. So I finally sat up in bed, expecting this unusual behavior to vanish. The cardinal did not leave. Very slowly and carefully, inching closer to the screen, he still was not disturbed. Is he blind? Becoming bold and placing my hand gently on the glass window, the cardinal remained clutched to the screen.

I was astonished to say the least. How could this be? I quickly retracted my hand from the window and jumped out of bed. I recalled the last conversation with Alberto and quickly glanced in the direction of the clock. The clock read 6:33 a.m. I blurted right out loud in wonder, "Alberto, what are you up to? Oh, such a fun thing!"

Elated with the incident and practically skipping downstairs to prepare breakfast for the children, I found the cardinal perched at the kitchen window, adding to my already peaked astonishment. Standing in this astonished state, staring at the window, the need to test the situation arose. So I moved to a different part of the house. The cardinal appeared in the window of each room I entered. I went outside, and he followed me around the yard. The last test to erase every bit of skepticism occurred as I headed into the woods. He followed me, flitting from one tree to the next, relentlessly chattering the whole time.

Of course, I did not wait for Alberto to call me. I called him.

"*Hellooooo*," he said.

Half jokingly, I said to him, "Who do you think you are, Merlin?"

He laughed and laughed. I was thrilled to have this sense of closeness.

The cardinal stayed with me every day, promptly waking me up at 6:30 a.m., until ten days after Alberto's death. There was only one time that this cardinal was not there in the morning at the bedroom window. On Valentine's morning, the ritual of waiting to hear the scratching and chatting of the cardinal was absent. Nothing came that morning. I admit I pouted. After reluctantly getting out of bed and entering the bathroom, there he was perched outside on the power line, giving me a real scolding. Exhaling a laugh of relief, I was comforted to know that his presence was still with me.

Alberto gave his time and deliberate attention to the moment at hand, and it showed. He was focused and in the present moment, and as a result, he could connect with people—and nature—on a personal level. His intuition was astonishing. For some, this ability was alarming or uncomfortable. For Alberto, it was the essence of being human. Gifted as Alberto was in accessing the mystical interior of the universe, nothing exceeded his capacity to love.

Alberto had a strong premonition that his mother was near death. He felt strong enough to make the journey to Brazil. He knew that I had concerns for his traveling to Brazil. The several episodes in Brazilian jails had wreaked havoc with his physical health. The phone call finally came saying he had made arrangements for a trip.

"I am only going to see my mother and to dismantle my apartment and all my business things in Brazil. Then I will come back to rest and use holistic ways as well as the medical system here in the United States."

"I know your favorite color to be peach like your mother. I will have a room ready for you."

"This is nice."

My children were on visitation with their father, and I was alone in the old farmhouse. My attention and prayers were a constant for him to make a successful trip. Shortly upon arriving in South America, he fell critically ill and was hospitalized. In feeling his distressed presence, I could not eat, nor do any work, or leave my home. Falling back on all the things that he had taught me with Ama-Deus, I sent healing energy.

Remembering in one class, Alberto had pleaded, "Please, if I should be dying, I beg you to send this sacred symbol to aid me. This is the one *most* important thing in the world you could do for me." Alberto was speaking about the use of a specific sacred symbol that assists a person during their transition. In receiving the strong message of his failing health, I proceeded to invoke Ama-Deus specifically using the sacred symbol for transition.

The first step was to clear my mind and light a candle to help create a sacred space. I had numerous experiences using this specific sacred symbol for transition for others, but not with someone personally close. The experience in connecting at this level to aid his soul was enlightening to say the least. In the afternoon, during the first session of tapping into Ama-Deus, several hours had passed, yet only seemed like minutes when opening my eyes and registering darkness. I came out of the session in such a state of feeling expansive Love, that my spirit was calm and at peace. This feeling gave me a sense of what he must be feeling. Not only did I sit for hours sending the sacred symbol to aid his soul during transition, I continued on after he passed, using a different sacred symbol used to assist the soul to move to the Light in peace. In this final process, there was a direct sense that he was surrounded in the glory of God.

He did not get to see his family. They were unaware of his death until someone called them. Coming from a good friend, who was with him close to his transition, Alberto's last words were, "I am silver . . . I am leaving before the marriage is complete."

As I learned from Alby, who never said *goodbye* to me: "There are no goodbyes, my dear. I am not leaving you." Instead, he would always end our conversation with . . . *Ciao*!

As news spread, the world mourned the passing of Alberto Aguas. I mourned the transition of my friend, my heart, and my mentor.

CHAPTER 2

What You Do for Others Lasts Forever

Nothing is too hard for me—it is too hard for my ego.
—Alberto Aguas

In July, during the summer of 1992, I was lost in some unfamiliar world. It certainly did not feel like earth. I had not been eating for almost three weeks. Communications were coming from Alberto that left me dazed and forlorn, especially during sleep. Once, I found myself suddenly waking, holding the phone, and realizing the conversation was really in my sleep. The scenes were that real, and I was that lucid.

Being awake only brought the feeling of a deep hole in my chest, as though my heart had been ripped from my body. I had no other feelings and no will to do, think, or feel anything. I was limp with grief emotionally, mentally, and physically.

Simply sitting in the old farmhouse and staring at nothing were all I could do. This was an alien feeling to me, since I am usually a person of great passion and much energy. In spite of this reality, deep inside, there was a sense of light at a very far distance. This image gave me a sense of understanding that, at some point, I would return to myself. I did not know how to cope or how long this "no feeling" state would last. Concerned friends had stopped by offering their compassion. One day, a dozen red roses arrived, delivered by one of these caring friends.

"These are from Alberto," she said. I stared in disbelief. How did she know these were his favorite flowers? She answered my quizzical expression with, "I got a message in a dream." Then another friend, who had no idea what was transpiring in my life, gave me a gift of a small hand-carved red cardinal for no reason. She said, "I saw this and thought of you and do not know why."

Two weeks into the ordeal, another concerned friend offered food. I was sitting on the floor of the small living room as Kathy entered the room. She had prepared a wonderful vegetarian dish and set it down on the floor in front of me, gently encouraging me to eat. Mechanically, I did as she requested. Not feeling or tasting the wonderful food, somewhere in my being, a strong sense of thankfulness for this friendship was stirring. A day or two later, another friend named Sally came to the house. She did not enter the house, but she handed me a book through the half-opened screen door saying, "I just thought you might like to go see this holy person with me. I have hotel reservations. The people that were going with me have backed out, so there is room in my car and room at the hotel. The book is on the life of this holy woman from India. Read it, and if you would like to go, let me know."

I do not remember speaking to Sally, only watching as she drove out of the driveway. Then looking at the book in my hands, I moved to the back of the farmhouse in the shade of a large oak tree and sat on the step to the back door. In the first pages, I became immersed in the life story of a unique woman born to serve the world. Her early childhood was filled with tremendous hardships. Her name was *Mata Amritanandamayi*. People called her Ammachi, and in her presence, simply Amma. This word, *Amma*, was familiar to me, and my constant reading of the word *Amma* was soothing and all so familiar to my Ama-Deus connection, which was constantly in my mind of late. I did not move from that back step until the last page. By then, it was late into the evening, and the shade from the tree had turned into the darkness of dusk.

The next morning, in a short conversation with Sally, I accepted the invitation to go with her to Chicago to see this holy person. The ride from Michigan to Chicago was a blur. The first recollection of this trip was encountering a steep driveway that led to a Hindu temple set on a small knoll in the Chicago suburbs. The architecture of the temple drew my attention to the many fascinating figured details. Upon entering, we were swept into the presence of a different culture through the smells, sounds, and sights that filled our senses. Western clothing was not dominant, and neither was the English language.

I spent my time observing the protocol so as to be respectful of the tradition. We learned that this holy person would be arriving soon. Several hundred people were present to receive her in the hall located beneath the temple. Two lines of people began to form from the entrance into the hall in preparation for receiving the revered guru. Suddenly, the hall erupted in song, and Amma, with a big smile, entered amidst the singing devotees who showered her with flowers. Amma, dressed in a pale lavender sari, was reaching with both her hands, touching the many extended hands and children's heads as she quickly passed to the front of the hall.

Taking her seat in front, Amma led everyone in devotional songs. After an hour of singing, people lined up in front of Amma. We learned that each person could greet Amma and receive her generous special hug. Waiting in line behind the others, I watched how to act and be with this guru as she blessed people with her grace through a hug. The devotees surrounding her quickly moved people in, and then out so that all could personally touch and connect in a timely manner with this great soul.

Specific key moments during those three days stand out for me. The first moment was my initial experience in her arms as she hugged me. Approaching her on my knees, she bent forward and brought me tightly to her chest while chanting a prayer. I felt her arms pulsating as she sang and held me tight. After the hug, she pressed her finger into some sandalwood paste, which she applied to my third eye in the center of my forehead. She held my head with her free hand as her finger applied the paste. My head tipped back from an unseen force, accompanied by the feeling of something warm flowing downward, inside the length of my spine. This held a calming essence, and I felt the tension in my body fall away.

The normal course of a hug with Amma ended after this sandalwood application. She would then present each recipient with a chocolate kiss candy mixed with a handful of blessed flower petals. Then her aides would hurry that person to the side, clearing the path for the next participant. Amma, however, said something, and everyone was suspended as she took an extra step with me. First, she sat back a little with outstretched arms, holding me at the shoulders. She was looking all around me, tilting her head side to side while speaking tenderly in her native tongue. She gazed into my eyes, and I lost the awareness of her speaking as the magnetic presence poured from her eyes. She took one of her hands from my shoulder and, in a wiping motion, swept the area of my physical heart. She did this wiping motion several times, gave me another firm hug, and put the chocolate kiss and flower petals in my hand.

This experience was very moving, stirring some life inside me. Did she have the ability to see my present life situation? I watched and observed that, on occasion, a change from her normal hugging routine occurred to accommodate other individuals' needs. I felt very blessed to have received Amma's love in this special way. This loving hug and blessed feeling moved me to participate with my surroundings and eased my sense of being out of touch. Maybe she was my light at the end of the tunnel. A sense of renewed strength that I perceived to have been received from her hug felt very welcoming.

My new willingness to participate sent us to inquire with the organizers about additional details for the different ceremonies with Amma. We found there were specific traditions in participating with Amma, and everyone was kind in directing us and giving us special attention as first-time participants. There would be three more opportunities to have a hugging session, an opportunity to receive a mantra directly from her, and the last evening would end with a *puja* ceremony. We were delighted to hear of all these opportunities, even though we were not sure what any of these ceremonies entailed. Moreover, Sally was delighted to see some new life come around for me.

Surrounded by a new language and customs, we attempted to move and integrate with the crowd, while Amma sat for hours and received individuals and families until everyone was seen. This is when the second memorable moment unfolded. Those who had already received a hug sat around her on the floor or on chairs set up further back in the hall. Some sang, others fervently chanted a mantra, and others simply watched Amma.

Sally and I joined the floor observers in front. My mind took in all the details of how the devotees worked with the crowds of people seeking to have a hug. All kinds of situations were occurring. Some people had special needs such as wheel chairs and were woven into the receiving line from the left side. Whole families had to be accommodated in one large group hug. Then I noticed a second line of people sitting on the floor to the right side of Amma. While she hugged people from a line in front of her, she would also talk to those people by her right side. I leaned toward a woman in a beautiful green and gold sari sitting crossed—legged on the floor next to me and, in a half-whispering tone, asked, "What is this second line of people doing?"

She replied with a warm smile. "Oh, this is when Mother will talk to you about any question you may have."

"Really?"

"Oh, yes. She will hug all these people you see in line, and in between or even during the hugs, she will answer questions to the people on the side."

"But I cannot speak the language."

"Not to worry. See the swami next to her?" I followed her eyes and found a large man in saffron robes standing somewhat behind Amma with a crowd of people around him. "He is doing any necessary translation from your question on a card for Amma."

"Ah, I see. Thank you so much." I rocked back from a cross-legged posture to gathering my legs tightly around my chest.

"Do not be nervous for your first time, Amma is so wonderful!"

"Okay." I smiled into her deep brown eyes that recognized my apprehension.

Shrugging my shoulders to Sally and without thinking, I approached the line for questioners. The line was short with only three people ahead of me. Sitting and being lower than the guru is the respectful posture. I wrote my question on a 3 x 5 card asking for Amma's thoughts concerning the passing of my dear friend and teacher Alberto. Surely, she saw something when wiping my heart area. Moving forward on my knees to the position of second in line, I watched the person in front of me having a direct conversation with Amma, as the swami reached for my card. When the person in front of me left and I was taking my position closer to Amma, everything began to happen very quickly. The swami was translating my note as Amma was reaching forward to hug a man. She abruptly stopped and broke into the swami's translation and turned to give me her full attention. Her eyes poured into mine as she spoke quickly. The person in her arms was momentarily suspended as she leaned down close to my face. Shrinking down and looking up at her presence in that moment was overpowering, and I looked to Swamiji for help in translation.

When Amma finished, the swami looked at me and replied, "She says that *YOU* are to carry on his teachings?" Swamiji's intonation of "you" seemed to be a question as he looked at me. I looked at Amma for further clarification, only to find that she had returned to being fully present with the man she was hugging. Clearly, she was complete in answering my question. I looked back at the swami, and he raised his eyebrows, cocking his head a little to one side, and returned my 3 x 5 card. The volunteers for Amma were moving me forward. I crawled away on my knees until I could stand respectfully out of the way.

I was perplexed with this answer, as I was expecting to hear something about Alberto's soul being freed, or a comforting message from him, or perhaps a few words about my heart that she had so carefully worked with during my hug. I felt numb and confused with this information. In a stupor, moving further away from the line and returning to sit down on the floor, I wedged in tight between the woman in the beautiful sari and Sally. Both were joyfully engaged with all the people singing bhajans. For some time, I listened to the songs and simply watched the rapture scenes of Amma continuing to receive everyone. I lingered on Amma's message and allowed the music and singing to blanket me as Amma continued her blessings. The translation of Amma's message could wait for another time. Closing my eyes, I entered the singing and swaying with the music—a most enjoyable feeling.

Amma finished seeing everyone several hours later into the early evening. She departed the hall for the night and returned in the morning to repeat the entire event the next day. Everyone sang as she left in a wonderful parting ceremony, and then people left. We did not want to leave the temple, as her presence seemed to linger in the air.

In fact, when Sally suggested departing for the hotel, I was reluctant to leave the temple grounds. So we sat on a curb in the parking lot, digested the events of the day, and shared our feelings of awe. Darkness came, and we ended up sleeping in the car. In fact, for the three days that Amma was there, we did not leave the property. The last evening was a *puja*, which is a ceremonial offering that lasted late into the night. Also, the event offered an open opportunity to receive a mantra. We stayed and participated in both events.

Sally and I headed home in the early morning after a short restful sleep in the hotel. How dazed and amazed we were at our magnificent encounters. Our four-hour return trip was effortless, full of conversation, and included my words of gratitude to Sally for giving me this opportunity. The weekend with Amma lifted me out of my deep sadness so that I felt my heart again.

The further we traveled from the temple, however, the more I was aware of descending into a heavy heart. I was exhilarated to be aware of this direct experience. My whole being in this moment comprehended a process. Amma's healing love inspired and lifted me up in order to move on. Contemplating this experience highlighted my understanding of how people could easily become attached to a guru by being in the energy of an advanced soul. One could choose to stay in their energy and not feel pain and not change, or one could continue their life knowing that, with practice, advancement on some level of spiritual understanding would occur from this experience. The intention of this guru was not to hold us, but rather to give us the support to move in a self-directed way to heal.

In addition, we were clearly fascinated by the turn of events with Sally that allowed me to attend. Truly, there is divine guidance. The feeling of love and the similarity to Alberto's Ama-Deus energy was very comforting, even the similarity in the words, Amma and Ama-Deus. Like Alberto's quoted expressions of love, Amma is quoted often also for she is viewed as the embodiment of Love, as with the following: "God realization is nothing but the ability and expansiveness of the heart to love everything equally."

Today, thousands of people go to see Amma, and she will sit for days until she has seen everyone. To be in the presence of the loving Amma seemed more than synchronistic; it was heaven-sent.

This beautiful gift of love from the Universe helped mend my grief-filled heart, lifting me up and giving renewed focus in my relationship with the Ama-Deus healing method. This foundation with Ama-Deus helped recall my experiences with this healing method, such as Alberto's words: "Nothing is too hard for me; it is too hard for my ego." This recent experience with Amma demonstrated this for certain: my ego was in pain, not my soul. Revitalized by Amma's loving presence, I returned home with renewed motivation to focus my attention on Ama-Deus.

For now, learning to trust and staying very grounded and comfortable in my relationship with Ama-Deus was a priority. My greatest gift became holding on to Ama-Deus, which was so dear to Alberto and so familiar to me. In my state of being renewed, Amma's message about teaching compelled me to revisit all that I had learned in the previous three years, especially Alberto's acknowledgements of my progress that transpired during his last seven months.

I realized that I had attended all the classes Alberto taught in the three years he came to Michigan. I had utilized the sacred symbols over and over in my daily life as well as in practice with others. I heard all the stories, as well as knew by heart all his meditations. This sacred oral tradition was imprinted in my heart, and I could recall it orally. After several months of reverent consideration and mindful intention, I now accepted my personal mission of teaching this sacred healing method in the exact manner and format as Alberto had taught me—with respect, integrity, and love.

Each of us creates paths in our life. At times, the feeling is like the stepping-stones are precast, landscaped, and invited our footsteps. Other times, there is struggle as though the ground is wet and slippery, sloping ever upward. Inch by inch, we struggle. Always, when we look back, our paths have meaning and purpose. They are uniquely ours and imprinted on our souls. Little did I know that, early on, all the classes I attended with Alberto and all the subsequent healing sessions were to equip me for this one profound choice. I was thankful to all who shared their concern and love during my grievous time and to Amma who put me back on track.

The Past Lights the Present

In addition to being precise about the delivery of sacred wisdom for the Ama-Deus classes, I also found the need to reconstruct Alberto's past. People were curious about Alberto's personal past, and with his passing, I felt a need to research the legacy of his life's work. Since most of our conversation revolved around spiritual work and present events, I had little knowledge of his early life. Even though he found ways to make you feel important in his life, Alberto was still a very private person. So the investigation started with searching out all the information in his personal files and speaking with the many people that knew Alberto.

In leafing through his personal files, I found a marketing ad that referenced a book in the numerous listings of Alberto's media coverage. My immediate reaction was to place a call for a search at the local library. Brilliant luck came through. A small library, thirty minutes from my home, had *Psychic Healers* on their shelf! I immediately reserved the book and drove straight away to retrieve it. I approached the desk and gave my name to the attendant for the requested hold. She reached for the book on a back shelf. As the attendant checked this book out to me, she glanced at the cover and, hedging for a moment, asked in anguish, "What is *this* about? Psychic healers!"

"Uh, yes, it is," I responded, feeling a little sting of intolerance and hoping to quickly move through the process.

"Well, we certainly are not in need of this book anymore!"

Holding my breath in anticipation of not knowing what she was going to do, I watched as she brought out a large stamp and marked the book, in big black ink, WITHDRAWN. She then marched, with the book in hand, over to the card catalogue. Still not knowing what was transpiring, I followed the woman, turning and smiling with delight in my eyes to my friend who accompanied me. The librarian turned from the catalogue cabinet and thrust the book and card into my hands. She brushed us out the doors as I was trying to ask if she needed any payment. There I stood with a big grin on my face outside the building in the evening darkness. Crossing the parking lot and heading to the car, I cried out in joy, "Thank you, Universe!"

I was thrilled to have the book in my possession, and it was mine to keep! However, after searching the contents later at home, I was dismayed to find the chapter on Alberto was missing. This was an earlier edition. So what were my next steps? Recalling from Alberto's conversation that the author's mother lived in the Midwest, I searched the yellow pages. The recently deceased author, David St. Clair, had been a close friend of Alberto. St. Clair helped him come to the United States in the early seventies and get started with spiritual lectures and healing career.

After further investigation, I found that St. Clair's mother actually lived close to my home. The phone call to Ruth St. Clair turned out to be a delightful occasion. She was pleased to receive the phone call, however, sad to hear that Alberto had passed. Ruth St. Clair was very gracious, and we had a wonderful chat on the phone.

"I am sorry to hear this news," Ruth said. "You know David has passed?"

"Yes, Alberto told me this."

"I remember so many funny stories of Alberto while he stayed here at the house. One time, he decided to go on a health kick. He was on an all-fruit diet and running long distances every morning. One morning, David and I were quite concerned for him as his coloring became so strange. But he assured us all was okay, and nothing happened."

"I knew that he loved to run but did not know of his all-fruit diet. I only knew his love of gourmet foods, and he loved to cook."

"Oh, yes, that too. How, may I ask, did you know Alberto?" I proceeded to give her a quick summary about Ama-Deus and my intention to continue the teachings.

"I have a paperback book here of David's that has the chapter on Alberto. I will send this to you. I would like you to have this last copy."

"Oh, wonderful, that is so kind of you, Ruth. Locating a copy of this edition has been difficult. I am really thrilled that you are willing to part with it! I would gladly return it after reading."

"Oh, no need." She hesitated for a moment, and then shared, "There is mention of Alberto, but not by name, in an earlier book by David. This gives a clue to how they first met while David was on assignment with *Time* magazine in South America."

"You mean *Drum and Candle?*"

"Yes. Let me see if I have an extra copy of it also. This book gives an interesting perspective of the Brazilian people in the subject of healing."

"This would be very helpful. Again, thank you so much, and please keep in touch. You are not far away. Maybe we could have a cup of tea sometime in the near future."

"Oh, that would be nice. If you have any other questions, please do not hesitate to call. I am not sure if I can be of some help, but I would try. Let me know also when you receive the package."

Shortly thereafter, in my hands were two books by David St. Clair filled with information about Alberto. Most of the information was familiar to me as I recalled previous topics in conversations with Alberto. However, careful details of his family background filled in the gaps—just what I wanted. One chapter in *Psychic Healers* filled in Alberto's personal family background. Also, in St. Clair's first book, *Drum and Candle*, a small but noteworthy paragraph indicated the beginning of their friendship. Ruth was right. This section also gave more insight to the Brazilian culture and the connection on how Alberto came to the United States.

I learned that St. Clair first met this "unusual" young man in the late sixties when living in Rio de Janeiro and writing his book *Drum and Candle*. St. Clair was introduced to Alberto through one of the country's best-known actresses. Alberto opened the doors for St. Clair's work by introducing him to the top Brazilian mediums. In *Drum and Candle*, St. Clair stated, "If it hadn't been for his [Alberto's] know-how and his reputation in the psychic field in Brazil, I would never have had the personal experiences and seen the fantastic ceremonies that I did."[2]

In *Drum and Candle*, Alberto is referenced in the end not by his name, but as an "actor friend," as follows, "then an actor friend came from another town to spend a few days with me. He was to start a soap opera on TV and to finish shooting a feature film. He is a good person and a good actor."[3]

Alberto specifically came for dinner to warn him of a curse that was put on him and also strongly urged him to do something before a catastrophic event occurred. St. Clair had no idea that Alberto was a healer when he invited him to dinner. He only knew him as an actor. *"He is also a spiritist. I didn't know that detail."*[4] St. Clair was reluctant at first to believe that he was in any danger from writing about the psychic and spiritualist movement in Brazil.

However, Alberto got right to the point of this visit after receiving information from a renowned medium, who had described a curse that was placed on St. Clair, blocking all of St. Clair's paths or venues for information. He listened and took heed in Alberto's warning. St. Clair said that his American mind dismissed such possibilities; however, his Brazilian mind told him the curse was real. Vivid details for the unraveling of this situation were convincingly portrayed in *Drum and Candle*, turning St. Clair's life around, allowing him to regain health and leave unscathed from South America.

This intense scenario set up a close friendship between Alberto and St. Clair and led me to understand how Alberto came to the United States from Brazil. Piecing together from Alberto's personal notes and conversations with his friends, we know that he left Brazil in the early seventies in a hurried fashion. Alberto became so embroiled with a group of influential people opposed to the military regime at that time that he was ordered to leave the country or else he might lose his life. Alberto did flee Brazil with nothing but his suitcase and entered the United States through the aid of St. Clair. In Alberto's personal tape sent to a dear friend, he described his feelings of leaving his country.

> I lost my country, my position, my identity, all my money. I had to learn all over again that I am not rich or have thirty-two servants or a limousine at my service, or unlimited funds. I cannot fly first class or be self-indulgent. I had been tortured mentally and physically by the government with electric shocks, and [they] had attempted kidnapping to kill me even when I was in San Francisco. I take this all with a grain of salt and I am happy doing my work here. I am very busy and there are extreme highs with this work, and there are lows. It is okay to feel the lows, as there are always the highs [sic].

In the United States, St. Clair initially housed and introduced Alberto to the psychic world in California. Besides being an author, St. Clair was very active in the psychic healing world, holding office in the *California Society for Psychical Research*. This involvement helped establish Alberto as a healer in the United States, eventually taking him on lecture tours in Europe as well. Alberto pressed St. Clair to republish his book to include a chapter about him in *Psychic Healers*. Finally consenting, St. Clair wrote a second edition inserting Alberto's story. This most certainly contributed to spreading Alberto's fame.

St. Clair's chapter is the only known written background of Alberto. As his reputation grew, numerous newspaper articles and television interviews featuring Alberto in the countless cities to which he traveled on his circuit of lectures and healings contribute to the authenticity of St. Clair's book chapter. These accounts can be found across the United States, throughout Europe, the United Kingdom, and Ireland, and across the Scandinavian countries from his back-to-back lectures on the spirit world and healing. Wherever he went, the lecture halls were packed, as his reputation grew for being an outstanding healer.

Furthermore, St. Clair's book gave assurance of accuracy because of the direct communication and review from Alberto. In his strong desire for St. Clair to republish his book to include his personal chapter, this must have been what he wanted the world to know. As we learn of Alberto's rich heritage contained in this chapter, one can understand how he could move and why he liked to move in the most elite of crowds, whether this was in Hollywood, London, or staying with counts in mainland Europe. But most important, St. Clair gives us a vivid glimpse at the foundation for his healing mission, which embraced all levels of people with all kinds of situations. Knowing his roots and early childhood helps to make sense out of the steps shaping his later years. Let's take a look at his personal background taken mostly from *Psychic Healers* and from some lectures.

In lectures, Alberto described his mother and his maternal grandfather. He spoke of his mother with great love. He recounted how she would take him, at a very young age, with her to an Espiritus Center in São Paulo as she did healings, sometimes allowing him to participate. He described his mother as being similar to that of a doctor of psychology. She came from a wealthy family in the north of Brazil. Her father was a surgeon and director of one of the largest hospitals in the area. Alberto's maternal grandfather was also interested in healing techniques and incorporated the knowledge of herbs he learned from neighboring indigenous peoples. At a very early age, Alberto was exposed to his life's mission as a third generation healer.

Alberto shared that his parents taught him about love and spirituality. As he spoke, he would close his eyes and describe so lovingly different personal exposures with his parents. For example, his father Octavio would take him outside at night, point to the stars, and tell him stories. Alberto became very emotional when he spoke of his parents, saying in the end, "My mother used to look like Susan Hayward, and my father looked like Clark Gable."[5] Anyone could see and share the intense feelings when he spoke of them.

The courtship of his parents was an instant love affair. However, in later years, this changed and was an emotional upset for him. His mother became bitter from the lack of a peaceful relationship. His father would go away for long periods of time even though they remained married. Alberto resorted to speak of the beautiful times proud of his heritage.

Alberto's paternal grandfather was a count and minister to Carlos I, King of Portugal. When the king was overthrown, revolutionaries pursued the family. His paternal grandfather put Alberto's father and siblings on a boat and sent them to Brazil, in the rubber rich state of Para. Mariquinhas was the oldest sibling at eighteen, who became the sole support to her two younger brothers and one sister, as they never saw their parents again. Mariquinhas quickly established her own home and bank account after a stay with a wealthy uncle in Para. "She was a beauty who knew how to make men squirm in her presence."[6] Alberto recalled being in her mansion when crates of goods came in from all over the world and witnessed her lavish entertainment. Alberto described his aunt Mariquinhas like the character in *Auntie Mame* and *Travels with My Aunt*.[7]

Mariquinhas, in this new country, became self-sufficient through business in oceanfront property, manufacturing, and imports. She was fluent in several languages, entertaining and traveling extravagantly; at one point, even coming to Hollywood to star in several silent films; nothing was too good for her living life to the fullest; keeping a watchful and protective eye on her younger siblings, even seeking out a bride for Alberto's father, Octavio. When Octavio presented the bride of his choice, Mariquinhas strongly disapproved, claiming he was marrying beneath him. This must have been a ploy, as Mariquinhas had been impressed with Alberto's mother's background. What most worried her was the political pressure that had come to the bride's family. She calmed down eventually and approved of the marriage, financing several factories and businesses for Octavio.

Alberto's mother Idalía was related to the Brazilian emperor with many of his aunts and uncles buried in the royal cemetery.[8] One of Idalía's brothers insisted on getting involved with politics, stirring people up against the central government. He was eventually captured by soldiers and taken out to sea, never to return. Soon after this event, the government exercised pressure on the rest of the family. Taxes were raised, friends avoided them for fear of their own lives, and these pressures resulted in Idalía's father losing his position at the hospital.

Idalía's father, Dr. Joaquim Felipe da Costa, eventually found work as a company doctor outside of São Paulo with a group of Englishmen building a railroad. Idalía helped to bring in money by teaching elementary school in São Paulo that was a two-hour train ride away. On one of these rides, she had noticed a man staring at her from another window. At the next train stop, she got off and so did he. After introducing himself, Octavio gave Idalía a chain that was around his neck . . . they were married ten days later.

Alberto shared that his father was an astute businessman and soon increased the value of the businesses that his sister, Mariquinhas, invested for him. Alberto described his life as abundant with maids, gardeners, fancy cars, and the very best schools. However, in the late sixties, unscrupulous partners and mismanagement forced his father to the edge of bankruptcy.[9]

Whether influenced by his Aunt Mariquinhas, the many famous mediums and celebrities that graced their home or both, Alberto was drawn into the world of film. Somewhere in the later sixties, Alberto emerged as a successful actor, starring in two known TV films: 1968 *Libertinas*, as directed by João Callegaro and Antonio Lima; and *O Terceiro Pecado*, directed by Sergio Britto. He won the Brazilian film industry's equivalent of the American movie industry's Oscars three years in a row.

His rich and opulent life did not hold him back from seeking truth, stepping forward, and speaking out. Alberto must have had a little of his mother's uncle in him as he also became involved in activities which opposed the political party. Alberto needed to quickly remove himself from the notice of Brazil's military dictatorship and the poor economic situation because of his ties with the opposition. As we learned earlier, the friendship with St. Clair was Alberto's ticket to the United States.

Once in the United States, Alberto settled with St. Clair in San Francisco. He practiced English and revived his healing skills. Very soon, the Metaphysical Bookshop on Sutter Street asked Alberto to lecture on Brazilian spiritism. The success of this lecture opened the door to private healing sessions. As a healer, his fame quickly spread, and he became booked several weeks in advance for appointments. People called at all hours of the day and night seeking help. St. Clair's dedicated chapter on Alberto in his revised book describes in wonderful detail the depth of Alberto's healing ability. The details not only demonstrate Alberto's natural ability to heal, but also his love for people and passion for his mission.

This quick success took Alberto to Europe through the help of St. Clair, who had arranged interviews with *Psychic News* in London, with the intention to find sponsors to host Alberto abroad. Also, at this time, Don Galloway, a medium from England, shared the stage with Alberto in 1978 in the United States at a Midwest Spiritual Frontier lecture. Galloway recognized Alberto's strong healing abilities and charismatic personality. As reported in London's *Psychic News*: "Alberto Aguas will be in London and several other cities [in the UK], thanks to the kindness and foresight of one of our nation's best-known mediums, Don Galloway. He was in the States in April and shared the platform with Alberto at the Spiritual Fellowship Assembly. He heard Alberto lecture, saw him channel the healing energies, and watched the results."[10]

Soon, Galloway had Alberto rearrange his busy schedule to include six weeks in and around London. Articles in major newspapers across the world continued to feature him in Germany, Austria, Switzerland, Denmark, and Sweden. He made several television appearances and documentary films and spoke on radio shows. Physicians called him from around the world to seek his advice.

Alberto was building a vast network of connections because of his renowned ability to heal. Sometimes he would drive several miles to help someone. When asked why he put himself out like that, he answered:

> People need me. We are moving into a strange period, a period of much unrest and confusion. People need to know the material world is not the only world. They need to have hope in the darkness. If I can act as one small light to make their darkness less fearful, I will do it. The time has come when all of us in the spiritual world must come forward and be ready to help.[11]

With this background information and myriad of stories, a rich tapestry of his private world was pieced together. Most assuredly Alberto loved life like his beloved Auntie Mariquinhas. Yet he was always an agent of truth. He had strong human desires like all of us to have a family, to raise children. Yet he gave his life first to helping others.

This life of helping others began as a small child of five. While his parents and grandfather were out of town, he feel seriously ill and was rushed to the hospital. From an interview in a London newspaper, he describes:

> I became dehydrated and was unconscious for three days. Later I woke and the whole room seemed to be coffee-colored. It was brown and gloomy. Then in front of me I saw little gold light moving up and down. I noticed it was 1:00 a.m. The next thing I remember was the morning light coming through the curtains. The clock showed it was 6:00 a.m. Five hours had lapsed. I found my hands on my head and solar plexus. I was well. I jumped out of bed and went home.[12]

Shortly after arriving home, a friend of his mother visiting the house was plagued with migraine headaches. Alberto confidently said he could help her. Placing his hands on the woman and reenacting what happened for him in the hospital, the woman was astounded and announced that her pain was gone. This act was the beginning of accompanying his mother to the healing center. As he grew, so did his ability.

Truly, Alberto's healing ability was exceptional. This was his claim to fame. More than an idea or belief, he took possession of his spirit nature and lived within it. From his notes, his lectures, news reports, he repeatedly described how he could see himself during a healing session.

While in a state of trance, Alberto would lift up, become separated from the confines of his body, and watch the metaphysical interactions below. The following is his description:

> First I have a very brief period of dizziness. My heart starts to pound very fast. Then comes a feeling of lethargy. Next I am not in my body. I'm up by the ceiling. I have left my physical body and see myself working. I watch myself place my right hand on

the patient's solar plexus, the left on the forehead. I believe that all healers work with the same energy. It is God's energy for all to use.[13]

Reports of great heat, calmness, and mental relaxation dominated the experiences of his sessions during which many fell asleep claiming miraculous healings. Accounts of smelling camphor during a healing session were also documented.

Miracles are random, although in the eyes of many, his healing method defied logic, the relationship he had with energy was not random. He said, "This healing power is all around me. It is an *Intelligence* that is always there. It is not because I want it to be there. It just is." Again and again, he insisted that miracles are not prevalent, and he strongly supported people to stay with their medical advisors.

He knew he existed as a spiritual being first and, from that reality, understood his purpose in the material world to be spiritual and to be a giver of Love. "I like to think that one hundred years from now, I will have been instrumental in putting one paving stone in the road to great things to come in healing."[14]

All in a Picture

In many cases, those in the medical field who knew Alberto's success rate referred patients to him. From his view of the person in need of healing, there was no competition with doctors and scientists, for he believed that "Love and healing can come from many sources. I have many people who come to me one time, and they are healed. Others come six times, and they are not. I will send them to other healers just as others send people to me when they cannot help. Most of the time, I am able to help."[15]

Also, there were scientists who shouted declarations of "Fraud!" toward Alberto and healers like him. With thousands of documented healings supporting his work, this was unjustified, and Alberto never attempted to duck from scientific review—quite the opposite. He said, "If scientists would come to me and admit they do not yet have the proper machinery, but were open-minded enough to see what would happen, I would work with them. They would give a little, and I would give a little, and possibly something could be born of that investigation."[16]

Months spent pouring over Alberto's notes, lectures, and newspaper interviews, and recalling personal conversations repeatedly brought to my mind his deep-seated sense of obligation to prove or demonstrate the validity of energy healing. Can we know or must we know for certain that our health—our mental, physical, emotional, and spiritual health—is fully dependent on Love, on this intelligence that surrounds his healing sessions? If it is true, we must know. To reach the Western mind especially, truth needs to be presented within a framework that is accepted in order to impact people's belief systems. In Western medicine, there is an obligation to seek evidence to support curative treatments, and nothing is true until put into a scientific framework.

The constant flow of questions from truth-seekers and the closed-minded jabs by mainstream scientists no doubt drove Alberto to seek researchers willing to explore energy healing through the tools of the scientific method. There are small news bits that Alberto had been involved with a study at Kent University. However, the event in the United Kingdom came closest to his dream. Here's the story.

Among his effects, I found photos with matching slides that showed hazy orbs and fuzzy oblong shapes surrounding unidentifiable people. The date on them read 1979. Among the photos were handwritten notes with a name underlined: Walter Kilner, St. Thomas Hospital, London. I looked up Kilner, thinking that he and Alberto had had conversations. Indeed, there was a Dr. Walter Kilner—the British Professional Medical Association replied to my correspondence. However, he died in 1920 at age seventy-three.

With this new information, my investigation was not over. What was his interest with this doctor? Kilner's book and several written papers point to Alberto's interest. Dr. Kilner performed some of the earliest photographic investigations capturing images of the human energy field.

So where did these pictures in Alberto's file come from? And what did they prove, if anything? I continued to dig and found something in a bundle of *Life Spectrum* newsletters. A photocopy on the cover page matched the ones in Alberto's file, and the headlines read "*Electronic Revelations in Healing.*" The article claimed the images to be individual slides taken from a video of Alberto performing a healing in the United Kingdom, and the technological details were still being analyzed. Below the images in the newsletter, photo credit was given to an electronic engineer named Trevor Stockill.

I was ecstatic. What did the video show? And where was it? Did anything ever come from it? Feeling there was something important here,

I could not let it go. Visual proof is such a powerful tool. Take X-rays for example; imagine a physician explaining the need for surgery without them. If Alberto found a reliable method for visually demonstrating the presence of energy specific to healing, I not only wanted the details, I had great ideas to replicate it! The photos depicting energy lines on a prone body found in his personal notes were definite beginnings, demonstrating that something significant took place in his healing sessions. There was no doubt Trevor Stockill could fill in the details, and I turned my keen attention to locating his whereabouts.

My luck was anything but good in finding people through his address book as it was twelve years since his passing. So using the address book to find Trevor was last on my list. People moved, died, changed addresses, and changed landlines to cell phones; all of which complicated the search. After retreating from several dead-end attempts to locate Trevor Stockill on my own, I contracted a private investigator, who found him within one week living serenely in Britain. As soon as the address was read from the investigator's report, the urge to check the old address book came through. Sure enough, the address was listed. There was something about the act of spending money that makes people suddenly intuitive. Sometimes fortune smiles, sometimes she shrugs her shoulders. I am pretty sure I heard Alberto laughing.

At first, Trevor was somewhat guarded around the reason for my interest. How could I blame him after being greeted with first introductions via a private investigator? After a couple of phone calls, he agreed to meet. The excitement was building in the prospects of getting closer to the search of the truth behind the photos. My son agreed to accompany me, and so flights were immediately booked to London. Ten years ago, practicing Ama-Deus, I never would have thought of myself on such a mission.

Sitting with my son outside in a crisp springtime morning breeze on the steps of the British Museum in London, we waited for someone I had only spoken with on the phone. Trevor was coming with his daughter, and we had agreed to meet on the steps of the museum at 10:00 a.m., and it was now ten minutes past. I pulled my scarf closer around my neck and looked at Christopher.

"Maybe we should try to call them?"

"Let's just give them a few more minutes."

Looking at every face that went by, I wondered which one was Trevor, and I never stopped to think how strange it was to fly three thousand miles to have lunch with a complete stranger. Intuition was running too strong and overriding any strange feeling for such action. Suddenly, a young woman appeared out of the crowd and caught my searching eyes. Keeping eye contact, smiles ensued as she approached the steps.

"Beth?"

"Yes?" She was beautiful, tall, and slender with graceful poised movement. Her kind face put me instantly at ease. She radiated warmth and kindness and seemed exactly the kind of person Alberto would have as a close friend.

"I'm Julia, Trevor's daughter."

"And this is my son Christopher."

Exchanging pleasantries with Christopher, Julia continued, "A little change in plans. Dad is coming from outside the city and will be here shortly. He was running late and asked if I would find you and determine a place to meet."

"Christopher and I have a special restaurant just down the street we thought would be a nice spot."

"This sounds wonderful. Let me phone my father and give him details."

A block away from the museum, the three of us entered a small Greek restaurant smelling of oregano and other pungent spices. We were early for lunch and had the restaurant to ourselves. As we settled into our seats, the door opened, and I looked up certain this was Trevor. Julia stood to greet her father with a warm hug and kiss on his cheek as he joined us at the table. He was a tall, large-framed man with a gentle countenance and dressed in a dark business suit. Julia introduced us, and after all the formal introductions, the waiter, who was singing "Opah," brought out bread and a large dish of *saganaki*, deep fried cheese doused in lemon juice. As the waiter flamed the cheese dish, an instant flash of light and heat projected on all of us. Setting the cheese dish on the table, we enthusiastically reached for a portion. Sitting directly across from me, Trevor was looking down and fingering his fork. He seemed to be intent on speaking rather than eating the appetizer. He looked up, met my eyes, and got right to the point.

I will never forget the first thing he said to me. He began, "I have had great hesitancy in meeting with you as you probably felt from our phone conversations. My wife is the one who had a strong connection with Alberto. She has passed away. Ever since Alberto died, many people have tried to contact me, to claim some part of his life or the other. I have politely ignored all of them. I do not know why I returned your call or why I agreed to meet. I just felt that it was right."

Riveted on his every word, my insides relaxed in hearing that it felt right. "I was also a little uneasy." Laughing away some of the tension and turning to my son, I said, "Which is why I brought Christopher! And yes, I did feel your hesitancy on the phone. However, I felt so strongly to meet with you." I hesitated for a second before saying, "I am sorry to hear about your wife, Trevor."

"It was difficult, but things are better now." Sensing from his tone and body language, this area of conversation was complete.

I turned to my satchel and pulled out a folder. "Here are the photos and slides from Alberto's notes." Trevor's countenance completely transformed. His eyes opened wide in delight when reaching for the photographs.

He excitedly started right in explaining. "Ah, yes, you see, here are the energy lines, and here is the orb. These are taken from the film. I would like very much to have a copy of these."

Answering in bursting enthusiasm, "Of course! Trevor, I am so thankful for your time and this opportunity. I feel like I need to do this, that Alberto would want me to, that it's important that this information is shared."

He paused for a moment, looked deep into my eyes, and said, "I'm going to share with you the original tapes. I had to dig through, find, and work the old Betamax tapes over to CDs. Some of the quality is lost, but the images are certainly all there." Trevor fished around in his briefcase to produce CDs in plastic cases.

Finally, the evidence was in front of me. I could hardly believe my eyes. "Oh my! Please tell me all about this story and let's celebrate with wine and food. I hope you like Greek food."

Together, Trevor and Julia responded, "Oh, we love Greek food! This was a lovely place to meet." All the tension of a first meeting and initial conversation melted away. Christopher and I smiled at each other, acknowledging our decision to eat at the Greek restaurant and for the wonderful unfolding with the meeting. The appetizer quickly vanished, and we ordered our lunch. The time together went too quickly as we immensely enjoyed each other's company and shared commonalities about our families.

I better understood Trevor's reason for being hesitant to meet with us after he explained his background with the situation. His relationship with Alberto was more than professional; they had a friendship. Alberto had stayed with Trevor and his wife Ruth many times and for several weeks at a time. Ruth had a passion for the occult. She opened her home to Alberto during his tour in England and assisted in scheduling healings. The Stockill's home became a respite for Alberto, and his presence there left long-lasting impressions. It was clear from his descriptions, Alberto felt comfortable in their home, and his playful nature captured the heart of the Stockills, especially their young daughter, Julia, or as Alberto called her, "Bananas." No longer a child, Julia still carried with her vivid, colorful memories of Alberto.

With laughter in her voice, she told me of one of her first memories. "From the very day I met him, I adored Alberto. I would sneak around the house watching his every move. To me, he was mysterious and wonderful. Alberto played right along. In my mind, I still picture him wearing beautiful magical robes, but I think those are the fanciful memories of a child. One morning, I crept as quietly as I could to Alberto's bedroom door and peeked into the keyhole to spy on him. Staring back at me was a very large eyeball. 'I see you, Bananas!' I heard him say, and then I ran, shrieking and laughing down the hallway. I pretended not to, but I loved that he called me Bananas."

During one of Alberto's stays with the Stockills, Trevor brought specialized equipment into his home office for an ongoing project. From a heavy large case, he removed and assembled a video camera, sensors, cables, and a variety of lenses designed to record infrared thermal energy. Alberto looked on with curiosity and undivided interest, and he peppered Trevor with questions. As Trevor described the camera's functions, Alberto pondered its potential, "If this equipment captures and measures energetic information that most people cannot see, I wonder how it compares to the things I see? Will you record me while I'm doing a healing? I'd like to see if the camera sees as I do."

That evening, the two men set up a room with the camera and a healing table, and Ruth, as the subject for the healing and recording, waited in the wings. The attempts that evening to use the recording equipment came up with nothing. Everything functioned as it should have, and Trevor made numerous adjustments, covering every aspect he could think of to bring about results of any kind. Alberto was disappointed. For so long, a big part of his identity had been encompassed by something that most people could not see or immediately relate to. He was gifted with an intangible relationship of great importance, and he had high hopes of being able to better share this relationship and the incredible good that it could do if others could better identify with it somehow.

A week passed, and in his mind, Alberto could not let go of the thought of filming a healing. Something inside him urged him to try again. He brought the matter up with Trevor again. A public lecture and healing session were scheduled at Stansted Hall of Arthur Findlay College, northwest of London, and Alberto, undeterred by the possibility of public failure, asked Trevor to once again set up the equipment.

"It's not going to work," Trevor said, confident that he had tried everything he could do the first time around.

Alberto grinned and put his hand on Trevor's shoulder. "It'll be different this time," he said.

In the stately and spacious meeting room of Stansted Hall, Alberto sat in darkness, his hands hovering above a woman lying on a massage table before him. Heavy curtains covered the windows to hide the glow of the nighttime streetlamps, and the only sources of light were small buttons from the electronics of the camera equipment and a stereo in the corner. The audience in attendance sat motionless, their eyes fully dilated to the lightlessness, and their ears captured every timbre, every musical note softly playing, filling the air around them. First was *Albinoni's Adagio in G Minor*, then the ethereal *Spectrum Suite* by Stephen Halpern. The electricity of anticipation touched each person like a shiver.

Moments before, while the lights were still on, Trevor removed the plastic wrapper from a brand-new videotape. He inserted it into the camera and recorder. Alberto had briefly explained to those in attendance that the healing would be recorded and carried out in dimmed light, and other than that, it would be no different from any healing he offered to anyone.

"I ask that you be silent and focus your thoughts to a single point of Love," Alberto said. With a smooth poised stride, he walked over to the stereo and started the music. Then he sat down next to the woman, looked into her eyes, and smiled lovingly. He closed his eyes, tilted his head back slightly, and took in a deep breath through his nostrils. The look on his face expressed pure peace and serenity.

"Please turn down the lights," he said. As he was raising his hands over the woman, the visible vibration of light left the room. Minutes passed in semidarkness. The attendees were now relaxed. Regardless of their ability to see it, all sensed the energy of healing and of Love in the room. It had always been there, only now their hearts acknowledged its presence.

Trevor concentrated entirely on the camera's viewfinder. Every few minutes, he averted one eye in the direction of Alberto, bewildered and praying that what he saw through the modified lens was being recorded to the videotape.

After twenty-five minutes, Alberto expelled a deep breath and spoke calmly, "There, that's it. You may turn the lights back up." He walked to the stereo, turned it off, and then approached the woman. Putting his hand on her shoulder, he softly said, "Please lay comfortably as long as you like, and when you're ready, you may sit up." She nodded her assent.

As Trevor rewound the videotape and set up a television monitor in the center of the room, Alberto slid the healing table off to the side. "This table has more miles under it than most of the automobiles parked outside, I dare say. But I don't think it has ever seen a massage." Alberto laughed out loud, as he often did to his own humor. The spirit of his laughter was hugely infectious. "I try always to call it a healing table, but I just get blank stares. No one knows what a healing table is. There has never been a table made for healing, as you know, because healing is a spooky thing. We need to change everyone's minds. Hit them in the pockets. Everybody go buy a massage table and say that it is for healing! Eventually, they will surely change the name." There was a ripple of acknowledged laughter from the audience.

Trevor and Alberto sat next to each other, off to the side, but near the monitor. The lights were dimmed once again, and the recording of the session played. For the first minute, the screen displayed a bright white; the lights of the room were still on at this point, overpowering the sensitivity of the camera's lens. Through the monitor's tiny speakers, the recorded sounds of the serene music could be heard. And then Alberto's voice saying, "Please dim the lights."

Near blackness filled the screen. Barely visible, the silhouette of two human forms blushed a subtle grey. Minutes passed. Nothing. The gentle melody of Adagio in G Minor continued to play uninterrupted by any visual change. And then at minute six on the tape, an anomaly appeared. Hardly noticeable at first, a small circular orange shape hovered above what were surely Alberto's hands. As moments passed, the shape glowed with increasing intensity and definition, and around the orange circle, a separate, distinct aura appeared.

"Oh my, oh my god," whispered Alberto. His was not the only astonished voice. All around the room, murmurs circulated like electricity through a live wire. The orange ball or sphere suddenly zigzagged erratically on the screen, and then stopped.

Trevor turned to Alberto and said, "That was my fault. I thought I might try to get a clearer focus, and I jolted the camera accidentally. This is as sharp as I could get it."

"Oh, it's wonderful," said Alberto.

Around the body of the woman, colored lines shimmered softly. Gradually, this curtain of light grew brighter and pulsated. It seemed alive. The brightness and coloration of the lines changed and moved in waves along with the tones and rhythms of the music in the background. Gasping sounds were heard from the audience. It was beautiful and staggering to watch.

Alberto leaned closer to Trevor and said, "Do you see how the colors shift and get stronger over the different areas? The energy moved exactly like that! There is meaning to the colors."

From the left edge of the television screen, streams of white light appeared. Within the rivulets, brighter droplets of light sparked and swirled and entered into the curtain of rainbow colors that surrounded the woman. Although an exact entry point could not be concluded, it was plain to everyone that the greatest amount of light was directed at the woman's abdominal area. The streams of energy maintained this state for nearly ten minutes before it dissipated.

Everyone was astounded with this physical demonstration. The room erupted in joyous enthusiasm. The stunning display of energetic lines marked a historic moment for all in attendance.

Neither Trevor nor Alberto willingly drew any firm conclusions from the recording, save one: more study was needed! The video was shown one other time before an audience in the United States. The audience's reaction, as in the United Kingdom, was overwhelming. It was not a decision made lightly, but Trevor and Alberto chose against ever displaying the video again in a public forum.

In a return trip to London, I had the privilege to review the recorded session in Trevor's sophisticated home office. While we reviewed the computer monitor, I asked questions.

"Why were the two of you hesitant?"

"At that time, the intention for requesting access to this work was not coming from a spiritual or scientific gain. We did not have the right connections in those fields of study. About the only thing we would have gained would have been popularity, and that was not our goal. An explosion in popularity would have been disastrous to the work Alberto was accomplishing in his own quiet way."

"Whoa!" I interjected, turning our focus back to the monitor in a gasp, "Look! That is the same image from the photo, the sphere of orange-gold light."

"Yes, it is."

"Trevor, do you know that in a news article in a London paper, Alberto described the image of a gold orb that he saw when he first healed himself at five years old? Perhaps this orange-gold orb that is captured on this film is what he was referring to. Wow, how remarkable is this!"

This hazy gold orb was an enlivened image on the screen as Trevor continued to narrate and walk me through the remainder of the film. The original Betamax recording was carefully restored and digitized, but because of the age of the film, along with the transition from a less-revealing low-tech format, there was no good way to derive conclusive data. With or without evidence, Trevor still held the opinion that the images of energetic lines were a direct result of Alberto's healing. The discussions moved to the idea of replicating this study as the technology for imaging had improved. Fired up in reviewing the data, I could see that the thrill of discovery in Trevor's scientific mind reignited every time he contemplated the memory of that day. He expected certain failure; instead, he walked the line between science and the unexplained.

In the years following the recording of the healing, those fortunate to be present continued to talk of the momentous event. I heard from people in the United States who were present for the showing in the United States as well as those attending the initial showing in England. Some months after this trip, I answered an unexpected call from a foreign student. This student shared about a manual of his uncle that referenced this event from an institution in the Middle East. The manual was mailed to me, and in reading it, I found that in attendance at Stansted Hall was Moiz Hussain, a professor from *The Institute of Mind Sciences and the Reiki Spiritual Foundation* in Pakistan. Professor Hussain wrote of the recorded healing in academic detail in his teaching manual as a means to support the scientific investigation of energy healing for his students. I am not sure if Alberto ever knew of this reference.

Although Alberto's dream to validate energy healing had taken very small steps forward, he was encouraged by the growing interest of researchers worldwide in this field. Today, there are several scientific investigations in imaging human energy fields with encouraging results.

Harry Oldfield, one such researcher, agreed to meet with me in London during a subsequent visit to pass Alberto's photos through his imaging device. Immediately, upon seeing the enhanced image, Harry exclaimed, "Oh my god, you need to keep these in a very safe place. I would not even let the queen have these!" Again, a spiritually minded scientist laid bare the importance of the photos. Alberto would have loved Oldfield's comment.

◊ ◊ ◊ ◊ ◊

Having answered the story behind the photos and still slides of the energy currents, the next step was to make sense of the remaining files that were crammed with lectures and presentations on Ama-Deus healing. His life was traveling the psychic circuits of global conferences that were open to his kind of work. He was always asked to lecture, to lead a healing circle, and do healing sessions. This he did all over the world.

After several years of being in self-exile, Alberto yearned to return to his homeland. The eventual change in the Brazilian government opened the way for Alberto to return to his roots. His files and travel schedule indicated an abrupt turn of events that occurred when he returned to Brazil.

Suddenly, he made a trip to Brazil and, in a short order, became involved with this particular Guaraní tribe. He reconstructed his work to be half the year in Brazil and the other half on the road in North America. He was developing Ama-Deus and was only doing the tour in the United States and in Canada.

No longer on a yearly lecture schedule in North America and Europe, he devoted half the year to living in Brazil. The other half, he continued to travel his familiar circuits. However, his lectures changed to incorporate his new experiences in meeting, studying, and working with the Guaraní from the Amazon. Taped lectures, as well as his personal lecture notes written in Portuguese titled *The Amazon Kingdom of Healing*, are clear, beautifully descriptive, and moving accounts of his journey with the Guaraní. In these early lectures, he speaks of a healing method that he called Ama-Deus and was learning from these wonderful people. In the short time that he had to learn, and then share, Alberto was only able to teach Ama-Deus in North America.

My own probing further into the Guaraní gave astounding evidence of their spiritual nature, and I realized more fully Alberto's sudden shift in his life to be with them. Something seemed to be precast with his involvement—the Guaraní knew he was coming. His last strong mission was to stand up for the human rights of an indigenous people who were losing their way of life. More importantly, before Alberto passed from this life, with encouragement from the Guaraní, he preserved an ancient healing system—a precious piece of sacred wisdom. I sense it was his greatest accomplishment and gift to the world.

CHAPTER 3

The People of the Forest

True religion is real living; living with all one's soul,
with all one's goodness and righteousness
—Albert Einstein

Before Europeans gave them this name, the Guaraní simply called themselves "*Ava*," meaning men. Alberto used the European-given name of *Guaraní*, meaning People of the Forest. He lectured that the Guaraní could be included and ranked as one of the oldest existing indigenous peoples in the world and estimated their cultural history as spanning more than six thousand years.[17]

My first glimpse of these people came in listening to Alberto during classes. One could picture a simple people who lived a highly spiritual life and who were willing to share with a white man their sacred ways. I found more details of Alberto's experiences in his files of personal handwritten notes in English and some in his native Portuguese.

Alberto described in more depth the people's way of life, as well as his experiences in working side by side with the pajé—shaman. The Guaraní received him with unconditional love, never questioning—always giving and always sharing. He spoke of how deeply spiritual a people they were, having reverence for all life. Alberto said, "The rivers, the vegetation, the trees, the mountains, the stars are *all* regarded as their home. Everything is unconditionally spirit and soul."[18] This unconditional relationship with all life is what maintains their spiritual balance; it gives a healthy earthly life and peace of mind.

He strongly pointed out the reverence and respect that is especially extended to all the children, as they are understood to be reincarnated souls. Reincarnation "is fundamental to the life and existence to the tribe."[19] Children are held in very high esteem with the Guaraní. Alberto completely subscribed to this life view and loved to talk about how the Guaraní related to their children.

My firstborn brought this perspective to life hours after my father passed away. During the last three months of my father's life, my two sons and I were living under the same roof with my parents. A special bond unfolded between my father and my three-year-old Michael. They had an uncanny way of completing each other's thoughts. When my father was hospitalized and drawing near to transitioning, I made arrangements for a family friend to stay the night with Michael. Michael slept, while my mother and I left for the hospital, taking my two-month-old along and planning to stay until my father's passing.

We returned home at 5:00 a.m. to the presence of family members and all their conversations, which woke Michael. I quickly went to his room, picked him up in my arms, and held him tight while walking back to the family room where everyone was gathered. While walking, I carefully found the words to speak of his grandfather's passing. We had been preparing for this moment by reading some children's books that related stories of losing a grandparent. As my father became weaker, Michael understood how the stories we read related to his grandfather. Holding my son tightly, I said, "Michael, grandpa has passed away."

Instantly, he was upset, shouting out, "You did not take me with you. You did not take me to see him! I needed to say goodbye, Mom!"

"Oh, Michael, I am so sorry I did not help you with this." He held my neck tightly and cried. Fumbling in my mind, I wondered how to soothe his soul and find an adequate response.

He lifted up his head, touched my face with both hands, hesitated for a split second, and then spoke in complete confidence with a tender, sincere voice, "Do not worry, Mom, Grandpa will be born again."

I stopped walking, looked deep into his eyes in complete wonderment of where this thought came from, and finally answered, "Yes, Michael, Grandpa *will* be born again."

My mother responded to this small interaction, "Out of the mouths of babes." From that point on, Michael held the entire funeral event as a celebration. He loved being with all the people and talking about his grandfather.

This was only one significant time of many that my children reminded me of how wise and thoughtful they can be. When Alberto first met my children, he straightened his composure as he spoke in a reverent tone, "Hmm, two very old souls." Attempting to keep this fact in mind in birthing and raising my children, I know I am only the caretaker for these beautiful incoming souls.

In my role as loving caretaker for children, I was captivated in how the Guaraní relate from a soul perspective with their children. According to Alberto, the parents taught their children that home does not end at the entrance of the door; the earth, trees, vegetation, birds, animals, lakes, rivers, seas—all are a continuation of their home. Several Guaraní families slept and gathered as one family unit under a wooden dwelling with palm-thatched roofs. Within the structure, a fire was always lit. When I eventually visited the Guaraní myself, I rarely heard a crying child, which is common in their communal culture.

The Guaraní teach the children meditation, as they, like everyone, are presumed to have the ability to work with healing energies. Some children chant to develop a recognized natural ability to become pajés or shamans. Those children who study to become a pajé learn about healing plants from the elder women who specialize in keeping knowledge of the plant kingdom. Some examples of these plants are the *crues* vine to help the liver, the *pipi* for cold and flu, *carqueja* to aid the stomach, and the pink flower (*pau d'arco*) for cancer.[20] Other plants are used for preservatives, compresses, and teas as the Brazilian Amazon Basin houses hundreds of thousands of species, which are healing in their medicinal properties.

The pajé is the spiritual leader and guide for the Guaraní community. In his training, he learns how to be calm and sweet with people—he is not like a dictator or judge. From this training, he learns to "respect other forms of cultures, governments, and white men."[21]

The house of prayer has the same construction as their homes and serves as the place the entire community meets unconditionally every evening. Alberto spoke of the nighttime gatherings and how mesmerized the people became as they fixed their focus on the stars and the moon.

The Guaraní house of prayer serves as the spiritual center for the village and the people's center of focus. When Alberto lived with the Guaraní, he joined the entire village every evening without fail to pray, meditate, and perform healings. The women would prepare two drinks. One was sweet for social commemoration called *kangui* and the other, *kanguijy*, is bitter and only used by the pajé during healing. The men used instruments like guitars and play them like violins. Of great importance to the forest people is the belief that music helps their meditation—music keeps them close to God, to the Source of healing.

The singing of sacred songs created a sense of closeness to the spirit world for the Guaraní. Everyone in the village sings as the pajé moves into trance. The pajé begins each evening ceremony by lighting his pipe and creating lots of smoke. He will sing, dance, and chant, while all in attendance support him in singing sacred songs.

Alberto noted that when the songs were sung, he had felt an unmistakable physical vibration, some unexplained sensation that was palpable in the body beyond normal hearing. When the connection was felt or physically perceived and a vibration was established, the pajé started the healing ceremonies. He then became the *Ñande Ru*—the Guaraní term for the most sacred form of being their "Father." Alberto also noted the pajé drank a lot of tepid water and repeatedly said or prayed the word *Ñandéva* as he worked. Ñandéva is a Guaraní word for the love aspect of God (it literally means all the people), the essential ingredient in the Guaraní healing process.

After two and a half years of living with them and gaining their trust, they finally allowed him to participate in ceremonies and granted him free access to the *Opy*. Alberto had the honor of being at the side of the pajé, watching and working with him during the healing. Alberto revealed, at the end of a healing ritual, how the entranced pajé as Ñande Ru honored and touched him at the core of his heart by calling him Ñandéva—the love of God.

The Guaraní do not believe in illness; they see everything as spirit and believe that outside forces cause imbalance. If the outside force or unwanted spirit or energy is removed, the effect upon the physical, emotional, and mental state of a person will be released and balance will be restored.

Many people from outside the village came for healing; some stayed for twenty-one days. Special diets for healing were observed by the pajé as well as the people who came for healing. The Guaraní understood the concepts of meridians and used bamboo shoots in the earlobe as a practice of acupuncture. During the twenty-one day healing sojourn, community members lovingly brought sacred water from the Amazon, shared special foods to aid the healing process, offered massages, acupuncture treatments, information from their dreams, and the Ñandéva—all unconditionally shared.

At the time that Alberto was working together with the Guaraní, the social impact of the loss of their land was a primary concern. He observed many times that the tribal members became annoyed and sad because "the white people were always looking to take something, and they always brought illnesses on purpose and not on purpose."[22] Alberto worried about the younger generation and the psychological impact from deforestation and the literal loss of their home. Alberto was so concerned for their well-being he orchestrated for psychologists to come to the village to help with the situation. This was during a time when the Guaraní adolescents were hanging themselves due to the pressures of a culture losing their identity and facing relocation and the loss of their land.

During one of these very stressful times in the village, Alberto approached an *enchanted woman*, who had the ability to see into the dream state. As he approached this one, in tears, he poured his heart out to the dreamer. She replied to him, "If you create your own reality, you have nothing to worry."

Alberto passionately declared to his later audiences, "Here was someone who was watching the destruction of her home and culture and still had clear understanding and great spiritual awareness."

Alberto became an extreme activist for the Guaraní rights and joined such organizations as *Save the Rain Forests Foundation, Greenpeace,* and *Amnesty International.* The outspoken demonstrations and struggle to help the Guaraní sent Alberto several times to a Brazilian jail. These encounters with the Brazilian government forces brought jail time and severe torture; one of which was electrical shocks that resulted in physical trauma, another was the contraction of diseases such as cholera. The police confiscated all of his notes, herbs, and any material related to his experiences with the Guaraní. This inhumane treatment and the ravages of diseases contracted in the Brazilian jails led to the breakdown of his health; however, this did not sway his determination to help the Guaraní.

Throughout Alberto's presentation lectures, the passion to save the Guaraní and their homeland was unmistakable and gave insight to his beautiful relationship with these people. Alberto did not share the location of this particular people. Finding indigenous peoples of the Amazon not known to the world at large quickly reached the news.

Interactions with the indigenous are of public interest, and this would never happen through Alberto.

Alberto expressed the danger involved with indigenous contacts. There was the physical environment to consider, and the indigenous struggle for land with the government in the early eighties was intense. I found this quote in a taped lecture in which Alberto explained this struggle in his broken English,

> I will be starting this year in my tour doing a shut off, [meaning that he would change his travels] to spend time with the tribe that I have adopted. Of course, I am not an Indian . . . I wasn't born in the Amazon jungle. What they have taught me. They are very selective. They do not like to teach the white man because they think the white man only comes to take from them, never to give or to divide [share]. And when the chances, and this is just circumstantial, that I could get there in the heart with them was because my uncle and because my cousin are very life threatened if you start to expose these to the outside world [sic].[23]

At one point, when Alberto left to come out of the jungle, the cacique touched him on his heart and simply said, "Do not forget the Ñandéva." The cacique once told Alberto they were willing to share all their cures, herbs, and Ñandéva. Their only wish was to keep their land—the gift of the great father Ñande Ru for the forest people to maintain a spiritual life.

Even though the government had confiscated Alberto's notes during his imprisonment and all earthly possessions relating to the Guaraní, they could not take away his initiation on the banks of the Amazon. He held tight in his heart their sacred ways for healing. The passionate Alberto taught their healing method in respect to the Guaraní who appealed to him to share the Love, the Ñandéva, with the world. In reverence to preserving a sacred ancient oral tradition, Ama-Deus healing method is a gift from the Guaraní and a sacrifice from Alberto Aguas.

Before moving into any further descriptions of Alberto's teaching of the Ama-Deus method of healing, I have provided an in-depth look into the Guaraní, caretakers for thousands of years of this sacred oral tradition. Alberto's stories were more than confirmed. Recordings over the past several centuries of mystical stories of Guaraní life confirmed their culture carried an oral history of immense spiritual significance. Certainly, this gives a clearer understanding of why Alberto was so enamored with the People of the Forest.

PART II

A HISTORY OF THE GUARANÍ

♦ ♦ ♦ ♦ ♦

Mbaracambri hastened to the side of the dying elder pajé. The pajé in garbled, whispered tones expressed in earnestness for Mbaracambri to pray, "Do not stop! Do not stop! Mbaracambri, you must pray and dance all the time. Do not be weak in your prayer. Prayer will keep you on the right path. Pray and dance to receive the sacred luminosity. You must now be the main pajé to bring forth the word souls for the good of the forest people." As he finished his plea, Grandfather Pajé closed his eyes and relaxed his body in the hammock. He smiled and mumbled a sacred chant, a song that would lead his way to the land with no evil. Mbaracambri buscó su maraca cerca de la cabaña desde la que había presenciado el ataque. Necesitaba su instrumento sagrado para rezar como había pedido el anciano.

Mbaracambri searched for his rattle near the dwelling where he encountered the attack. He needed his revered instrument to pray as the elder had requested.

Tangara came to Mbaracambri's side and exclaimed, "We must retaliate, Mbaracambri!"

Mbaracambri spoke directly to Tangara, "Go and look upon the suffering people and return after you have done what is needed. I now must sing to Grandfather Pajé's departing soul." Tangara watched with compassion as his friend, who lost his wife and son, retrieved his sacred instrument, his mbaraká.

Mbaracambri turned in the direction of the failing pajé, as Tangara respectfully moved to do as he was bid. Several people already gathered around the elder pajé. Mbaracambri raised his sacred gourd to begin his farewell song to the elder's soul when suddenly he heard his name.

"Mbaracambri! Come close, do you see? It is so bright. I see the luminosity. My heart is swelling with the love of Ñandéva ... I am hearing beautiful word souls ... Listen as I speak these beautiful words!" Mbaracambri lowered his raised arm holding the mbaraká and leaned his ear close to his grandfather's face to better hear the elder. "The forest people will take a journey, where the beginning and the end are different but the same." With his voice trailing softer with this last message, the elder whispered, "The stones, retrieve the sacred stones, Mbaracambri," and then he took his last breath. The women *wailed in grief. Mbaracambri took to heart the elder's last message and started singing.*

Opening his arms wide, Mbaracambri sang in great feelings of love to Grandfather Pajé. Others joined him. He could feel the energy building as the singing eventually took hold through the entire village. With his eyes closed, Mbaracambri watched as a silver cord released from the elder's body, and a twinkle of light moved in a scintillating stream toward the path where the great light of Kuarahy rises. He then witnessed a showering golden light descending upon the forest people, filling him with the ecstatic Love. Mbaracambri knew he and his people of the forest were not alone. As he received this energy of Love, he poured out from his heart to the elder and all the people, even Tupanchichù and his warriors. This golden blessing he knew to be his support and strength; without it, there could be no life and no direction. And so his heart poured out songs of gratitude to Ñande Ru.

Mbaracambri slowly opened his eyes. For a moment, he was not aware of the length of time of the chanting. He located the position of the great Kuarahy, which now had traveled little more than halfway across the sky. Tangara was there near his side; women were still wailing at the loss of their elder pajé and others that were lost in the skirmish. His son Veraju had a long gash on his leg but was well. Mbaracambri felt himself back in his body and spoke to the village people asking for their help to wrap the elder pajé in his hammock and carry his wrapped body into the house of prayer. Veraju nodded his willingness to help.

Tangara took a moment with Mbaracambri to share the news of the village, "Mbaracambri, there are only two others who were caught with arrows and few with slight injuries."

Mbaracambri sighted those families who had slain members and spoke directly to them, "Let us help the souls and prepare the bodies for travel to the land with no evil. Women, please gather all the personal items of your loved ones, and, men, reverently place your loved ones in two kangui jars. In your dwelling, dig a place in the earth to hold the earthen jars. When this is done, we will all gather in the Opy with the resting of the great light and sing to the departed souls for a safe journey. We will sing and dance until darkness to then follow the light of Jesyju."

Of all the people in the village, Mbaracambri had received the greatest number of sacred songs. He had demonstrated many times to the community his ability to speak with Ñande Ru and the minor gods, receiving songs and visions for several seasons now. He worked alongside the deceased elder pajé. The people now looked to Mbaracambri for leadership. Mbaracambri felt his heart heavy in thinking of his wife and son. He had lost his first wife, the mother of Veraju and Kitu, by a great cat as she was working in the fields of manioc and maize. His present wife Yyvkuaraua was the elder pajé's daughter. She apprenticed as a healer with her father since a young age. She received her song for healing in a dream as a young child. As was their custom not to extend into intimate relations when studying the sacred ways, marriage for Yyvkuaraua came later in life. She chose Mbaracambri several moons after the passing of his first wife.

A full season of maize passed after their marriage, when Mbaracambri, after several days of dance and chanting during the harvest celebration, received a wonderful dream. The gods called him to follow to a place of great beauty. He was shown of an incoming great soul that would arrive soon to him and Yyvkuaraua. In preparation for this incoming soul, Mbaracambri and Yykuaraua changed their daily routines to a special way of eating certain foods and restricting actions of work, as this was the way of the forest people. The incoming soul was held in high esteem, and this reverent regard continued through inception, gestation, birth, and for several months after the soul is born.

The birth of Arapotiyu brought great joy to their family and to the community of forest people. Grandfather Pajé presided over the naming ceremony that brought forth the powerful message when he received his grandson's name, Golden Flower of the Day. Mbaracambri watched as the elder pajé gave close attention in the raising of this child as he could see the special abilities and the role he would play for the forest people. As the child grew and came to reside frequently with Grandfather Pajé, it was announced to the community that Arapotiyu would also be involved in any healings needed by the village.

All this flashed through Mbaracambri's mind as he surveyed the village. He was brought back to the present with the many concerns and questions from the dazed forest people. He fought off the melancholy feelings and returned to his song and heart, feeling the golden light. Taking on the elder pajé's role, Mbaracambri directed people to carry wood to the dwelling where the bodies were interred in the kangui jars. Wood was needed to keep the fire lit for the two days of singing. The feet of the deceased were placed in the direction of the rising light to help the soul find the path to the beyond. The fire illuminated the path for the ascending soul to the land of paradise. To the forest people, it was important to aid the soul to move to the land of paradise, the land with no evil. Death to Mbaracambri and the forest people was not fearful or sad, as the soul does not die and may be reborn.

The only fear of the forest people associated with death is the anguêry or wandering souls. They are more feared than their attackers. Mbaracambri held strong to prayers that led the community in support of the transitioning souls to the luminosity and not to be left to wander the forest. The forest people in great sincerity of heart and devotion followed Mbaracambri in song to assist the souls to the luminosity, toward the land with no evil.

As Mbaracambri organized the ceremonies and the gathering at the Opy, Tangara came to his side and indicated again his willingness to track and regain their people.

"We are close friends, Tangara. As a youth, you were attracted to the dances that make the body quick, strong, and agile in flight for hunting. This day, you are the leader in the sacred songs and dance for hunting. On the other hand, I always looked to develop my poriee. The elder is gone. Our good friendship with our many songs between us will help the village to gain mbiroy. The village needs your strength here in the Opy. This is the way of the forest people to listen to the gods, as their messages will give us true guidance." Just as Mbaracambri finished speaking, Kitu softly approached and placed a gentle hand on Mbaracambri's shoulder.

He turned from Tangara to his daughter and spoke to her in a gentle soothing tone, "Do not worry, my dear child, for your second mother is very wise, and she was not harmed. We must pray for a safe return. The great light Kuarahy is showing signs of resting, and we will be entering the Opy soon. Kitu, could you please aid your brother?" With downcast eyes, she nodded in consent and listened to further instruction, "Keep your thoughts in healing prayer as you attend to your brother's leg. Seek out the healing herbs that your second mother taught you. I will need you to be at my side to help sing later in the Opy."

With the last rays of the golden sunlight diminishing in the forest, Mbaracambri continued to organize the needed activities and provided strength through his voice to the forest people of the village of Takuaty.

Everyone understood the preparations for the departing of souls ceremony would last for two nights and days and were willing with renewed energy to quietly follow Mbaracambri's instructions. They yearned for the nighttime of singing that brought them closer to the beautiful Source. Dancing and chanting always opened their hearts, and their minds and bodies felt lighter. As they sang their sacred songs, heavy worldly feelings slipped away.

The ceremony was set in motion with the sharing of a special drink. The kangui was passed around for all the forest people, while the kanguijy was specially prepared and reserved for Mbaracambri. As he was drinking his special kanguijy just before entering the Opy, Mbaracambri felt a soft warm *wind caress his check. He briefly looked up to the sky, and with closed eyes, he could sense Yyvkuaraua. He could smell her, and his senses relaxed into this comfortable presence. He knew she would be singing for her father's soul and for the good of all her village.*

Mbaracambri entered the Opy with a lighter heart and with great focus to lead the ceremony, and for a brief instant, he could hear the elder's words ring in his ears. He knew he must keep strength. He could not give into the evil feelings from the attack and the loss of his family. He must pray and dance for guidance. Mbaracambri knew, from past experience, that he was always tempted before he received a great song. Spiritual gifts always came with a challenge, and now, before him was his greatest challenge. With turmoil and great disruption of mbiroy in the village this day, Mbaracambri faced his inner feelings alone and trusted completely in the sacred ways of his people.

In his past dreams, the spirits instructed him how to heal, dance, sing, and live. Mbaracambri knew, if he listened to the fear in his people, he could lose his connection to the spirit world. In order to prepare himself to receive a special dream or vision, he needed to pray and dance for long hours. In this way, he would support his community as the elder pajé through communing with the spirit world to bring peace and love. Through their sacred songs—the word souls—they would be guided, and this gave great comfort to the small village of forest people.

As pajé, Mbaracambri smoked his pipe and hummed a low sound while moving his feet with the singing of all the villagers. With Yyvkuaraua gone, Kitu now supported her father with her takuá and singing as he moved into trance. Men on one side would sing out, and the women would answer while beating their takuá on the ground to create a rhythmic earthly sound. As the singing intensified, Mbaracambri danced, sang, and prayed with his rattle and did not stop until two nights and two days had past.

During the long ceremony of prayers and dancing Mbaracambri had a vision of the Grandfather Pajé who spoke to him, "Mbaracambri, the last instructions are word souls for you. Listen again! The forest people will take a journey, where the beginning and the end are different but the same. Remember this, and retrieve the sacred stones."

After the last night of ceremony, just before the gold rays announced Kuarahy's coming, the spirits came to him in his dream. The lesser gods, instructed by Ñande Ru, the One Father, shared with Mbaracambri to continue to live in the sacred way. He was encouraged to take the village on a journey along a path in the direction of the rising Great Light. They showed Mbaracambri the new space for the forest people to relocate, a space for mbiroy to flourish with the celestial world. He was shown simple foods of wild roots, berries, kungui, honey, and water along the way for all to eat. The beautiful beings also commended the village for their singing to assist their elder pajé and loved ones safely to the land with no evil.

Mbaracambri moved out of his deep trance to share the word souls with the forest people. Relocating the village when someone dies is their way. So the journey came as no surprise to the village; however, where and how they would travel came from the word souls. The village looked to Mbaracambri to hear the beautiful world souls, and so he spoke to the people, "Our departed family members are safely to the land without evil in the care of the celestial beings. We are now instructed to make a journey. All will prepare now to depart after the next rising of Kuarahy. Please gather this day those things that will not burden you for the journey. Take time to nourish with manioc and maize and cleanse in the river."

After answering questions and watching everyone disperse to begin the preparations, Mbaracambri tipped his face skyward with eyes closed and shook his mbaraká as song burst forth in thanksgiving for the guidance. Soon, he felt gentle warmth flood his body, and a strong gold light presented in his inner vision. This light moved into a vision of the space under the altar in the Opy. He followed the vision into the house of prayer. He knelt down and moved the dirt with his hands as his inner vision instructed. He dug a small hole and encountered two stones. The two stones, one amethyst and the other rose quartz, were the size of a child's fist. Hesitating with the stones in his hands, he recalled the elder pajé's message. He put the sacred stones in a small hand-woven reed pouch, and placed it around his neck and close to his heart.

Still kneeling in the dirt, he took a moment to connect with his breath and uttered a prayer of gratitude as he clasped his hand over the pouch. He followed the word souls given by Grandfather Pajé in his last breath, and now, he must prepare for the journey.

CHAPTER 4

For the Love of Nature and All Her Inhabitants

We cannot do great things on this Earth,
only small things with great love
—Mother Theresa

The season is winter of 2009, and the water level of the Amazon River is low enough to expose a sandy bank. A group of twenty-five people, including me, crossed the river in canoes to a stretch of exposed beach.

Wrapped in a blanket, shivering from the cold, and excited for the adventure, I searched the night skies while lying on my back on a thin mat on the sandy Amazon River bank. Looking up at the exquisite night sky, the constellations of stars were so mesmerizing, so bright and countless, and so different from my usual view in the northern hemisphere. They looked and felt so close.

Between the fascination and wonder of the night sky and the cold nagging at my body, my eyes become heavy as the song of the *curandero* overtook my senses. Closing my eyes in surrender, my conscious self drifted with his melodic voice and attempted to focus on my healing intention.

I came here to the banks of the Amazon for my lifelong love of indigenous ways and for my continual journey in healing. My childhood dream, over forty years earlier, was to study ancient cultures as a career, well before Ama-Deus and Alberto Aguas. So dear to my heart is a clear image of the childhood day on which I chose that path.

As a twenty-three-year-old, I was lying on the living room floor leafing through the newspaper-sized university curriculum to organize my next semester of courses one late summer evening. My father sat in his chair reading the newspaper and having an evening cocktail. I had made the decision to declare archaeology as a major with geology and French as minor studies after returning from a year-long study abroad at the University of Grenoble. In looking through the syllabus, another college major pulled on my curiosity.

"Okay, Dad, how about astronomy?

"Really?"

"Sure! Maybe that has a better financial career than archaeology. I could go all the way for my doctorate. I would then be Dr. Cosmos!" We both had a good laugh at this idea.

Reading further, I exclaimed, "Oh my gosh! Astronomy is out! The courses presented in this syllabus are *all* mathematics. This is definitely not going to work. Gosh, why would I need math to study the stars?"

My father laughed at my outburst. Even though he was partial to archaeology, a career he felt would not bring financial security, he did not dissuade me to change; instead, he only offered his opinion. The appeal and heartfelt fascination for any course in archaeology gave strength of conviction to not switch majors; and so the final year of courses were selected to complete my degree.

Seeking to understand human existence was prominent in my life early on. So-called lost cultures were fascinating to read about and decipher, like spiritual detective work to the incessant questions of life. My reason for taking a year to study abroad during college was not only to visit Greek and Roman ruins, but also to experience different cultures that were living before studying them as dead or lost. Growing up, the Midwest American suburb offered a protected cultural environment. I felt the need to live within other cultures and learn how to observe through other people's perspectives and traditions.

Being an only child, raised within the proverbial social etiquette of being seen and not heard, created ease with personal inner dialogue. Observing my environment became natural. Of all places, nature was most comforting. Nature held so much to observe, the small and large, the plants, the animals, the water, and the mineral kingdoms, which many times ended up in my pocket as real treasures to carry home. Nature inspired my imagination and encouraged deeper insights to universal principles. To be outside was to be in heaven. God, or what I now call interchangeably the Universe, the Uncreated Light, Divine Love, Source of all that Is, was alive for me everywhere.

76

A book about a Native American hero captivated my attention in grade school and started my journey of seeking any story containing indigenous ways. Their lifestyle was appealing, being so in balance with nature. This first book titled *Geronimo* also became my nickname in grade school after the boys in class discovered my reading material.

The name-calling and embarrassment did not stop my looking for any material on indigenous or *first* peoples. This search continued, and the small collection of grade school books eventually led to the discovery of other lost cultures in *National Geographic* magazine. I became fully absorbed each month reading about ancient cultures in the Mediterranean area, Middle East, or early dynasties of the Far East. However, the most appealing and captivating were the Mayan and Incan cultures. This Central and South American indigenous focus stayed strongly with me through the years.

During my first year in college, my uncle offered the chance to join him on a trip to Mexico to visit Akumal on the Yucatan Peninsula. Akumal was a small beachfront community between the towns of Playa del Carmen and Tulum. *Akumal* means "place of the turtles" in the Mayan language.

I acquired wonderful memories of the Mayans in small villages and following footpaths through the jungle prior to the development of this area for tourism. From this opportunity before throngs of tourists and divided highways, I walked through the ruins of Tulum and Chichen Itza, falling in love with the idea of not just studying indigenous cultures from textbooks, but immersing myself in the remnants of past cultures. And so I did.

I graduated from college, and the best news for my father was my landing a job in New Mexico with Solomon Ruins Museum for contractual archeology. This paying job was very exciting and satisfying work, and my father was pleased, as this presented an application of my studies and interest in a career that would be life sustaining.

The small museum dedicated to the first white people who had homesteaded the area was located in a stretch of uninhabited land between Bloomfield and Farmington, New Mexico. The curator for this small museum was an archaeologist. In the seventies, the oil and gas fields were booming with drilling activity, and a large area of this activity was located on reservation lands and Bureau of Land Management (BLM) lands. Any activities on either lands required an archaeological survey according to the Federal Antiquity Law. The curator was overwhelmed with needed clearance surveys to satisfy this law. My coming on board helped to alleviate her backlogged requests and offered me direct field experience.

For close to ten years, I was contracted by the three major oil and gas companies to perform archaeological surveys and worked in the fields on the different reservations. This fieldwork also brought my interactions with the different tribal governments in the area, such as the several different Pueblos, the Mountain Ute, the Navajo, and the Jicarilla Apache nation's governing boards. The interactions with the different tribes, as well as the numerous land surveys, proved rich in experience and satisfied my thirst for being close to and learning indigenous ways.

My background of consistent deep-seated interest and experiences of indigenous ways ignited the strong sense to eventually inquire beyond Alberto's notes and lectures concerning the Guaraní. This deeper investigation clarified why he became so enamored with these people's way of life. More so for me at this stage in my life, the investigation into the Guaraní mirrored a clearer understanding for all mankind's natural roots and a clearer understanding of all peoples who carry traditional indigenous practices. My childhood quest for answers from "lost" cultures was richly rewarded later in my life in discovering the Guaraní way of life.

CHAPTER 5

Historical Recordings of the Guaraní

I find hope in the darkest of days, and focus in the brightest.
I do not judge the Universe.
—Dalai Lama

With passion and focus, I took a good year to single-mindedly investigate the main sources for information on the Guaraní. I found a wealth of written material in books, manuscripts, and dissertations about the Guaraní in all aspects of their social lifestyle. My goal was to sift out and locate accounts that coincided with Alberto's experiences. The results more than confirmed his descriptions. My eyes opened to a fascinating indigenous culture very much still alive.

"The Guaraní of Brazil and Paraguay live in some of the largest subtropical forests in the world, inhabiting an extensive, though discontinuous, area ranging over four thousand kilometers, from the Amazon River to the River Platte Basin."[24] Keep this environment in mind as you read next some of the history of this tribe and their original encounters with men and cultures.

Most of the numerous accounts of the Guaraní were written in Spanish, Portuguese, German, and French. These languages dominated the first written accounts because the explorers and missionaries in the sixteenth and seventeenth centuries were from Europe. These first accounts of the Guaraní provide glimpses, as there is no known written documentation or archeological finding that describes pre-Hispanic indigenous life.

Some of the first expansive reports documented the impact from "reducciones," a type of settlement created by the Jesuit missionaries for the indigenous. Further chronicles from the missionaries and numerous ethnohistorical accounts delve into the impact of colonizers. From the fifteenth century to the present twentieth century, chronicles reported waves of epidemic diseases as measles, small pox, and pneumonia; the encroachment of fur traders; the rubber boom; ranchers; loggers; hydroelectric dam projects; nuclear projects; mining, roads, and airstrips— all of which posed threats to the social fabric of all the indigenous peoples of South America.

I could have been easily caught up in the difficult social morals of this historical unfolding of events, not unlike many other expansionist movements of human habitation on earth. My task at times was distressing as I struggled to stay focused on exposing descriptions that demonstrated the spiritual nature of the Guaraní. These recorded accounts have the capacity to stir up personal as well as global questions for needed change.

Early chronicles in the fifteenth and sixteenth century were substantially about the missionaries' daily routines of moving quickly through villages and baptizing as many natives as they could. Later, in the eighteenth century, many of the missionaries cohabitated within the different villages. Jesuit missionaries, such as Montoya and Dobrizh, who lived among the Guaraní people, offered a more descriptive narrative of forest living, which was in contrast to the earlier missionary accounts of conversion.

This trend of living within the different villages continued into the nineteenth century. German-born Curt Nimuendaju, who worked for the Brazilian government, lived with a group of Guaraní called Apapokúva and was formally baptized and adopted into their community. Nimuendaju, meaning "he who knew how to clear his own road in this world and win his place," was his given Guaraní name. He compiled the first comprehensive accounts of the mythology and the spiritual practices of these people. Others who were eager to learn about the Guaraní followed Nimuendaju's example, adopting his fashion of living among them in order to witness and record their traditions and way of life. Such contributors as Alfred Métraux 1948, Egon Schaden 1962, anthropologist Leon Cadogan 1962, Jesuit Bartolomé Melia 1977, and Vivieres de Castro 1986 attempted to capture the true cultural essence of the Guaraní. Some of these above-mentioned contributors' works have been translated into English, and the elements of these translations are discussed later in this chapter.

After personally pouring through mounds of translated manuscripts, dissertations, and books, I thoroughly enjoyed Richard Reed's *Prophets of Agroforestry*. Reed's work corresponds to the same time of Alberto's experiences with the Guarani in the early 1980's. Reed lived, studied, and wrote a full account on the Chiripa Guaraní in the forests of eastern Paraguay between 1981 and 1984. Reed pulled together into a most comprehensive book the most accepted historical documentation to support his own rich personal accounts.

Another recent book, ten years after Alberto's work, Bradford Keeney, a psychologist and editor for "Ringing Rock Profiles," wrote accounts about the present-day Guaraní in the book *Guaraní Shamans of the Forest*. Keeney shared personal experiences and gave testimony to the Guaraní way of life through the voices of present-day pajés or shamans. These pajés' personal accounts still reverberate the same sacred story held in the previous major themes of all the ethnographic and anthropological accounts on the Guaraní. This book illustrates and brings to life the accounts detailed in Alberto's stories.

In all of the recently written accounts that I have come across, only Keeney's experience compared to Alberto's. Their intention for interaction came purely from a spiritual quest. Both Alberto and Keeney approached the Guaraní with spiritual eyes, not with an evangelical quest or for historical documentation. This is not to say that the Guaraní have not received other people who observed and experienced their sacred ways. Rather, these are the only accounts I have encountered that suggested the initial purpose of seeking the Guarani was for spiritual intention.

Like today, the early accounts surfaced repeatedly on how some of the early explorers in the 1500s were touched when meeting and interacting with the Guaraní. On the other hand, others were blinded.

From Savages to Mystics

The first written accounts in the sixteenth century of the Guaraní came from the Jesuit missionaries. The descriptions made apparent that the Jesuits' intention was to baptize and convert the "savages." Missionaries had the primary aim to evangelize the world and "the Jesuits were major instruments in God's hand."[25] The savages were indeed a seemingly suitable group to save. In their first encounters, the most zealous missionaries did not have the eyes to recognize the spiritual nature of these people. The missionaries were on a religious crusade for which they had been trained and instructed. We are, however, indebted to the authors of these early recordings who did capture some descriptions tucked here and there of spiritual practices that are described in the next sections.

The following descriptions combined several Spanish chronicles taken from John Monteiro's *The Crises and Transformations of Invaded Societies: Coastal Brazil in the Sixteenth Century.* Monteiro's presentation of the different observances made obvious the leadership roles in a given village, provided early accounts of an oral tradition, and suggested strong community spiritual practices.

> Oratory skills figured in the making of a great leader among the Tupi (Guaraní) . . .what caught their attention was not only the rhetorical methods, but also the contents of the frequent speeches. According to Fernão Cardim, every day before dawn, the headman "preaches during half an hour, reminding [the villagers] that they will work as did their ancestors, and distributes their time among them, telling them what they are to do."

> Father Manual da Nóbrega, writing from São Vicente in 1553 accounts, "Every day before dawn from a high place the [the principal] sets out the day's task for each household, and reminds them that they must live communally."

> Magalhães Gandavo commented: "These people do not have a King among them, or any other sort of justice, except for a *principal* in each village, who is like a captain, whom they obey by choice and not by force."[26]

These chronicled references gave us a glimpse of the people's strong spiritual way of life. These "headman" preaching in the morning were the shamans or pajés and, according to the accounts of Yves d'Évreux, a French historian and explorer (1577), "exercised multiple functions such as healing the sick, interpreting dreams, and warding off the main outside threats to local society, including spirits and demons."[27] Later accounts give the foundation to the structure of this leadership within the community. We learn that the community chose and designated who would fill this spiritual leadership. The pajé earned his place in the community as a spiritual leader by demonstrating his power with words or word songs that he received in a dream state.

This type of leadership posed considerable challenges to the early observers, as they were more accustomed to the division of political and religious leadership. The Guaraní later adapted what is called a "cacique," a patrilineal leadership in addition to, but not stronger than, the pajé, most likely in response to Western domination. This importance placed on spiritual leadership and the power of the word was clearer in much later recordings.

One tale recorded by early missionaries was a narration of a great flood. Why did this finding not register any notion by the missionaries to look further into the Guaraní cosmology? Because, "the Jesuits were all consistent in their accounts, finding no idolatry and form of worship, however, any tales accounted during their observations, alas myths, were considered amusing tales or if they did not fit into their own understanding of 'cosmogonies' were works of the devil."[28]

Later reports account and give evidence of several destructions on earth in the Guaraní's oral history. In addition, the natives' fears of spirits were mentioned in numerous documents. These accounts of the pajé facing the rising sun in prayer, a flood story, and descriptions of earth-bound spirits gave helpful hints that the "savages" had some beliefs in the spiritual realm.

Of particular note is their acceptance and patience sustained even today. Nimuendaju stated that one main principle of Guaraní daily life is tolerance, "Even though, the Guaraní, within his soul, is convinced about the truth of his religion as the most ardent Christian, he never is 'intolerant.'"[29] Tolerance is demonstrated in many ways. To the Guaraní, past and present spiritual knowledge comes from the Great Father uniquely to each of his children. So the etiquette of listening or being tolerant when someone is speaking is an act of sincere *reverence* toward another. Listening was hearing another's soul speak, and this was of great importance in their world. After much listening and observing of the "foreigners," we find recordings of how the Guaraní did not feel less fortunate, but rather they felt sorry for their intruders who seemed to be dominated by their animal nature.

De Léry shared in 1578 how he observed the Guaraní receiving them: "I have observed among them that just as they love those who are gay, joyful, and liberal, on the contrary they hate those who are taciturn, stingy, and melancholy."[30]

Twentieth century anthropologist Jonathan Hill also clarified this concept: "Sadness and 'seriousness' are negatively valued. In fact, one of the things that most surprised [them] . . . about the behavior of the white people was their inexplicable fluctuation in mood and spirit. To not laugh is a euphemism for rancor . . . the notion of 'joyfulness' or *tori* has profound philosophical resonances . . . the cognates of *tori* designate ritual activity."[31]

In order to authenticate themselves from the intolerance and moodiness of others, the Guaraní use the phrase "the Guaraní way of life" with dignity and humility. *Ñande reko* is an expression of their identity that means "our way of being," "our present manner," "our law," "our customs," and "our behavior." Meliá, in his careful analysis of Guaraní language, takes the meanings from the oldest dictionary *Tesoro de la lengua guaraní* (1639) compiled by Fr. Antonio Ruiz de Montoya. He describes the Guaraní character in two expressions "*ñande reko katú* and *ñande reko marangatú* [our true and authentic way of being, and our good, honorable and virtuous way of being, with respect to the religious side of the person]. How this religious side of the character develops and lives in the present is the same as asking about the Guaraní religious experience."[32]

The development of the individual's religious or spiritual side is of utmost importance. Each individual learns to add to the unity of the community through constant poetic expression in song to the Divine. In summary, no division exists between the Guaraní's two concept of the material and spiritual world.

To most of the earlier colonizers, explorers, and members of the religious orders, the simple exterior way of life in the forest masked the rich interior of the sacred relationship between the people and the land and the understanding of their place in the Universe to eyes that only saw and valued the material world or preconceived religious matters. The Guaraní kept life simple in material ways and surrounded themselves with riches in the spiritual realm.

The later ethnohistorian accounts recorded a more detailed lifestyle that revealed a spiritual life. Metraux described them as "men [who] yearn to live in the company [of the spirit world]."[33]

Egon Schaden, as quoted in Hélène Clastres's works, wrote of the Guaraní, "My kingdom is not of this world. The entire mental life of the Guaraní is turned toward the Beyond."[34] So many researchers, who studied the Guaraní, became captivated with their soul level of understanding and perspectives of life. They went from being savages in the first recordings to what Clastres described as mystics and assigned to the Guaraní the title "theologians of South America" in later academic accounts.

The Land and the Home

Early documentations merged with recent accounts of Guaraní village life provide the texture and color of their lives. They were swidden (slash and burn) agriculturists and rotated planting as needed by moving the community to allow the regeneration of the soil. The Guaraní had a system of sustainable agroforestry,[35] which they regulated by the stars. Earlier observers noted cultivation of different varieties of vegetables: corn, manioc, squash, and beans. A later ethnographic account in 1948 describes:

> The early Guaraní seem to have been proficient horticulturists . . . [they] supplemented their diet with all kinds of fruits, and with game and fish . . . the whole community, among both ancient and modern *Guaraní*, cooperated in clearing a large field by the slash-and-burn method in a thick forest and then subdivided it into family plots. Planting and sowing were regulated by the course of the Pleiades. The main agricultural tool was the digging stick. After five or six years of cultivation, fields were considered exhausted and were abandoned."[36]

Other observers noted that inside their houses parrots, whose feathers were valued for personal adornment, were kept.[37] They grew cotton and yerba mate and domesticated the Muscovy duck.[38] [39] The cultivation of primary importance was manioc and maize. Their diet was supplemented by hunting, fishing, and gathering wild fruits and such things as honey for subsistence, which occurred between crop productions.

Today, even though they are unable to move in the forest, the Guaraní still observe sacred ceremonies revolving around the planting and harvesting of their maize and manioc with the movement of the planets and stars.

Musical Instruments and Dances

For the Guaraní, ancient to present-day peoples, all life is a ritual. There are ceremonies for conception, birth, naming children, puberty, parenthood, sickness, transition, eating, hunting, planting, and harvesting. All aspects of life were sacred, and so the tools used for a ceremony are also of importance and have specific roles.

Musical instruments, mainly the gourd rattle, and the rhythm sticks are important sacred tools. The men use the rattles, called *mbaraká*, during ceremonies, and the women use the takuá (or *takuará*), stamping rhythm sticks. Males mark the rhythm through songs, rattles, and footwork, and females answer in song while rhythmically pounding the takuá and using dancing footwork. Flutes were used among the ancient Guaraní as noted in early accounts, whereas string instruments have been introduced in more recent times.

The "voice" of the rattle or "the sound is believed to be endowed with sacred power. The rattle communicates with God. The seeds inside represent the sons of the community. Shake it and the whole community prays."[40] "The rattles are made from small gourds that are filled with seeds, and then fitted with short bamboo handles."[41] They are usually decorated with feathers that are attached to a cotton cord. Shamans are capable of shaking rattles, creating the most varied rhythmic patterns.

"The stamping tube [about a meter in length] is a bamboo section closed at one end, trimmed with feathers, and engraved with checkerboard designs. This instrument is reserved for women who pound it against the ground to produce a dull thud which marks the cadence of their dances."[42] Tamped on the beaten earth, a resounding tone can be heard for kilometers in the forest.[43]

Dancers stand in a line—women in one line moving up and down and men in another line throwing their feet forward in rapid succession. Dances involve a line of people, who are facing east, and if there is movement, the line revolves and moves north, west, and south.[44]

Schaden, author of *Fundamental Aspects of Guaraní Culture* wrote, "All the different prayers that accompany the religious dances and that extend through the night until the break of day . . . are nothing but paths that lead to the presence of the gods. Without a path, one does not arrive at the place that one intends to reach."[45] Dancing is a technique used by the Guaraní to lighten the body. By lightening the body, one has more inter-dimensional access.

Planting with the course of the Pleiades, sacred instruments used to commune with the spirit world, and dance to lighten the body for inter-dimensional travel, all begin to demonstrate intense spiritual practices, which lead the aspirants to connection with and eventually home to the Land with No Evil.

Language and Soul

In early accounts of the colonizers, important events such as the morning communal activity of gathering around the headman were recorded. The community followed the "headman" by choice, not by force. We learn these headman were the shamans or pajés and the community followed because of their *word souls*. Word souls are divine language and were sacred to the Guaraní. This importance was insightfully depicted in Nimuendaju's following explanation of the linguistic meaning for soul:

> The Apapocúva [Gaurani] do not refer to the soul as *ang*, as do other tribes of the same linguistic family, but as *ayvucué*. I'm not sure about the [meaning of] beginning of this word "ay," which may correspond to the term *ang*; *vu* means to "spring forth" and *cué* means "language" [it's the simple past tense form of the verb "*ayou*," which also means to make a sound].[46]

Soul and sound are synonymous. Word soul is the translated Guaraní term used to describe song and language. The larynx gives the incarnated soul a voice and the power to express the language of the soul through song and beautiful words, while the lips are simple portals for passing these sounds in to the earthly dimensions. The Guaraní, as a community, have had centuries of soul communing and maintaining a celestial pathway to the spiritual realm for balance and harmony during their earthly journeys. The beautiful language or word soul is language received from the gods. Schaden in 1969 says *ayvú* [meaning soul] "properly means language ... is of divine origin; that is, it shares the nature of the supernatural spirits. It is responsible for the desires, feelings, and the noblest manifestations of the individual. The basic, primordial function of the soul is to confer upon man the gift of language; thus the designation."[47]

Keeney's testimony in 2000 from present-day Guaraní shamans demonstrates an unbroken continuity corresponding to these earlier reports. Ayvú, "word soul," the principal aspect of Guaraní living is realized when the spirit touches one's heart and one is moved to express through speech. "It is so pure that when it comes to you through your body, it gives pure wisdom and truth. If you don't act right and therefore break the harmony between your body and the word souls, community, and nature, you may possibly die. The source of the word souls is from the main God and the minor gods."[48]

The Guaraní recognize two souls. One is considered the human soul *ayvucué* and the other an animal soul *acyiguá*. According to Guaraní belief, the human soul is "entirely good and is manifest immediately. The animal soul is more or less aggressive, depending on the type of animal involved, and begins to manifest when small children exhibit crankiness or dissatisfaction."[49]

> The human part of the soul is definitely always good—there is no difference between one person and another. The quality of the animal soul varies widely: anything from a butterfly to a jaguar. Since the animal soul dies along with the body, it is also not subject to judgment in the after-life. The seat of the human soul in the physical body is the heart; the seat of the animal soul is the head.[50]

In this belief of soul, the Guaraní have no room for purgatory or hell. The incoming soul is divine and is given all due respect by the community. This perception brings to mind Alberto's description on reincarnation and children. Nimuendaju gives one of the first accounts describing the soul:

> The *ayvucué*, the birth soul, soon receives an added element to complete the dual entity, which is a human soul. The new element is the *acyiguá*. This word consists of two particles: *acy*, which means "pain" and the rest, which means "intense." The *acyiguá* is the animal part of the human soul. Gentle and good actions are attributed to the *ayvucué*; evil and violent acts are attributed to the *acyiguá*. Restfulness is an expression of *ayvucué*, restlessness of *acyiguá*. An appetite for vegetarian fare comes from the *ayvucué*, a desire for meat is from *acyiguá*. The characteristics

of the animal, which a particular *acyiguá* is based on, determine a person's temperament.[51]

At death, the soul splits into the original two components. The animal soul dies with the body, and the human soul has the choice of reincarnating. This concept is so much a part of the Guaraní that there is no fear of death. Earthbound spirits are feared more than death.

The author Nimuendaju relates this through his personal experience with the dying process:

> The Guaraní fear the dead far more than they fear death.
> Once they're convinced that they've really reached the end,
> their imperturbability is remarkable. This has a lot to do with
> their temperament, to which is added their religious faith. The
> Guaraní fear neither Purgatory nor Hell, and where the soul goes
> after death is not subject to doubt. A dying person is therefore
> utterly level-headed in handing out final instructions to his heirs,
> which are carried out without fail; then he sings his medicine
> song if he has one, and brushes off all remarks about possible
> remission as well as refusing all further medication. If he must
> die, he wants to die—as quietly as possible. Even the thought of
> being separated from loved ones carries little weight as his belief
> in reincarnation guaranties that he will live among them again.[52]

These more recent descriptions revealed an image that language and soul are intricately linked. Comprehending this perspective provided more insight and importance to fully understanding the Guaraní way of life and their ceremonies.

CHAPTER 6

Viewing their World as Divine Souls

You must prove the existence of God first to yourself through our own direct experience ... at that point both faith and hope will be canceled out and what will remain will be love.
—Father Maximos

In 1986, Viveiros de Castro reports the Guaraní have the most elaborate "theory of the person ... developing the distinction between the celestial and terrestrial principles of human beings to the maximum."[53] Nowhere is this more evident than in the ceremony for naming an incoming soul. "A Guaraní's name is considered part of his soul, almost identical with it, and indivisible from the person. In their words, we don't say an Indian "is called" so-and-so; he "is" so-and-so. To misuse a name is to inflict harm on its owner."[54]

The Guaraní distinguished between a soul of divine origin and destiny, linked to the personal name, individual "prayers," speech, and breath and a soul with an animal connotation and a posthumous terrestrial destiny, linked to individual temperament, eating, the shadow, and the corpse. The first is given complete at birth; the second grows with the person and manifests his/her history.[55]

The naming ceremony gives a tangible example of their perspective on soul and how "word souls" hold so much power and importance in Guaraní daily life. A birth of a child is a birth of a soul. The entire community comes together unconditionally and partakes in celebrating and rejoicing for the incoming soul. The naming ceremony begins with the wife and daughter supporting the pajé in singing and using the sacred instruments. Eventually, the entire community joins the singing into the night, as the pajé goes into trance to retrieve the name of the incoming soul. The name has great significance to the Guaraní. Again, a wonderful account is found in Nimuendaju's report:

> When a child is born, the entire band assembles after a few days, and the medicine man begins his ceremony to find out, "Which soul has come to us." The soul could have come from the dwelling of Ñanderiquey, which is the zenith, or from "Our Mother" in the east, or from the abode of the rain god Tupa in the west. The soul arrives fully formed, and the medicine man's task is merely to identify it. This he does by addressing the various powers of these cardinal points with appropriate songs and asking them from where the soul came and what its name is. It takes a lot of effort on the part of the medicine man to connect to these heavenly powers, as this is possible only in trance. Usually, he sits down soon after dusk to sing and shake his rattle. At first, he is accompanied only by his wife and daughter, who sing and pound the dance *taquara* rhythmically. By and by, all the village's women and girls gather around facing east in a single row along the wall of the house. Men remain in the background. This will go on for hours. Meanwhile, the medicine man occasionally receives supernatural powers from the entities he's singing to which are then transferred to the child. These powers are considered to be quite tangible, albeit invisible. The medicine man appears to catch these substances with his hands above his head. He then makes a wrapping movement before spreading them out over the child . . . as the sun begins to rise, the medicine man's song becomes louder and more solemn as rhythmic accompaniments fall away and he gives himself over entirely to trance. He is no longer accompanied by other singers and his rattling fluctuates from barely audible to very energetic. This is the Ñeengarai, the culmination of any religious dance. Singing, the medicine man circles inside the hut a few times . . . the small procession walks west, south, east, and north . . . Finally, all those present line up with raised hands and bow to the rising sun. Thus ends this particular medicine dance, as do all others.[56]

This naming ceremony recorded at the turn of the century does not seem to have been lost or changed as seen in this present-day description by shaman Tupa Nevangayu.

> In our community we call everyone a child, no matter how young or old they are. When you baptize someone you ask God where the child comes from—East, West, North, or South. God tells you where the child is from, and then He tells you their Guaraní spiritual name. When you were conceived God gave you a spiritual name. God gives this to you. The shaman asks God what He named you, and in our baptism ceremony, this name is announced to the community. We dance and celebrate such an event.[57]

Well before I researched the background of the Guaraní, several opportunities occurred for me to visit Brazil. Christian Vianna, in 2005, was my first contact in Brazil and a most gracious host. He arranged a meeting with a specific Guaraní village south of Rio de Janeiro. Subsequently, during each return trip, I visited this particular village, and a certain sentiment and bonding happened for me with these people— *saudade* in Portuguese. In 2007, during my third trip to Brazil and visit with this particular village, I came across an experience with the Guaraní naming ceremony.

This trip occurred during autumn in Brazil, and the temperature was warm, and the foliage was beautiful green. At home in Michigan, the weather was a cooler springtime with just the hint of color returning. The warmth was a nice welcome. I traveled by car as a passenger and enjoyed the beautiful coastline along a two-lane road heading south out of Rio de Janeiro. Christian made arrangements with a close friend, Teodoro, to transport me to the Guaraní village. Like Christian, Teodoro had good relations with the cacique of this village, and he speaks fluent Guaraní. I had met and stayed at his home on my first trip to Brazil through my host Christian. We had become good friends.

I was returning to Brazil to further my investigation into Alberto's background and to make a third visit with the Guaraní in order to purchase some of their crafts. In anticipation of returning to the village, throughout the year clothing had been collected, which would be distributed among the village's children. All the clothing and some personal items for the cacique were packed into a large suitcase. The plan was to give the cacique the contents as well as the suitcase. The previous year, when I brought clothing to the village, the cacique seemed a little disappointed that the suitcase was not included. This year, preparations were made to present him with everything.

"Teo, I would like to stop and purchase something fun for the children, as Christian suggested in my first visit."

"Yes, this is good etiquette. I know a market that will be easy to access and have some nice choices for you. I too would like to bring the cacique something."

We stopped along the way at a market that was twenty minutes from the village to purchase several packages of cookies for the children. I remembered vividly the children's joy in the previous visit when the same cookies were distributed; I expected they would respond joyfully again. The village was poor in terms of material goods.

The main goal for this visit besides delivering clothing was to replenish my collection of their crafts. The entire ritual of looking at many earrings, necklaces, baskets, and bracelets from each of the women created an exciting visit, as they loved to show their handiwork. Purchasing directly from the women aids the village to maintain their way of life.

When we returned to the car and headed down the two-lane road, Teodoro explained why he was excited to be on this visit and speak with the ninety-three-year-old cacique. "Earlier in the year, I had business in a city near the village. So I took the time to visit with the cacique. He told me how he shared with his people that I was a true friend. I even speak their language. He told me that he wished to share a true Guaraní name for me."

"Really? How wonderful! How does this happen?"

"This is a good question. Each time I visit, he tells me it is not the right time. I believe the right time will be in about a month, when they have the important harvest ceremony and celebration for the maize. I was very taken by his gesture, but I think I am impatient in waiting for the right time!"

We turned off the paved road onto a winding dirt road through the Atlantic rain forest. The road followed a small meandering river. There was a lot of dust flying around as he expertly navigated the vehicle around large potholes in the road. Teodoro explained during the bumpy ride that the road was impassable during the rainy season. After twenty minutes of Teodoro intensely steering and me holding tightly to the door, we arrived at the edge of the village.

He stopped, turned the car off, and said, "Please wait here while I go to search for the cacique. He will tell me if it is appropriate to visit."

I saw no visible human activity and heard only the sounds of the forest birds and insects. I waited in the vehicle as Teodoro disappeared down a small dirt path winding between thatched roof houses in search of the cacique.

In no time, Teo returned, walking and talking and smiling with the elder. This ninety-three-year-old elder, who moved well and looked more to be in his seventies, must have anticipated our arrival. My heart was happy as I opened the door and stepped from the truck. We were welcomed.

My previous two visits occurred in this same manner. All meetings took place at the entrance to the village in the presence of the elder cacique. Greeted with a gentle hug and big smile from Cacique Tata Ti (White Smoke), pleasantries were exchanged while other community members appeared and gathered around us. We presented our gifts to the cacique only, as this is their tradition. The duty of the cacique is to fairly distribute to all members of his village. The cacique opened the suitcase on the ground in a clearing on the edge of thatched dwellings. A big smile erupted on his face as he inspected the contents and learned that the suitcase was included in the gifts to the village. Tata Ti gestured for someone to move the large heavy suitcase to his home.

Teodoro whispered to me, "The cacique said he would determine how the clothes would be distributed later at another time according to each family's direct needs."

I asked, "When can we give the cookies to the children?" Teodoro looked from me and turned to the cacique speaking in Guaraní.

Turning back to me, he replied, "Let's do this now," he says. The grocery bags holding the packages of cookies were brought to the feet of the cacique. He sat down and handed out the cookies to a few children nearby the cacique. There seemed to be a telepathic line to the children as they came running out from every angle of the rain forest to receive the cookies. They wore big smiles and squealed with delight. As Tata Ti worked the pressing small adults crowding around him, his wife helped the smaller members who were shyer to receive their fair share. Quickly seeing the numbers grow, Teodoro called out to me, "We need to break these in half so there will be enough for everyone."

"Okay!" I started gathering up the packages surrounded by excited smiling faces. "Here, I have my knife. You pass them to me and I will cut them in half." It seemed the numbers of their children had grown since our last visit!

Some other adult members were lingering around as if to observe the action. One middle-aged man sitting off to the side held an instrument that looked like a small ukulele with three strings; however, he was playing it like a violin. He was discreetly on the side, repeating a specific song that drew my attention.

With the cookies passed out, Teodoro moved a few feet away with the cacique and, half turning to me, explained, "We are going to make plans for his birthday in a month." He turned back laughing and joking with Tata Ti.

I moved and quietly positioned myself next to Tata Ti's wife. She affectionately hugged me while we listened to the men and watched the children as they ate their cookies. All the while, the music played softly. Simply observing the interactions and being with the people was enjoyable, while Teodoro was making plans for Tata Ti's birthday.

Teodoro eventually led the cacique back to where we were standing. This was the moment to give Tata Ti his gift. Teodoro translated for the cacique the reason for the additional personal gifts. A handmade pipe was gifted for Tata Ti from an Ojibwa in the United States. Before receiving the gift, he spat on the ground all around the pipe. Then Tata Ti was presented a large bundle of white candles and a large package of organic tobacco—a small gesture of thankfulness from me. He had a large smile and repeated, "Aguyje," which is thank you in Guaraní, and I stumbled in response, "Tere guahe porâite." You are welcome.

Our visit produced a slow gathering of people from the village. As the formal etiquette and gift giving was complete, I searched the small crowd for the women who made and sold the crafts. They were normally out around the informal gathering waiting for their turn to interact.

I looked to Teodoro with a questioning face.

"Teo! Where are the women with their crafts?" Teodoro gestured for me to go further into the village. "Are you coming with me?" I asked.

"They say it is okay for you to go to them. I will be there in a moment."

With apprehension, I moved into the interior of the village in search of the women with their crafts. The prospect of moving deeper into the village unescorted was new and I felt a little unsettled but soon I felt lightness and an ease of acceptance as I walked further into the group of thatched houses. Stepping up a small hill and spotting the women with their shawls spread out on the ground, I wondered how they knew I was coming to this spot. I did not see anyone run ahead and announce my arrival.

They smiled and gestured for me to come closer and look at their work. Approaching, and then sitting on the ground with the women, they talked with me and presented their crafts. The women with their infants wrapped on their bodies returned to nursing or playing with their babies, as my eyes and hands sifted through and selected from all the wonderful colorful handiwork of wooden carved animals, woven baskets, beautiful feathered earrings, intricate beaded necklaces and bracelets. Teodoro eventually joined me to help choose from the many items and to translate the transaction.

"So which ones are you going to buy?"

"I don't know. There are so many wonderful pieces to choose from, and I have to decide what people will accept at home."

"You'd better hurry because the sun is going down."

"Okay, then please ask them how much for all of this, as I pointed to my chosen wares."

Darkness descended quickly and we fumbled around in the semi-twilight, paying the women and helping them to pack their things. The women quietly slipped away in the darkness. As Teodoro and I turned from the empty space, I had no idea how to find our way back saying, "Gosh, I think we need a flashlight!"

"It is so amazing how quickly it becomes dark in the forest."

"You go first because I am not sure of the way out."

"Here, take my hand."

"Did you work out the details for the cacique's birthday?"

"Oh yes! I believe he is very happy. This year will be a special celebration." As we chatted and navigated slowly down the path to our vehicle, a young man approached, exchanged words with Teodoro, who then turned and shrugged his shoulders, saying, "He wants us to follow him."

I was grateful that someone appeared to guide us. We descended the low slope carefully in the dark, and I realized that we were near a large thatched dwelling. As we rounded the corner to the structure, the young man gestured for us to enter. I held my breath as we passed through a small door and entered a large room that I knew instantly to be the *Opy*, the house of prayer. Neither Teodoro nor I spoke; we only looked at each other in amazement. I had no idea of the reason for this occurrence or what was going to happen next.

I was touched to be here, to be included in this gathering.

The Guaraní hold the Opy to be sacred and usually, outsiders are not allowed inside. My heart was pounding as I quickly scanned the dimly lit space. My eyes quickly adjusted to the candlelight, and Teodoro and I followed the gesture from our escort to sit. The interior room had simple low wooden benches along two sides and an altar at the opposite side of the entrance. The altar was about five feet high and composed of a narrow board set on two posts. On the altar were candles, rattles, and other musical instruments—including the one I witnessed earlier being played by the man during our welcoming visit.

We moved silently to the far corner near the altar and sat on the low bench. I quietly set my bundle of crafts at my feet. A young boy, who seemed to be around ten was smoking a pipe and praying while circling the circumference of the room and passed in front of the altar and each person sitting on the benches. We both fixed our eyes on him to understand the meaning of his intentions.

As this was happening, the Opy was filling with children and adults who positioned themselves on the small benches on either side. The man who had been playing the small guitar earlier came in and picked the instrument from the altar and sat opposite us. He began singing softly while playing.

The young boy made several full circles around the inside while chanting and smoking a pipe, passing close by all who were seated. Each time he passed the altar, he directed a forceful stream of air on each item on the altar and also on the larger musical instruments, the takuá (that looked and sounded like rain barrels) that lay propped below the altar. This boy was performing a preparatory cleansing ceremony. Soon after, everyone gathered and the door was locked from the inside.

The chanting youth then commenced the ceremony, beginning at the opposite side from where we sat. He inhaled from his pipe, then directed a forced breath directly on the top of each person's head at the fontanels spot of the cranium. The benches were low, which allowed the young boy to easily perform his cleansing movement—even on my friend who was of his taller height.

Many of the gathered children were lined up facing the altar. The boys standing closest to the altar began to sing; some used rattles, the mbaraká. The girls lined up behind the boys and used the takuá by rhythmically pounding them on the ground in synch with the singing. The girls answered loudly to what the boys sang out, and both moved their feet in specific ways and differently to different songs.

Cacique Tata Ti placed a jar of water with tobacco leaves on the altar and then returned to the end of our bench and began smoking a pipe near the door with another elder. As the children sang he smoked and prayed.

As Tata Ti continued to smoke his pipe and pray, the children sang many songs. Some were serious about their task, and others were smiling and having fun. The young boy who performed the cleansing ceremony was now among the young boys who giggled and were playful, yet respectful while singing. He maintained a reverent composure throughout the ceremony, not bothered by the gaiety of his neighbors. Apparently, this young person was in a trance state, and he came and rested near a very old man in the corner seated next to us.

At one point during the ceremony, a young boy not more than five years old entered and looked for a place to sit. The only available space was a very small opening between me and another adolescent. This young child did not hesitate to squeeze himself in next to me. Expecting to feel a sense of repulsion when our skin touched, much like experiences with children at home when they had no choice but to sit by an unknown adult, this child exuded no feeling of strangeness. This experience was so endearing. The feeling in my heart grew large and warm.

This heart feeling was a combination of being allowed to participate in a ceremony, the comfort of the child sitting next to me, and the accepting nature of all the people inside the room.

At this point, I ceased being an observer. Closing my eyes and listening to the children sing, feeling the pounding sound of takuás coursing through my legs via my bare feet on the dirt floor and the shaking rattles explosive in the house of prayer quieted my mind and unified my senses. I surrendered to my surroundings.

The timbre of the singers moved to the different expressions of sound coming from the rattles and takuás and my body dropped all tension and naturally fell into their rhythm.

Recognizing familiar words such as Ñande Ru, I joined in and chanted in a loud voice with the girls. Very quickly I felt in harmony with the group. Our collective intention of appealing to a higher power was all too evident and we easily slipped into a strong feeling of praise and gratitude for life.

At some point during the devotional singing, which lasted for more than an hour, I became aware of a pulsating, loving presence expanding my heart-center. There seemed to be no separation, and the feeling of oneness permeated the Opy. The group called out to God—Ñande Ru—with great yearning to hear our prayers and, blissfully intoxicated, I felt myself floating beyond the boundaries of my body.

The music changed. Teodoro moved from his spot and I was partially brought back to my physical body. Without breaking from the singing I quickly scanned the room and located him with the cacique at the end of the bench by the door.

Cacique Tata Ti was praying over Teodoro's head, holding a jar of water and tobacco leaves. He dipped the tobacco leaves into the water and touched specific areas of Teodoro's body, particularly around the head and the back of the neck. He repeated touching these places while he prayed. Feeling peace and happiness for my friend, my heavy eyes closed easily and I slipped effortlessly back into the rhythmic singing.

Suddenly the singing abruptly stopped, and Teodoro returned to his spot. Resting there in silence, we watched as the instruments were placed on the altar, and everyone silently cleared out of the Opy. The last to leave, we stepped out of the house of prayer in a daze and found ourselves alone, amazed, and entranced. We stood in the light of a full moon in a cloudless sky.

The canopy of trees in moonlight silhouetted him as I looked around and spoke in quiet reverence my first words since entering the Opy, "I feel overwhelmed with joy. I have no words, I just feel so wonderful. My heart feels like it will burst, and I'm so humbled with the sharing from these loving people."

Dreamily, Teodoro responded, "Hmm, yes, it was so wonderful." Looking around, there was no one in sight.

"Where did everyone go?" I wondered aloud.

"I don't know, but we now have the moon to help us out of the village!"

"What just happened in there, Teo?"

"I received my Guaraní name, Karai Tupã."

I caught my breath saying, "Oh! How wonderful! I did briefly see the cacique in some form of ceremony with you. So this was your baptism? What an honor! What does Karai Tupã mean?"

"It means 'God helper.' You know I have to thank you for this happening. I did not know this baptism would happen now."

I replied in a burst, "Oh no, it is I who need to thank *you!*"

"Please listen, I need to say thank you, and I will explain why." Standing in the moonlight surrounded by thatched huts and the stillness of the forest, Teo proceeded to explain. "The cacique said to me the reason the baptism took place tonight was because *you* were singing. The cacique summoned me when he saw you become immersed in song, and this action allowed my baptism."

I was speechless as I recalled Alberto's explanation of how the people felt that song brought them closer to God. How they came together unconditionally every evening to sing. As soon as a certain feeling, or what Alberto explained as a specific vibration, was reached with the singing, then and only then would the ceremonies or healings take place.

I felt the unity Alberto described in surrendering to the pounding of the takuás, the shaking of the rattles, the smoke, and most of all, the singing.

In that moment, I understood that I would not comprehend the depth of all had taken place. However, I could embrace the genuine feelings of joy and exuberance in my heart-center. For me, this encounter was a spiritual gift, an authenticated experience of Alberto's story of how the people came together each night to sing songs of praise until a sense of harmonious connection was achieved before proceeding with the ritual. Communally, the participants tapped into a stream of consciousness that was love.

My humbling experience in the Opy was a direct knowing of the power of their song, more so, of the communal power of love and reciprocity. And this lives on in my heart. Alberto had begun every class by saying in his rich and passionate voice, "They are always giving, they are always sharing."

Teo and I walked away in awe of this beautiful evening spent with these gentle, giving people. This experience and the expansion of my heart-center opened me to better see the world through a prism of unconditional love. We drove home in silent wonder.

Alberto's messages were clarified, but I also realized another point about the musical nature of the Guaraní. In every Ama-Deus class Alberto taught, he had everyone sing, and he encouraged the people to watch the movie *The Mission*, which according to him was being filmed in another area during his visits with the Guaraní. This movie strongly demonstrated their spiritual nature; however, the natural musical inclination of this culture was also made obvious. The humbling experience in the Opy allowed me to encounter the power of their music firsthand.

For me, personally, all of these experiences were a continuation of my love for learning indigenous ways—a real treasure and far more than just an archaeological study. After reviewing substantial written accounts of these people and their naming ceremony, I felt a deeper love for this work and the Guaraní people.

In this celebration I attended with Teodoro, the cacique delivered the ceremony. The pajé at the time was one hundred and four years of age, and he ministered several villages extended over several hundred miles. He visited the villages in the most need. Many of the ceremonies can be officiated by the cacique or any person the community deems has demonstrated a level of spiritual attainment. Receiving a sacred song in a dream entitles the dreamer to baptize others. Pajé Tupa Nevangayu says soul perception and soul knowledge come from the spiritual or divine realm. "There is a great spirit in our chest near our heart. It protects us while we sleep. When we sleep, this spirit goes to heaven. This is how we dream and have communication with heaven. This is the path where the songs are sent."[58]

Teodoro and I agreed from our observations that the young boy singing in a trance state and performing the opening ceremony was preparing himself for the role of pajé for his community. This ceremony we experienced did not last late into the morning hours, as recorded from earlier accounts, but most assuredly, the power of the word souls were experienced as well as the community participation. The Guaraní today continue to practice their spiritual ways and continue to view their world from a soul perspective.

CHAPTER 7

Pajés are Masters of Divine Word Souls

Let your mind start a journey through a strange new world.
Leave all thoughts of the world you knew before.
Let your soul take you where you long to be ...
Close your eyes let your spirit start to soar, and you'll live as
you've never lived before.
—Erich Fromm

What constitutes a wise person in the Guaraní culture? Song defines or expresses a person's level of spiritual awareness—the song in one's heart, which is brought through the dream state. The number of songs or word souls determines how one participates in community ceremonies. The importance of song is the determiner for earning the role of the pajé—shaman. From the early accounts to the present day, the pajé or the *opara'iva*, which means the "one who sings," is the community's important spiritual leader. Again, Nimuendaju brought the first description that was also recorded by several observers since. He described four categories of spiritual attainment, and this ranking has been held in high regard in Guaraní society. He begins by saying: "The Guaraní medicine men are different from those of other native groups in that one does not become a medicine man by learning or by initiation but only through inspiration."[59] His four categories begin ranking those who do not have a song, to those who have received one or a few and use them in private context (in which most adults over thirty-five fit in this category), to those who feel the urge to assume a leading role in the sacred dances to serve the community, and those who have perfected their spiritual powers to the highest degree and become the pajés.

The community ultimately decides who will be pajé after many demonstrations by an individual. He must reveal not only his ability for receiving songs, but also the willingness to be of service to his community. Metraux added to this observation in his accounts:

> No amount of training can make an *Apapocuva-Guaraní* a shaman if he has not been supernaturally inspired with magic chants . . . Its possession confers a certain immunity against accidents. A shaman is a man who owns a great many magic chants, which he uses for the common good of his people . . . he must also have frequent dreams, because they give him superior knowledge and insight into the future . . . Legends and historical traditions both attest the extraordinary prestige enjoyed by some shamans of old who were leaders of their tribes. After receiving their inspiration, these great men retired into the wilderness, where they lived on celestial food. By constant dancing some *Apapocuava-Guaraní* shamans gradually subjugated their animal soul, strengthening their ayvucué, or peaceful soul, until they could fly toward the heavenly Land-Without-Evil.[60]

The following is Keeney's account from the words of a present-day shaman, Tupa Nevangayu, which confirms Nimuendaju and Metraux's work and also makes obvious that traditions are still strongly maintained.

> A child as young as seven to eight years old could have a spiritual dream and become a shaman. There is no age requirement for becoming a holy person. That is something God decides. I was twelve years old when I had my first vision. The owner of a sacred song appeared to me. He was dressed as a shaman . . .[61] If you didn't come to earth to be a shaman, there is nothing you can do to become one. God chooses you. You cannot make yourself become a shaman if you were not chosen to be one. No one can teach you how to be one.[62]

So it is with the Guaraní. The pajés were and still are the leaders of their community. The honor stems from their God-given natural ability to access the divine word or "word soul," the demonstration of great reverence and kindness, and the complete acknowledgement from the community. Those who could lead from this standpoint were in love with the divine realms. Viveiros de Castro relates his experience of the pajé's role:

> Every night . . . in the small hours of the morning, I heard emerging from the silence a high, solitary intonation, sometimes exalted, sometimes melancholic, but always austere, solemn, and to me, somewhat macabre. It was the shaman's singing the *Maï maraca*, the music of the gods. Only during the most acute phase of the influenza epidemic and for a period after the death of a middle-aged woman did these songs cease. On certain nights, three to four shamans sang at the same time or successively, each experiencing his personal vision. Sometimes only one sang, starting with a gentle humming and droning, gradually raising his voice, tracing a staccato articulation that stood out against the continuous, sibilant backdrop of an *array* rattle, until it reached a pitch and intensity that was maintained for over an hour. It then descended back slowly into the first light of sunrise the "hour when the earth is unveiled" [*iwi pï dawa me*], until it returned into silence.[63]

This experience by Viveiros de Castro supported Alberto's stories of how the community came together in the evening unconditionally to the Opy and sang with the pajé. The nighttime mesmerized the people. Through his great love for them, as well as his unshakable attention to the beauty of their life, we certainly could assume in the ten years of Alberto's interactions that he too was introduced and mesmerized through song and their poetic oral history.

Still today in the most recent accounts from Keeney, Pajé Tupa Nevangayu in his humble attitude shares the value of song and the importance of divine word souls.

> When I put myself into a prayerful attitude, I speak with great humility, acknowledging that I am nothing as a person. I confess that I am simple flesh made of dirt. This attitude helps to make me a cradle for the soul. For the Guaraní, the word souls are the main thing. I am only a medium for the spirits who carry the word souls. We bring forth word souls for the good of the world . . . whenever I'm about to receive a new song, something evil

usually comes to distract or tempt me. Every day I have to grab my rattle and pray, "Great God, you must protect me. My true father and true mother, please help me." You, too, must pray for help. Spiritual gifts always come with an evil that challenges you. Always ask the gods for help.[64]

The picture presented from older accounts and the more recent indicate the all-encompassing spiritual life of the Guaraní and clear insight as to Alberto's attraction and dedication to these people. All the numerous accounts that focus on the spiritual aspects of Guaraní life found great joy in recording their discoveries and demonstrated that all those who really took the time were deeply touched and even changed by these people. The pajés are still finding hope in their *words souls*, and they are still singing. From a present pajé, Ava Tupa Rayv:

> It is said that we are strong shamans.
> We are the Ka'aguygua
>   the "People of the Forest."
>
> The forest is not simply
> the place where we live.
> We are the forest.
> It is our life.
>
> Our greatest gift is voicing
> the spirit of the forest:
> The sounding of the word souls.
>
> Someone dreamed that more
> and more people
> are talking about shamans:
> saying we ascend and descend
> into the Vision,
> saying we have helpers of spirit,
> saying we seek power,
> saying that the rattle,
> independent of any God, is sufficient,

saying it finds lost souls,
saying all kinds of things.

KNOW THIS:
We, among the strongest who see spirit
and experience its power, say that
many who talk about such things
have not seen, heard, or been touched
by what is most essential.
We are thereby called to speak
our simple truth:
A shaman is someone who
prays to their God.
Prayer is the instrument, the link.
All other paths only pretend.
It is prayer, prayer, and more prayer.
This is what gives you flight,
Brings you the purest sight,
And reconnects you to
the web of light.

You will know a shaman by
the sound of their prayer.
They carry the word souls.
No song, no shaman.
Songs of prayer come from
a serving heart.
They cleanse, forgive,
and rekindle hope.

There is no other way
of the shaman than
prayer and song.
It is the way we know God,
It is the way we become the forest,
It is the truest way.[65]

Word souls', the songs that come from the spiritual realm in dreams, keep the Guaraní in a present state of mind. Pajés continue to be masters of word souls and the spiritual leaders of the Guaraní, looking for guidance outside the earthly realm to this very day.

Dreams as Pathways to Receive Songs

We now understand that the pajé's access knowledge from the trance states is induced through song and dance and that the dream state is held in high esteem and contained invaluable knowledge for the community. Anyone in the community was eligible and may receive a sacred song in the dream state. Alberto lectured on what he called "enchanted women." They brought forth information received from their dreams to the community in the Opy each evening. Altered states of consciousness, whether trances or dreams, were normal and accepted by the Guaraní. The early accounts of Nimuendaju state:

> As far as dreams are concerned, the Apapocúva [Guaraní] agree with all other Indians [villages] that these are real events of great significance. Even if a dream is not connected to an immediately tangible result, dreams are still experiences that can impart knowledge and skill. Those who dream know more than those who don't; medicine men therefore cultivate dreaming as an important source of knowledge and power.[66]

Metraux's notes support this importance: Dreams are experiences of the soul and are paid great attention, especially by shamans, who derive their supernatural knowledge and power from them.[67] And during a period of cohabitation in the mid-1980s, Reed recalls his experience:

> Elder leaders provide religious direction for their families. This ability increases with age, as older residents accumulate experience in communicating with the supernatural. Knowledge is seen or heard while asleep, ikérupi. For example, it was not uncommon to enter a community after an absence of weeks or months and to be met by children proclaiming my arrival with excitement but not surprise: "He's arrived!" rather than "He's

back!" After the first greetings, their leaders would explain that my coming had been dreamed and word spread through the community. I had been expected.[68]

The Guaraní community rejoices in the individual who shares the dream he or she receives, as this is a sign of continued access to divine guidance for the community. Meditative chants can also be avenues for supernatural knowledge. Reed described the *poraé* as literally meaning "to sing," and it is often received in a dream state "through personal inspiration that is neither solicited from nor taught by religious specialists. The chanting is used by individuals in search of guidance ... after a period of intense *poraé* which can often last several days, the intonation becomes part of that individual's tool for accessing the supernatural."[69]

Schaden eloquently states: "Without any exaggeration, it can be said that the Guaraní ceases to be Guaraní when he ceases to feel the necessity to apply himself to his religious devotions, that is, to the *porahêi* (song)."[70]

There is no educational format for receiving information in dreams; this is a naturally occurring event. Life close to the earth in rhythm with the stars, cultivating spiritually based cycles of food production, community support, and reverence to dreaming—all lend a nourishing environment. Schaden points out once again in this description the Guaraní view of life a soul perspective is foremost. God teaches you about God is the Guaraní theme:

> Regarding the soul, that is, the psychic and moral individuality, there are some practices of magic—educative treatment, but of secondary importance. The soul is born already finished, or at least with certain qualities, so to speak, embryonic. In general, therefore, no attempt is made to force the development of the psychic nature. Several magical remedies developed by the culture in order to influence the formation of the personality of the immature ... The Ñandéva told me that prayers are not taught to the children for, being individual, they are sent directly by the deities. . . . [One of the elders in an air of contempt told me] "We do not need money, nor any school for God says so. A child does not need school, because knowledge comes from God."[71]

One example of receiving information in the dreams, as related earlier in the naming ceremony, the incoming soul is identified and given a name for his or her earthly journey. Alberto spoke often of how the children were adored and respected by the community, as the people believed in reincarnation. The "extraordinary love" that he witnessed was for the loved ones who have returned to them. The father is usually the first to receive the information that a child will be forthcoming in a dream. He tells the dream to the mother, and she becomes pregnant. "Therefore, the child is sent by the gods . . . the ideas concerning the connection existing between conception and sexual relations are obscure," as recorded by Schaden.[72] Life is given because of the spirit world. Specific precautions in preparation for the incoming soul are adhered to by the parents for prenatal and postnatal care. Diet and work schedules and emotional states are considered. "A pregnant woman should not become angry because the rage would pass to the flesh, the bones, and the spirit of the child."[73]

Complete soul awareness is involved in all aspects of life. Later in the chapter on Ama-Deus, the importance of "soul" level healing is evident and adds reinforcement to the thought that "soul awareness" is the key to understanding the Guaraní cosmology. Through Alberto's lectures, we first learned of their spiritual nature. And now these added accounts from centuries of descriptions seem to indicate "unanimous agreement that the mental framework of the Guaraní is suspended in the spiritual world."[74]

Word Souls to Share

Keep in mind, all this information cited from written sources originally comes to us in oral transmissions. The Guaraní language is rich in images and expressions. The illustrations of Guaraní poetic language allow the opportunity for the Western mind to absorb the beauty and the potency of their divine world. Their word souls demonstrate a manifestation of their spiritual refinement.

From the earliest accounts, de Léry recalled his experience of their songs;

> I received in recompense such joy, hearing the measured harmonies of such a multitude, and especially in the cadence and refrain of the song, when at every verse all of them would let their voices trail saying *Heu, heuaure, heura, heuarue, heuta, heura, oueh*—I stood there transported with delight. Whenever

I remember it my heart trembles, and it seems their voices are
still in my ears.[75]

Reading this account, could de Léry have felt the same vibration
that both Alberto and I experienced? Nimuendaju spoke also of his
experiences in hearing their songs as mystically moving.

The word souls collected in *The Guaraní Religious Experience* by Melià,
a contemporary Jesuit anthropologist (songs are cited from Cadogan's
1959 work) gives a wonderful glimpse of their songs. Even though the
music from a human voice is omitted, it is a privilege to read and feel the
dream song—the following word souls with the intention to exalt and
give praise, as seen in these two songs which petition the greatness of
heart and courage:

Around the houses where they say beautiful prayers
I go walking, dispersing the clouds
(the smoke of ritual tobacco smoke).
to preserve it so I shall learn numerous words
To strengthen my inner being.
So that the true Father of my word will see it;
that in a not too distant future they will cause me to
say many, many words.
Although we love one another sincerely
if we allow our heart to be divided,
we will never reach a greatness of heart nor be
strengthened.[76]

◊   ◊   ◊

Oh, Our First Father!
it was you who first knew the rules of our way of being.
It was you who first knew within yourself that which was
to be the basic word,
before opening and showing the earthly dwelling ...
Towards greatness of heart, some among us, from among the
few that remain, we are trying hard ...

To those of us who remain erect in the earth,
grant that we may live, standing straight,
with greatness of heart.[77]

I recall Alberto's passionate descriptions of how the Guaraní saw the sacred in all life—the trees the vegetation, the hills, the rivers, the animals. The following outpouring of love exhibits their sacred world in giving praise to their beautiful earthly experience.

You yourself are the Creator.
Now we are treading on this shining earth, said the Creator.
Now we are treading on this evocative earth, said the Creator.
Now we are treading on this thundering earth, said the Creator.
Now we are treading on this perfumed earth, said the Creator.
Now we are treading on this shining, perfumed earth, said the Creator.
Now we are treading on this evocative, perfumed earth, said the Creator.

. . . .

Beautiful they are when they open
the flowers of the gates of paradise;
the flowers of the brilliant gates of paradise;
the flowers of the evocative gates of paradise;
the flowers of the thundering gates of paradise.[78]

In singing of beautiful life, their philosophy, the Guaraní way of life, Melia captures the song's essence in this expressive passage: "A people that has lived in such an environment for centuries has had to think of its true land in terms of light and sound for not only the birds, the insects and the waters talk, but also the trees like the cedars from which 'the word flows' (*yvyra ñe'ery*).")[79]

Immersing oneself in the details of the Guaraní way of life, a song takes on a new and expanded meaning. As I pondered the reason for the power in a song, attempting not to draw from scientific validation of the benefits of harmonics to life, the so-called discovery that all life is vibration; I called out to my youngest son who was sitting within earshot in another room, "What makes singing so powerful?"

"It is a higher form of communication," he responded instantly.

"Of course!" I said out loud to myself in response. My pensive mind then drifted to the impressions of all the current songs that speak of getting, losing, and then finding love in limitless variations. People obviously seem ravenous to sing about love. What would happen if people did what the Guaraní did and extended their awareness to Divine Love? To sing about an ecstatic experience from the heart brings to mind other indigenous peoples who chant in community. How about our singing and chanting for Divine Love, especially if the song came in a dream, and our friends and family were anxiously waiting to hear it?

In summary, the Guaraní measure a person by his or her inspired song, which indicates a treasured connection to the spirit world. This value is held higher than any measure of economic production or any material gain, resulting in the absence of individual and collective competition or separateness and the presence of shared heart in community balances and maintains the village unity. The Guaraní see their songs as divine links to a realm that shares the truth and gives them ultimate sustenance. In the form of prayer, they came together in small groups in the Opy and reverently listened and made approving exclamations.

The true Father Ñamandu, the first,
of a part of his celestial being
from the wisdom contained in being celestial
with his knowledge which is opening up,
made the llamas and the clouds reproduce.
Having begun and stood erect as a man,
from the wisdom contained in his celestial being,
with his expansive and communicative knowledge
he knew the basic future word for himself.
From the wisdom contained in his celestial being,
in virtue of his knowledge that blossoms into flower,
Our Father caused the basic word to be opened
and it became as he is, divinely celestial.

When the earth did not exist,
in the midst of the ancient darkness,
when nothing was known,

he caused the basic word to be opened,
which became divinely celestial with him;
this is what Ñamandu, the true father, the first, did.

Already knowing for himself the basic word that was
to be,
from the wisdom contained in his celestial being,
in virtue of his knowledge that blossoms into flower,
he knew for himself the basis of love for another.

. . . .

Having already caused the basis of the word that was
to be to blossom into flower
having already caused a single love to blossom into
flower,
from the wisdom contained in his heavenliness,
in virtue of his knowledge that blossoms into flower,
he caused a mighty song to be spread abroad.

When the earth did not exist,
in the midst of the ancient darkness,
when nothing was known,
he caused that a powerful song be spread abroad for
himself.

. . . .

Having already caused the basis of the future word to
blossom into flower for himself,
having already caused a part of love to blossom into
flower for himself,
having already caused a powerful song to blossom into
flower for himself,
he carefully considered
who would be made to participate in the basis of the
word,

who would participate in this singular love,
who would participate in the series of words that
would make up the song.

. . . .

Having already considered deeply,
he caused those who were to be companions of his
celestial divine being to stand forth,

. . . .

he caused the Ñamandu of great heart to stand forth.
He caused them to stand forth with the reflection of
his wisdom,
when the earth did not exist,
in the midst of the ancient darkness.

. . . .

After all of this,
from the wisdom contained in his celestial being,
in virtue of his wisdom that blossoms into flower,
to the true father of the future Karai,
to the true father of the future Jakaira,
to the true father of the future Tupa,
he caused them to be known as divinely celestial.
The true fathers of his own many children,
the true fathers of the words of his own many children,
he caused them to be known as divinely celestial.
After all of this,
the true father Ñamandu,
to she who was before his very heart,
to the true father mother of the Ñamandu
he caused her to be known as (divinely) celestial.
(Karai, Jakaira and Tupa in the same way placed

115

before their hearts the future mothers of their
children.)
Because they had already assimilated the celestial
wisdom of
their own First Father,
because the had already assimilated the basis of the
word,
because they had already assimilated the basis of love
because they had already assimilated the series of
words of the powerful song,
because they had already assimilated the wisdom that
blossoms in flower,
for this same reason, we call them:
sublime true fathers of words,
sublime true mothers of words.[80]

These songs help us feel the beauty, reverence, and sacredness the Guaraní have for life. And I agree with Nimuendaju, theirs is "poetry in a metaphysical universe."[81] This profound spiritual presence created in a song, as well as their giving nature, seems not to have changed over the centuries.

My personal experience in the Opy was a direct experience of the power of their song, but more so, of the communal power of love and reciprocity. Alberto started every class saying, in his rich and passionate voice, "They are always giving, always sharing."

CHAPTER 8

Reciprocity, Love, and the Land with No Evil

God-realization is nothing but the ability and
expansiveness of the heart to love everything equally.
—Amma

The Guaraní validate, fortify, and sanctify their community within ceremony, identifying their connection and relationship with all of life. All is held sacred to the Guaraní as we heard from Alberto, "The land, the water, the sun, the moon, the vegetation are all a continuation of their home." The land is beautiful and bountiful because the great God orchestrates this. They strive to live in communal harmony, rejoicing in the gifts of the land.

The Guaraní live with the principle that "cooperation is strength." They share work in kin groups and among friends, usually with tasks that are boring or arduous. Reed observes that as the yearly food cycle can be a "picture of scarcity and abundance sharing among the family is an inborn responsibility."[82] The spiritual orientation of the culture, as seen in all accounts, indicates that there is no division or separation in lifestyle, for spirituality is in all aspects of Guaraní life. The economic cycle is determined by the ecological cycle that is determined by the spiritual world, a kind of "ecclesiastical year," described by Schadon.[83]

From the numerous accounts we have come to know, there is little social distinction. More importance is placed on the "way of life" for the community. Reciprocity establishes alliance with the gods, as the gods give, so too does the incarnate soul in a natural outpouring of love. To the Guaraní, a person reaches perfection, explained Schaden, in the following:

According to modern day expressions the virtues are goodness [*teko pora*], justice [*teko joja*], good words [*ñe'ẽ jpja*], reciprocal love [*joayhu*], diligence and availability [*kyre'y*], deep peace [*py'a guapy*], serenity [*teko ñemboro'y*], and inner purity without duplicity [*py'a poti*]. These practices and ways of being do not actually refer to individual or personal behavior, but to relationships with others. These virtues are mainly envisioned and given their social context in political meetings and in the religious feast. They are closely connected to speech: the word that is heard, the spoken word, and the prophetic word. These words are made possible by the practices of reciprocity.[84]

I related to this inherent practice of singing and reciprocity from my first encounter with the Guaraní village of Cacique Tata Ti in 2005. The third visit with the village demonstrated a growing acceptance, allowing me to partake in a ceremony. The first visit, however, was not without experiencing the Guaraní way of life. Communal sharing and giving were very much alive, from my first observation, and was an inherent natural extension of their beingness.

The first trip to Brazil came about when Christian Vianna's, a native of Brazil, searched the Internet and eventually called me to inquire about the background of Alberto and the Ama-Deus healing method. The conclusion of our conversation was to teach a class in Brazil in 2005. This would be my first visit to this country and to Alberto's homeland. I was overjoyed to learn that there was the added bonus of visiting a Guaraní village arranged by our gracious host, Christian. He had an established relationship with this particular village and the cacique, Tata Ti, and he knew the proper etiquette. Christian met with Tata Ti to seek permission for a visitation. On the third day after the two-day class of Ama-Deus arrangements had been made for a visitation to the Guarani village.

To uphold the etiquette and to demonstrate *our* reciprocity, Christian brought enough soccer balls for all the children in the village—more than eighty brand new soccer balls were packed into his small vehicle. I had several packages of tobacco and white candles for the cacique, along with some small items for the children brought from home. After arriving in Brazil, Christian helped to select another item—cookies—for me to share with all the children.

Nearing the village after traveling several miles through the Atlantic rain forest, we saw people gathering at the edge of the village as we arrived. Looking down into the ravine to a meandering river, we saw children splashing in the water. They ran up the embankment to meet our vehicle.

Christian stepped from his vehicle and motioned for us to wait as he went into the village first to meet with the cacique. My son and I waited at the vehicle for their return. After a few minutes of eager anticipation, we saw Christian with an elder emerging from a grouping of thatched-roof homes.

At the edge of the clearing, Christian formally introduced my son and I to the cacique in Portuguese. He went on to show him the gifts. Christian continued to discuss something as my son and I listened in silence. Christian finally turned and winked at me as the cacique gathered all the children. Christian came to our side and explained that the children were going to sing for us.

The children formed two lines, the girls on one side and the boys on the other, forming a large V shape around us as we stood to listen. The boys sang a song, and the girls followed up in repeating a refrain. Both performed slightly different footwork as they sang. One male teenager, at the point of intersection of the two lines, played a guitar. From teenagers to toddlers held in arms of the girls, they all sang several songs for us without nervousness or reservation. When this was complete, the children raced toward the cacique, who dispersed the gifts to the children with a big smile.

Sitting around after the soccer balls and the cookies were passed out, Christian explained to the cacique that we were from the United States and had come for this special visit. The cacique with a big smile extended his hand to us in welcome. I offered him candles and tobacco. He smiled saying aguyje, *thank you* in Guaraní several times. Then he turned to speak to Christian.

Christian now had the big smile on his face telling us, "He says that you may take a picture with him."

"Really!" As we watched the cacique make a gesture to sit next to him, Christian continued to explain, "Yes, you know that you must have permission to film anything in the village. It is only permitted by the cacique."

"Okay, what are we to do?"

"Come, he wants you to sit here next to him." As I sat down, he was primed with a big smile at the camera. I was not sure of the etiquette, but was so moved to place my hand on his knee after he put his arm on my shoulder.

"And, Christopher, he would like you to sit here." Snap, snap went the camera. Then Christian and the cacique's son joined in the pictures. This little scene was his way of giving us appreciation for the gifts and special visit.

The cacique was leading his community in sharing and giving, the children with their role of giving and the cacique with his. We were blessed with a brief but momentous experience of life with these joy-filled people, who were gracious givers. We were briefly immersed in reciprocity born out of the interpersonal relationship in the revered attitude of community. This fundamental way of being is very much alive today. As we read earlier in the numerous ethnological and anthropological descriptions of these people, they view all life as sacred, upholding their earned title of the "theologians of South America."

The Land Without Evil—
Endangered Spirits in a Material World

A myth from past recordings that continues to be a central theme in the present Guaraní cosmology is the "land without evil." Reciprocity born from communing with the spiritual realm to maintain balance and harmony with the earth sustained the Guaraní on their sacred journey toward the "land without evil". There are consistent Jesuits' records of periodic searching for an earthly paradise. This myth, passed down through oral history, described a place where crops grow themselves, people never die, and they spend their time eating and dancing. One could get to this paradise or land without evil by finding the right path and observing strict practices of dancing, chanting, and fasting.

These migrations are led by a more "extravagant pajé" who does not live with any one tribe, but lives alone in the jungle and exhibits great feats of magic. These pajés could incite huge movements of people. What was not consistent was the location for this land without evil. Most times, the migrations were directed to the east across the ocean, where the land meets the sky, and other times, the migration was inland. Regardless of the location or direction, the "land without evil" is still strongly held within the Guaraní belief system.

The "land without evil" has been recorded consistently from early sources; ethnologists and historians have offered their opinions of the motive for these "messianic" migrations. Hélène Clastres dedicates an entire book, *The Land-without-Evil*, recounting several documents and offering her theory.

Another researcher, Melià suggests the idea that the "land without evil" refers to "intact soil, where nothing has been built."[85] Melià's theory was based on his readings of the Jesuit Antonio Ruiz de Montoya's *Tesoro de la Lengua Guaraní*. Robin Wright, with Manuela Carneiro da Cunha in *Destruction, Resistance, and Transformation—Southern, Coastal, and Northern Brazil (1580–1890)*, suggests that moving to a virgin forest had to do with ecological reasons.

Regardless of the interpretation, there seems to be strong consensus that the migration patterns to a land without evil had been intact prior to Iberian penetration in the fifteenth century and were not caused by the forced introduction of new social systems. Rather and more importantly, this rooted belief has been embedded in their spiritual practices.

Consequently, it is the driving force in their plea for land; as without land, the Guaraní "way of being" is lost.[86] So strong is this belief that even though a migration might not prove to be successful, great reverence persists in following the spiritual communication to this day.

This reverent attention to the land was also based on oral historical origins depicting epics when mankind became imbalanced, the results of which were calamities. The recorded flood story was familiar, but it was only one event. Reed described the following from his work with the Guaraní:

> It is believed that *Ñanderuguazú* created this world, destroyed it several times, and will cause the final destruction sometime in the future. Although the accounts vary greatly, there are reports that the earth was destroyed three different times: variously by fire, by water, by falling darkness . . . the world was recreated after each cataclysm.[87]

These cataclysms, stored in oral proclamations and sustained in many cultures, globally depict sound evidence to how life became imbalanced but subsequently rebalanced. Is there something to be learned from this information? From the two contemporary Guaraní pajés, the same theme reverberates globally today: the plea for spiritual awareness in order to circumvent catastrophe. From the interviews by Keeney with Ava Tape Miri and Takua Kawirembeyju, we learn:

> Several months ago I had another big dream. It said that all the things from the sacred dreams are not being respected anymore. In many parts of the world, people are not following the ways their grandfathers and grandmothers taught them. The spirits told me that this is why there is so much trouble in our world. They also told me that modern people think that they are very wise because of technological developments, but they have forgotten how to talk with God. They have fallen away from God. This is the biggest problem for the future, and it will get worse.[88]

> All the bad things that human beings do to the earth also go up to the sun and cause harm to it. The bad things we do always

hurt the sun. When we do something wrong, we may not feel it, but the spirits know it. This is because the spirits are more sensitive than we are ...[89] The world is getting worse, but if we dance and pray there is hope.[90]

"Right now the worst thing non-Indian people are doing is the destruction of earth. We all have to take care of the earth. We must face this responsibility together . . . the future is up to us. We all have to be together. There will be fire, big water, and darkness . . . We can make things better. It is up to each one of us, because we have always been one people."[91]

To these pajés, the evil in the world is not naturally occurring, but rather a straying and deterioration from the good way of being. The "land without evil" is a continual spiritual framework that is lived in and will cause a new land and beautiful people a place of reciprocity and mutual love.

These pleas from present-day Guaraní pajés are not different from other current indigenous people around the world. They all have a deep understanding of the importance of being in harmony with each other, with the earth and other realms, and with the Spirit. There has been consistent sound evidence in their oral histories of the consequences when humankind is not in balance with the earth and universal energies.

Alberto too in his association with a particular village responded to their plea to share healing with the world. He had to earn his way with the community even though they knew he was coming. For two years, he worked along side of the pajé before given the status of the pajé himself. This was a monumental event for a village to not only accept a white man, but also allowing access to working with their sacred wisdom. Initiated on the banks of the Amazon into the sacred healing ways of the Guaraní, the pajé granted Alberto permission to translate and share the sacred healing way of the Guaraní into an oral form that would be understood in the "outside" world. Sacred stones were unearthed and presented to him as a gift of love and a symbol of sharing this love with the world. Alberto wholeheartedly accepted and opened himself to new opportunities to what he called "new life, new views, new experiences."

In collaboration with the Guaraní, over a span of several years, Alberto learned how to access and heal with Love according to the Guaraní ancient ways. He created and organized an abridged format to fit into a several-hour long workshop. Abridged, meaning that condensed knowledge extracted from a "way of life" of the village people was offered. Obviously, not all teachings could be contained and formatted for a weekend workshop.

In 1985, Alberto taught his first classes in the United States and Canada. He named these sacred teachings Ama-Deus. He taught that the words *Ama-Deus* are Latin, translated as "to love God." Like the Guaraní, Alberto believed that without the component of Love, there could be no healing. He stated strongly how the Guaraní understood that everyone had the ability to pass Love into this world, always knowing "the power was God." After working alongside the pajé and the village people for many years, Alberto was honored and touched by the entranced pajé calling him Ñandéva—the love of God.

In an act of reciprocity, Ama-Deus was the Guaraní way of sharing through Alberto their call to action with the world, in hope to circle the world in Love—to teach and share love, to maintain the mbiroy, the harmony, for *all* life.

Alberto spent half of the year living in Brazil and managing several trips to work with the Guaraní, and the other half of the year, he carried his newfound wisdom to North America. He was excited and passionate about delivering this sacred information. He tapped into his network of conferences to lecture, teach, and offer healings using Ama-Deus.

The information from early to present-day accounts of the Guaraní, enriched with information from Alberto's recordings, reveals consistency, accuracy, and most certainly, a deep spiritual awareness. The Guaraní's mystic nature, after centuries of the outside peoples' encroachment on their way of life, survived and was self-evident from the historical progression of accounts. Alberto risked his life to not only preserve a way of life, but also to bring awareness to our destructive behaviors and ignorance of our oneness with all life. He did this through an act of love for the Guaraní and for humankind. In partnership with the Guaraní, he offered a simple yet powerful method for all people to access energy for healing. A piece of sacred wisdom has been preserved from the beautiful word souls so that all may journey to the "land without evil"—for we all are *one people*.

PART III
AMA-DEUS AND HEALING

♦ ♦ ♦ ♦ ♦

Ancient word souls guided Yyvkuaraua and her captives on their forest journey to the Tupinamba coastal village. Crossing rivers with precarious footholds, trekking long distances without food, watching for wandering souls from abandoned villages, all made Yyvkuaraua's heart break out into song, asking for the gods to illumine their path. This was the way of her people to commune with the spiritual realm for guidance on all earthly matters.

Even with the unsettling ending of this day, Yyvkuaraua, as was the custom of the resting of the gold light of Kuarahy, felt herself in the Opy with her husband and all her village people. She sang an ancient song given by Ñande Ru for her father's soul to move to the Light, to transcend the force of earthly energies and rest in His peaceful Love. Through the night, she sang, and the forest and the small band of travelers listened. Her voice, full of beautiful word souls, was healing to them. Arapotiyu, at times, sang with his mother, as did the others from the village, while the captors felt the music bring peace to their minds and hearts.

Tupanchichù also felt soothed with the singing, as this was not strange to his people. He understood also that his earthly strength was supported by his attendance to the gods, and a song was the link. He was particularly enchanted with Yyvkuaraua and her healing presence. Even though he had several wives, this woman captivated him. Perhaps he was mistaken with his mission to find Arapotiyu; he was beginning to think Yyvkuaraua was his real gift. There, in the quiet of the forest night, he slept with a peacefulness that he had not known for many seasons.

As the first light filtered through the tree canopy, the band of travelers prepared to begin their final journey to the coastal village. Arapotiyu quickly assessed the wounded of his own people as well as the warriors. Even at such a young age Arapotiyu held a strong presence. His eyes shone with intense brightness and always seemed he was in two places at one time. Even though he was walking the earth, he was communing with the spirit realm.

127

His first dream at the age of five was powerful, especially for such a young age. The spirits of the four winds revealed to him the importance of four principal forces. The four gods overseeing these forces gave him a song for each sacred direction where they resided. In another dream, he was instructed through a sacred song to gather certain feathers and a stick to make a wand to use for healing.

After demonstrating his first dreams, Yyvkuaraua made a mbaraká for Arapotiyu. Being gifted a sacred rattle by a family member, who has received a sacred healing song, was the way of his people. Living in the loving presence of his parents, grandfather, and the village of forest people, Arapotiyu had a beautiful mentorship that prepared him for the role of a pajé.

The injection of force from Tupanchichù and his warriors was new to Arapotiyu. The image of his grandfather receiving an arrow, and then leaving his village gave him his first feeling of a hurting heart. He observed this feeling as he walked through the jungle. He changed this feeling by singing with his mother, listening to the guidance and feeling the strong presence of the spirits. His heart warmed as he saw and felt this communion with the spirit realm. Singing was never so dear to him as it was this strange day, for song was the path to the gods and gave meaning to the situation.

He knew his captors were driven by acyiguá, their animal soul, not their ayvuquê, their celestial soul. Their ways of fierceness and eating of animal meat fed their acyiguá. Soon, with the celestial support, his heart opened with desire to help these coastal people, and his sadness fled.

Most pajés specialized in a particular gift. His father had a great ability for inner vision. His mother and grandfather received numerous sacred songs in their dreams for healing. Arapotiyu not only received healing songs in his dreams, but he had also received strong inner vision. He received much information on how to live in balance. His latest dreams were sowing new seeds of how to use animal energy. He found it easy and comfortable to slip into different worlds to learn how to live in harmony on earth. He saw and felt all life as sacred.

As the band of travelers trekked single file silently along the jungle path, Tupanchichù pushed past some of his warriors to move close behind Yyvkuaraua and remarked, "You are pleasing to my eye, mother of Arapotiyu. When we arrive, I will make you comfortable with your new family." Yyvkuaraua did not respond but walked in elegant dignity and moved closer to her son.

As she took his hand, she said aloud for all to hear, "Ñande Ru will guide us, my sweet son, through this mystery." Yyvkuaraua and Arapotiyu moved in a more relaxed fashion than the other village people who were tied around theirs waists by a long rope to each other. Arapotiyu sided up to his mother and said, "Mother, I am not afraid. I see these people are in need of healing." "Yes, Arapotiyu, your vision is keen. Let us continue to pray not only for a safe journey, but to send love to your father to support our village."

As they approached their destination, Arapotiyu could smell and taste something foreign in the air. When they broke from the forest, there was a huge expanse of blue so beautiful to his eyes. He had only come upon stretches of waters that you could see across and that flowed in one direction. This large body of water repeatedly crashed forward as if it were begging to walk the land. He slowed his pace as the water's sound and movement mesmerized him. As far as he could see, there was no land across the water. This beautiful intriguing scene held his attention until the noises of a distant people turned his head. The awe-inspiring scene quickly faded as the village came into view. He returned to his mother's side contemplating this rich experience.

The village people stopped their activities to view returning warriors. The wives looked for their husbands, and the children all ran forward to greet and hear the news. With a swift movement of his arms, Tupanchichù made way for the traveling party. He gave orders for the captives to be housed together and separate from the others. Yvvkuaraua and Arapotiyu were brought to Tupanchichù's dwelling. After all was secure, Tupanchichù and his warriors celebrated their victory with much drinking and eating through the night. It was midday before Tupanchichù showed himself.

He took his seat, motioned for a man to bring Yyvkuaraua to him, and said to her, "I am perplexed with this situation, beautiful mother of Arapotiyu."

"How are you confused, Great Chief of the Tupinamba?"

"How is it that I have two prizes?"

"Perhaps you are being given a gift for your great deeds and an answer to your worries," Yvykuaraua responded with no fear in her voice.

"So you think Tupanchichù is a worried chief? How so?"

"There is sickness here in your village. I can be of great service to you and your people."

Tupanchichù pensively observed Yyvkuaraua for several minutes. She was right in that they did have sickness, and their pajés were helpless as to the cause. The Tupinambas believed if you eat another with great abilities you can attain those abilities for yourself, and the sacrifice of her son was to bring abilities to his pajés.

"Mother of Arapotiyu, what other observances do you see in our village?"

"I see the loss of your songs. I see the sliding of spiritual ways and more energy is in fighting with your neighbors and celebrating your fierceness." Taking a deep breath, she continued, *"Surely, your pajés have guided you in the real meaning of the change in Jesyju. In several passes of the great sun Kuarahy, there will be the showing of shadow over the sacred moon Jesyju. This shadow at this time indicates the beginning of a long period of change. Our dreams show us great turmoil is coming to this land. People never seen before will enter these lands and rule over the existing people. So rather than fighting over land that you will possibly lose from strangers coming to the edge of the great waters, use this found treasure, as you say, to band together your people in spiritual strength. So you see, Great Chief, your treasure is amidst you, and you must change your focus to see the gift."*

Tupanchichù closed his eyes for several minutes before speaking. *"There will be two to sacrifice? Hmm, this I will not let happen, as I wish you for my wife."* He turned his head away like he was speaking to himself.

Yyvkuaraua gently continued speaking to the contemplating chief. *"I would accept with honor, Great Chief, only if you free my son. Think back to your sacred stories and know that pajés are vehicles of the gods. One attains great spiritual powers only through the will of the gods. Do not give reason to anger them. You do not need to eat my son nor me to gain knowledge. This will not feed your celestial soul. I will, with glad heart, help heal your people."* She paused, taking in a long slow breath. *"Let Arapotiyu be free. He will continue to prepare through his great ability to receive songs so that the spiritual way of life for all villages will not be lost."*

Tupanchichù waved her away. He needed to speak with the other chiefs, as he was concerned with this news of invading foreigners. Backing away, Yyvkuaraua left Tupanchichù in deep thought. Reaching the chief's dwelling, Yyvkuaraua found Arapotiyu listening to some women. She quickly learned he had been questioning the people about the sickness in the village.

He shared, *"Mother, we can help these people!"*

Yyvkuaraua believed her son and felt the tenderness in her heart swell. Stroking his hair, admiring his beautiful emerald eyes, she replied to the seekers, *"Go and ask permission of your chief for a ceremony in your Opy with the resting of the great Light of day, and my son and I will attend to you there."*

With broad smiles, the people eagerly left to seek counsel with their chief.

Yyvkuaraua said to Arapotiyu, *"My son, this will take more effort on our part as the mbiroy has been broken in this space. There are lower forces you have not yet experienced at work in this village."*

"*Mother, on our walk to this village, I heard in my ear, as you were singing, a soft voice that told of this disturbed place of the coastal people. This voice told me not to be afraid, and that you Mother, will bring change to these people. We will hear a new song that will help us. I felt my heart fill with strength from this beautiful voice.*"

"*You are truly a gift. I will be honored to follow your lead in prayer if the chief allows.*"

"*He will give us permission for this evening. I have seen this also.*"

Permission as seen by Arapotiyu was granted for the healing ceremony. Yyvkuaraua and Arapotiyu worked side by side in the coastal people's house of prayer, which was slightly different than they had known. The sides were open to the surroundings, and Arapotiyu could see the beautiful water. The light of Jesyju was a beacon creating a shimmering path across the water. Her light brought to his mind that this cycle of her reaching fullness indicated the time to harvest. This would have been time of great ceremony to protect food plants, animals, and people against evil influences for the coming season in his village; instead, he was standing in a strange village. Resting on the calm peacefulness his mother demonstrated and the message from the beautiful voice, he accepted his new surroundings. A rattle was presented to him from a small altar. He cleansed the rattle with a prayer while fanning smoke from a sacred plant. He turned to face the growing number of people gathering at their sacred space. He raised the rattle and his eyes to the sky to sing, and his mother accompanied him.

The village joined in the singing and dancing. Two women and a small child were helped to the ceremony. They came with trouble in their lungs and bodies on fire. Yyvkuaraua aided Arapotiyu as he smoked a sacred pipe. He danced and sang through the night. As Jesyju had reached the highest point in the night sky, and the village singing had become intense, Arapotiyu felt so light he could fly.

Together with his mother, they went into deep rhythmic breathing. They were listening to their inner voice and following the instructions from the celestial beings. Arapotiyu was singing a healing song. In their ecstatic trance, they used their hands as guided by the celestial beings to heal the people who sat on a low bench in the center, while the village people continued singing.

Coming close to the end of the healing ceremony, Arapotiyu heard a different song. He turned his body in the direction of the music and before him was a large jaguar. He felt her physically in every way. He found himself being pulled into her while listening to her melody. The jaguar felt strong as *he melded into her. He found himself looking through her eyes to all the people in the house of prayer. As he quickly scanned the area, he could see in a newer clarity the disturbances surrounding the people's bodies. He felt his body tensed as he made contact with their eyes. He heard a low growl come from his throat, and he felt his skin prickle. As he became focused on the vibrations in his throat, he heard the growling tone change back into the sweet song, and then he felt a surge of energy pass through him to the people. As quickly as this came on Arapotiyu, it left his body leaving him lapsed on the ground.*

Several coastal people, who witnessed the scene, were initially frightened; however, they experienced a beautiful feeling just before Arapotiyu fell unconscious. Those receiving the healing were instantly cleansed of their ailment. The beautiful feeling and the healings confirmed the potential of this young pajé with the brilliant green eyes, and all in attendance felt great joy. Tupanchichù moved to help Yyvkuaraua carry Arapotiyu back to his dwelling for sleep. Arapotiyu's eyes were still glazed, and he easily slipped into a deep sleep.

As the strong arms of the warrior chief laid Arapotiyu down, the chief spoke quietly to Yyvkuaraua, "The mother and this growing great soul in our presence have strong connections with the celestial world. I wish to keep both treasures for our people."

While bending over her son, Yyvkuaraua looked up and met the warrior chief's eyes; she could hear her son softly mumbling the new song. She looked away without responding and gently lay down next to her son on a bed of palms.

Just before the great sun Kuarahy sent gold rays to Mother Earth, Arapotiyu became aware of his mother breathing next to him. With his eyes still closed, he became keenly aware of his surroundings from outside his body. Again, the great cat returned.

"I have come to help you, Golden Flower of the Day." He heard her intoxicating song. Again, he found himself looking through her eyes. Together, they walked quietly outside through the village to the jungle. As they walked, he heard the familiar sweet voice of the great cat. Speaking to his heart, she said, "Your mother will be safe and guarded by her guides. You are to return to the forest people, Arapotiyu. You will find them in a new place, and you will live a long life. Your father is the carrier of the sacred stones that are to be protected through the coming dark cycle. Many generations from now, after changes to the land, the sacred stones will be unearthed. This will be the sign to share the forest people's spiritual gifts with all the villages to awaken them from their darkness."

In the morning, Yyvkuaraua found Arapotiyu was gone. Soon after her awakening, the others realized that he was missing. An alarm of voices traveled quickly throughout the village. All the men gathered to look for Arapotiyu, and all they found were the tracks of a large cat through the village leading to the forest.

Tupanchichu's eyes forcefully locked with Yyvkuaraua's eyes. She was standing motionless as feelings of gratitude flooded her body. Outwardly, she showed no emotion; however, inside, she smiled, while the village people erratically moved about and discussed the event. Tupanchichu was apprehensive of sending his warriors to search for Arapotiyu. They feared the jaguar. This certainly was an omen and needed special consideration of the other chiefs and pajés.

Yyvkuaraua turned to Tupanchichu. "You have me for a healer to your people. Let this soul go to be nourished in his earthly mission for all the people of these lands. I am here to sing to the Nandedjá, the celestial beings for mbiroy to return to your village to revive your taekópapá, your magic songs. Certainly, it is not the omen of the jaguar that you should fear as much as the will of the gods." Tupanchichu listened to Yyvkuaraua's words and took this message with him to the council of chiefs. He felt deeply that it was she who had performed this magical feat.

Arapotiyu woke from his deep sleep, disoriented at first, thinking he was moving into a dream, but then became conscious of his surroundings. He lay still, became more aware, and appreciated the feel of his body in the earth world. In opening his eyes, he was startled to find he had curled himself into the arm of a large tree several feet off the ground. The smells were of the forest, gone were the smells of the big waters and the coastal village.

As he lay trying to reorient and control his breathing, he naturally fell into singing the song in his dream with the large cat, revisiting the message given. This soothed his soul as he lay in the tree. A troop of monkeys came near and created a great ruckus over his head. He stopped singing and looked up, smiling at them from his tree bed.

He sat up and stretched. His thoughts went to his new situation. In such a short time, he lost his family and his great family. He had nothing with him but the feathered bracelet his mother had made for his recent birthday. For a moment, he was sad. While he was contemplating and turning the feathered band around on his wrist, he heard his grandfather call to him, "Arapotiyu! Sing, Arapotiyu, sing!" He was so moved in hearing his beloved grandfather's voice clearly. He spontaneously broke into a song, a morning prayer of gratitude.

When he finished, the forest became quietly still, and all of Arapotiyu's senses came alive. Through the stillness opened the sweet sound of the small brown bird, the Irapuru. He listened, as did all the forest, and his heart became lighter with joy.

Climbing down from the tree and looking around, his first impulse was to find certain feathers and a wooden stick to remake a sacred instrument to aid his inner vision. For certain in this moment, Ñande Ru had placed before him the path of complete surrender to his care. He felt confident with the sacred ways he learned from the celestial beings in his dreams; however, he knew the mundane things of the world would be a new and challenging adventure. He had always been cared for in terms of food and shelter from the forest people. That left him time for spiritual practice. Now, he must completely rely on his inner sense and vision for everything.

While making the instrument, he chanted his porahêi. When he finished, he looked around. Not knowing where he was, he proceeded to connect with his spirit guide for help. Arapotiyu closed his eyes to focus on breathing deeply while repeating the word Ñandéva for the great Love to fill his heart. Using an ancient sacred image given to his people from the celestial beings for connecting to their guidance, Arapotiyu listened for his guide to speak to him. He first felt the loving presence, and then he saw, in his mind, a beautiful celestial being approach him.

"Arapotiyu, you will find your people in three days. Your journey will be difficult, but you will be guided. Look for signs along the way. Avoid villages you may encounter. The forest will feed you." As soon as the being had said this, he heard a song, and an image came to him. He could see a particular plant, and the being was showing him the roots to eat, then berries from a small bush, and bees coming from an opening in a tall tree.

"Use this song, Arapotiyu, and the plants will show themselves to you." As the being faded from his vision, his heart filled with gratitude, and he breathed this feeling to the gentle being, bathing the image in golden light.

Continuing to look into the golden light, he brought his mother and father into his inner vision. He breathed the Love to them, and then to all the forest and coastal people. He could see in his mind's eye that his family was safe. This gave him great comfort. As he lingered on the image, a familiar feeling came over him, and the image of his parents faded into a brilliant scintillating light. Then he heard the familiar song and the beautiful melodic voice. He sucked in a large breath and asked, "Could this really be?" Then looking quickly at his body, he told himself that his body was not changing.

"Yes, Golden Flower of the Day, your thoughts and feelings are correct. I took on the image of the great cat as a vehicle for you. The coastal people have great fear of this beautiful animal."

"You are a wonderful being! Are you here to guide me to the forest people?"

"Arapotiyu, you are guided by beautiful gifted celestial beings. Stay strong with this. My presence is different. I was sent by the great Light and all-encompassing Love to give aid to you in response to your beautiful words and actions with the coastal people. This event marks the choice of a great path for you. Continue to follow your heart and guide the forest's people in love and harmony. I will be present for you at another great event many moons from now, marking another great choice on your earthly journey." As the dazzling light faded, he heard the beautiful voice whisper, "Always remember how much you are loved, Arapotiyu. You are a child of the glorious Ñande Ru."

As the beautiful voice trailed off, his whole being filled with beautiful light, and he felt one with the pulsating Universe.

Arapotiyu came out of his trance feeling light and totally immersed in the force of Love. Upon opening his eyes, the first thing he saw was a butterfly resting on a rock. He stared at the butterfly for several moments as it was fanning its wing until his stomach spoke loud enough that he thought the coastal people could hear. He scampered to his feet and searched for something to eat. Brushing aside large palms leaves on his path, he noticed the butterfly was darting around him just out of reach. The butterfly came to rest near a small bush, the same bush he saw mentally from his celestial guide. As he reached out, he found delicious berries to eat.

"How can I be alone?" Arapotiyu said out loud. "All the forest is my home. There will be difficulty, but I have such loving guidance from Ñande Ru and all his celestial helpers. All that I have to sustain me is within." In determined joy, Arapotiyu began his journey.

CHAPTER 9

Opening to Sacred Space

Love is the affinity which links and draws together the elements
of the world ...
Love, in fact, is the agent of universal synthesis.
—Teilhard de Chardin

The Guaraní people view life from an energy perspective, from a soul perspective, from a spiritual perspective that reveals all life to be sacred. The Guaraní people embrace a spiritual philosophy that reveals the sacred nature of our souls and the energetic connection to all forms of life. Showing respect to all forms of life through ritual and singing the beautiful word souls from the heart maintains the connection. Thus, their energy healing method called Ama-Deus embraces the soul perspective as the key in healing all dimensions of life.

The actual description of working with this heart-based healing method is reserved for a classroom setting replicating an oral tradition and physical participation as Alberto was taught and upheld in the trainings he provided to others. The initiation and sharing of sacred symbols are held in utmost respect, integrity, and love, being shared only with committed participants in a physical presentation. What can be discussed publically are the intentions for the various sacred symbols, along with understanding the importance in creating sacred space, and one's preparation for a ceremony of life.

Alberto emphasized the importance of creating sacred space to prepare oneself to meet and approach the spiritual realm for healing throughout his lectures, during his class teachings, and specific references to the Guaraní. In our modern day schedules, we approach a typical day with our rituals consisting of a cup of coffee, some vitamins, and a check-in with the Internet. We feel out of balance if we miss one of these steps! Our morning rituals or tools may vary, but each of us has a set of steps to enhance our ability to cope in mundane but hectic lives.

Most of us also have tools or practices to engage with the spiritual world. Yet the daily work routines often take priority over the spiritual practices. Therefore, these short-lived spiritual practices become obscure and are not as effective in our times of need. In other words, when we are rushed, stressed out, or upset, more often, we fumble around in the darkness, not remembering our spiritual connections for balance.

In contrast, the Guaraní continually engage in rituals that hold sacred intention and enhance spirit communication; these are of greatest importance as their "indwelling" spiritual practices are their coping mechanisms for any confusing and disorderly events. Their lives revolve around foundational common practices using breath, sound, or resonance, and moving from the heart, all of which open the doorway to the sacred realms.

The Breath and Spirit

The Merriam-Webster Dictionary's definition of "spirit" is "breath, a life-giving force; soul." During his lectures, Alberto's stories from his experiences with the Guaraní, along with what he learned as a young boy, depicted the importance of using breath in a conscious or directed manner to commune with the spiritual realm. To begin his own healing sessions, he first connected with his breath in what he called full abdominal breathing. The breathing altered his state of consciousness and opened his heart as he shared in the following statement from a lecture.

> When I was three years and a half that I first went through trance, the first thing to be learned was breathing, then the alignment of the spine and through breathing [he blows puffs of air] you can go to another state, you call alphabet or whatever. It's your state. My trance is my trance; Marilyn's trance is her trance. So on and on each one of us perceive and are in trance in a different way, with different "techniques." But the most important of them is the breathing; the body palpitation, the body heat, everything changes with the breathing. And you create a space for yourself and you can project to that the healing [sic] ...[92]

Breathing rhythmically brings you into the harmonious universal vibration with nature and with your heart. Be conscious of your breath, as well as consciously breathing fully on the in breath and exhaling deeply on the out breath. Breathing in this manner massages our heart and exercises our internal organs. Placing attention on the physical properties of breathing is good. However, the primary function of breathing is to circulate the Holy Spirit (Christian), Prana (Sanskrit for Absolute Energy[93]), Chi (Oriental), or the Vital Life-force (science) of the Universe.

The heart pumps the spiritually laden oxygen-imbued blood to our entire system. So too, the combustion that rises from the process creates heat. The by-product of impure blood brought to the lungs physically as denser energy and as subtler energy needs a full cycle of correct breathing to completely release impurities from the system. Thus, balance is ensured with a full complete breathing cycle. "Lack of sufficient oxygen means imperfect nutrition, imperfect elimination and imperfect health. Verily, 'breath is life.'"[94]

At the start of any Ama-Deus class, Alberto discussed the importance of breathing. He shared and demonstrated how the Guaraní began with deep abdominal breathing to invoke energy for healing purposes.[95] "Breathing consciously makes the magic," Alberto said when teaching a preparation step for accessing energy to heal. "It is the link between the physical body and the soul. *B-r-e-a-t-h-e* from the stomach," he sang out. "Claim the breath of God to your most holy temple. You can change in one minute with the breath of God."

Outside of class and during lectures, Alberto shared more descriptive stories of his encounters with the Guaraní and breathing. This following description from a taped lecture illustrates this.

> Since they are born they are induced, they are trained, and they are preparing all men and women to be healers. No distinction between sex, no distinctions of age, no distinctions if they are the sons, the grandsons of the pajé that is the general psychic healer of the tribe. They are preparing and this preparation involves dream analysis, involves relaxation, meditation, chanting, and meditation with music. But the most important thing that involves them, it is the breathing again. They open their legs, they spread apart, they open their arms, and they call on Ñhandeva

for the love and the energy of God to come to them. And they are in a trance like before they channel [the healing through the psychic surgery]. All of them know the art of [being psychic surgeons] or just doing the laying of the hands. But not all of them choose to do this in a daily basis. Some are fisherman; some are going to plant fruit; some are going to pick fruits; some are weaving, and so forth, so they have the pajé, the professional healers [sic].[96]

This form of breathing, coupled with intention, establishes relationships with the Spirit of life and allows one's personal awareness to move into a dimension of love. The next example from the same taped lecture depicts Alberto's interactions with the children and the same importance is placed on the breath:

Let me give you an outside example of some little children that are three, four, five, six, seven years old. They have tiny little guitars that they make with wood, local wood called cipó. The children play for them. And as they are playing and chanting one of them is performing psychic surgery. I have asked them, "How do you do this?" They say, "First the breathing, then the music induces us to have a blank mind and the music vibrations vibrate with our fingers. And we do with our fingers is a member of vibration." And right there before me I saw a lady that has had an enormous breast tumor. And they open her breast, this was a forty-year-old Indian, and they took it away, the tumor. And the breast was closed immediately without scars and you could not notice if you did not see right then and there, when the psychic surgery was being performed [sic].[97]

Breath is sacred. All cultures throughout time have indicated the importance of breath. The first thing we do as incoming souls is inhale, and the last thing we do as outgoing souls is exhale. Breathing moves the vital life force energy that keeps the physical body alive. Of course, we have sufficient understanding that oxygen supports the physical body. Equally important is to have the awareness and to place emphasis on the breath to maintain self-balance emotionally, mentally, and spiritually with good distribution of vital energy.

So think beyond the absorption of oxygen through the circulatory system and take into consideration that you feel and absorb the vital life force—the Spirit of life. Practice over time, will bring awareness to our daily activities and will assist in bringing balance and spiritual perspective to our lives. From the earlier accounts depicting the Guaraní way of life in using the breath for healing, Nimuendaju gives a personal account of his experience after first doubting their ability:

> My own source of gratitude requires me to mention that the Native healing arts really did save my life in 1907, when I was so run down with malnutrition, yellow fever and bloody dysentery that I had given up on myself and even wound up witnessing my own prematurely scheduled funeral rites. Actually the Guaraní have much more faith in the sacred songs of the medicine men than in herbal remedies, whether used internally or externally. Disease is made visible to the shaman by means of his trance and is then treated with his invisible energy. Here is an example: Fifteen-year-old Cuper, stepson of a medicine man, came down with a fever. After four days, his condition appeared completely hopeless. The stepfather began to sing, which went on for hours, while the boy lay in his mother's arms without a sign of life. The medicine man kept breathing his sacred energy across Cupres' body until about midnight, when he appeared to have caught a glimpse of the disease-causing energy. He carefully pried this energy from the patient's body as if it were a damp sheet, folded it together, and wrapped it around his right hand. Then he strode to the door, threw out the bundle, blew into his hands, and slapped them together. As he returned to the hut the young man opened his eyes, moaned and said. "What's going on?"[98]

As you use your hands for healing, so too *the breath* transmits life energy. Alberto told class participants in preparation for working with healing energy, "Claim the breath of God to your most holy temple." The Hebrew writer of the book of Genesis knew the difference between the atmospheric air and the mysterious and potent principle contained within it. He speaks of *neshemet ruach chayim*, which translated, means the "spirit of life."[99] The breath, along with intention centered from the heart in unconditional love, is the most important component for creating sacred space to invoke energy for healing.

Listening carefully to Alberto's instructions for entering into sacred space made me more thoughtful about the power of the breath. One early morning, after opening my eyes from meditation, this breath awareness gave me insight. I was alone on a beach before sunrise, feeling tingly from the meditative experience, and I let my vision blur as I stared over the ocean. The surrounding sounds from the birds and waves and the salty smells of the beach created a peaceful, serene environment. In profound gratitude for the day and the moment, a sense of Divine presence filled the air. Taking in a long draw of salty ocean air and feeling my lower abdomen, my solar plexus, and upper chest expanding, I envisioned the spiritually potent air filling and circulating throughout my whole body. As my gaze adjusted to the physical world, I smiled peacefully and breathed in Divine presence. In a suspended peacefulness, I first caught sight of a small tide pool and instantly focused attention on the diverse life forms contained in this small space. A small, speckled fish frantically darted here and there, and my thoughts drifted to the *water* as total life for this fish as the *air* gives life for me. In the action of breathing, I too was swimming in a medium that is completely life sustaining. I needed only to be aware of expanding my intention to connect with the Spirit of life with my breathing, especially in times of tension. I carried this all-encompassing peaceful feeling and awareness of breathing for the rest of the day.

In the continued search to learn and experience the power contained in the breath, a wealth of information turned up in *The Miracle of the Breath* by Andy Capinegro. He shared how the ancient "Hindu masters measured the span of a person's life, not in terms of how many years they live, but in terms of the number of breaths they take from the moment they're born until the moment they die. They called the human soul the anu, which means 'the one who breathes.'"[100]

Our culture has become numb to the simplest of spiritual habits like breathing. When we are without hope and feel alienated from society, like the fish in the tide pool who was constricted for a period of time from the greater part of the ocean, he still was swimming in a sea of rhythmic life. Benny Smith, a Cherokee Elder, spoke at a conference, "Where is the Great Spirit? He is always here! He is a stow-away on every breath you take."

Music and Sound as a Sacred Medium

In the Guaraní way of life, song defines a person's status in the community. This practice is not unique to the Guaraní, but common to all indigenous peoples, who understand that vibrations are the creative force in the Universe. Ted Gioia in his book *Healing Songs* states, "This deep faith in the transformational power of sound is so widespread in traditional cultures that we are perhaps justified in calling it a universal belief, in assigning it a role as an intrinsic value of music in the early history and prehistory of human society."[101]

The learning of sacred songs through the dream state is also not unique to the Guaraní. Again, this is a common practice of North and South American shamans, as well as other shamans around the world, in leading their communities. Songs are intrinsically basic to people, who have held on to sacred ways and the significant benefits of sound. In times of trouble or celebration, their songs fill the air, and it has been for millennia. "No culture so far discovered lacks music. Making music appears to be one of the fundamental activities of mankind," says Anthony Storr in his book *Music and the Mind*.[102]

During the summer of 2001 in the south of France, I was introduced to Kototama in a weeklong workshop on Sound, Color, and Movement with Fabien Maman. The Kototama Principle "was perfected 56,100 years ago. In that ancient time, our ancestors grasped the reality of the entire universe as sound rhythm."[103] Kototama literally means "spirit of the Word."[104] How well this concept syncs with the Guaraní passion for the beautiful "word souls."

In hearing this information, I could not help but reflect that perhaps Kototama was the "one" common language in the beginning that all humanity understood. Even in the King James Version of the Bible, there is a reference in Genesis 11:1, "And the whole earth was of one language, and of one speech."

In the practice of Kototama, you sound with the breath, and you feel yourself vibrate from the inside out. The structure of vowel and consonant orders creates a powerful electromagnetic activation of resonance. Vowels carry magnetic power and open space; consonants carry electric power and mark time.[105] Russell Paul in his book *The Yoga of Sound* also described an ancient language of sound from roots in India, "In ancient languages, the sound of a word contained the energy and essence of the thing signified by that word."[106]

Ancient traditions understood the science of resonance. They could hear the sounds of the forest, so too they heard the sounds of the universe and the heartbeat of their Mother Earth. They replicated these sounds, acknowledging their adoration for life and the desire to be in harmony with life.

In the previous section on breath, Alberto described the essence of breathing but also mentioned how music influences the Guaraní: "First the breathing, then the music induces us to have a blank mind . . . and the music vibrations vibrate with our fingers." Music is indicated to be the language of the gods and the forces that permeate our universe. To enhance life is to communicate through and synchronize with the rhythm of the universe. Indigenous cultures impart orally through song not only their history, but also the intent of the energy and essence of the song.

Oral tradition demands retention and memory skills, and the practice of music creates a specialized brain to accomplish this. The human voice, according to Maman's research, is more powerful than acoustical instruments. "The voice can be considered the premier instrument because its inflection carries not only the physical aspect [vocal chords, pitch of the note], and emotional colors, but also a finer, subtle element, which comes from the conscious and unconscious will of the singer. The human voice carries its own spiritual resonance."[107]

Of further interest about the voice is the recent rediscovery that you only speak what you hear. Dr. Tomatis discovered from his work with opera singers that the voice only reproduces what the ear can hear—the "Tomatis Effect."[108] This is interesting detail in discussing oral tradition. Dr. Tomatis made a distinction between hearing and listening. "Hearing is predominantly physiological and passive . . . Listening, however is an active process that relates to one's ability and may be psychological in that listening requires motivation, desire and the intention to take in, process, and respond to the information."[109]

Interesting how the timing of this understanding is occurring now when sacred oral teachings are being shared from traditional societies. Listening is a skill developed inherently within a society dependent on oral tradition. As Dr. Tomatis shared, listening is an active process related to one's ability to process information. Our world is replete with mechanical noise and conditioned book learning skills. No wonder we have atrophied listening skills.

As a small child, I experienced learning a song through oral transmission. Once a year, my family, along with my aunts, uncles, and yiayia (grandmother), attended a midnight Easter service in the Greek Orthodox Church. The entire service was in Greek, a language of which only three words were familiar to me, *Ti Kanis* (hello), *Efhkaristo* (thank you), and the repeated phrase from my yiayia, "Drink your *gála!*" (milk).

The service started at 11:00 p.m., and I was woken from sleep to dress and attend the midnight service. One of the fondest memories was witnessing the church lights being turned off and seeing the bishop through the candlelight holding three large candles bound together in the middle with purple ribbon. This blessed bundle was used in a ceremony of passing the light to each person in attendance. The congregation chanted, setting a wondrous environment for the Easter ritual.

I was not old enough to hold a candle, and soon, a mesmerizing exhaustion took hold of me with the inundation of candle wax smells and great bellows of incense from swinging incense holders and thunderous heartfelt chanting. Giving into sleepy eyes, my body curled up in the pew, and I would fall asleep listening to a repeated joyous song beginning with the words "Chri-sto-s A-nes-ti!" (Christ has risen!)

This yearly event stopped when my yiayia moved from Michigan to Florida, and our Easter family gathering retired to memory. Many years later, after absence from attending the Greek services, I took my own children, and joined the Greek Church. During their first Easter service I experienced an overwhelming feeling of welcomed familiarity, as the entire church was ablaze from the individual candles and singing. And at the appointed time as my children began to sleep, I burst into singing *Christos Anesti* with the congregation as if a conditioned response. I was fascinated at hearing myself sing every Greek word in complete pitch and without any hesitancy. I was caught in the power of the essence of communal singing, completely swept into and immersed with everyone at that beautiful moment after so many years.

For the Guaraní, singing their history was a sure way to capture, retain, and pass on the spiritual message. Let's turn the pages of history around for a moment and ask how did the Guaraní people perceive the coming of the Europeans? What an interesting document it would be to read the Guaraní's perception, a *holistic* perception that has been cultivated for thousands of years in ways of the forest, in hunting, planting, as well as interacting in nonphysical dimensions. Perhaps their listening skills from an oral tradition and their brains, enhanced from a dominant communication through song, allowed them to see the invasive intolerant foreigners as the more primitive ones. We can understand now what they meant when they described the Western world as having lost their spiritual sight.

Music appeals to the emotions. Emotions are of the heart. Science describes the heart as an electromagnetic field fifty times greater than any other organ of the human body, including the brain. The heart pulses outward this potent field of electromagnetic energy, and this energy field also receives information from other pulsating living organisms. The heart perceives and receives. The heart's "pacemaker cells" all work together beating as one unit, "synchronized in their harmonic oscillations."[110] The cells entrain to one another.

> If one pacemaker cell is removed and placed on a slide, [*what a horrible thing to do*], it will begin to lose its regular beating pattern and start to fibrillate—to beat wildly and irregularly until it dies. But if you take another pacemaker cell and put it close to the first fibrillating cell, placed next to a non-fibrillating pacemaker cell, will stop fibrillating and entrain, or pulse in unison with the healthy cell. The reason that these cells do not need to touch is that they are producing an electric field as they pulse, as all biological oscillators do.[111]

The Guaraní came into harmony as a group quickly in the Opy through their songs and dances during the evening of my friend's naming ceremony. What I sensed in the Opy was being pulled into rhythm by the musical instruments and singing with the cohesive surrounding group— an entrainment of hearts. Anyone who has experienced a live concert is familiar with an ecstatic reaction of the audience and the play back from the musicians creating a great *feeling*.

If an individual has a magnetic heart field fifteen feet in diameter, how glorious the thought or image of a large group moving from the heart and creating an immense magnetic field! This unity through song or vibration, no doubt, has much to do with the entrainment of *all* the hearts. As a group or homogenous community, the Guaraní create a powerful electromagnetic field.

We Are All Connected

Humans first experience their mothers' heartbeat in the womb. A mother and child are synchronized with this rhythm, which intimately continues after birth in the physical action of feeding, holding, gazing, or touching the infant, with its head resting at the breast near the heart. Mothers naturally have a *singing*, cooing sound to communicate to their newborns.

A mother's natural instinct to sing and create rhythmic cooing sounds is important in the first months of life. From a soul perspective, Corinne Heline demonstrates in *Healing and Regeneration through Color/Music* the value in daily bathing the new incoming souls with music, "Prospective mothers come to know and realize the great building and sustaining powers of music in the formation of body and character during these sacred months of preparation."[112] Heline goes on to share which specific harmonic tones are beneficial to use during the different stages of the first months of life. "Thrice blessed are the 'little wanderers from heaven,' who during the first three months of life among mortals can be surrounded with music in the keys of G-Major, A-major, and B-major."[113]

Reading Heline's reference to the first three months of life supports the knowledge in the Ama-Deus system, as there is a sacred symbol used to support newborns. Alberto conveyed that the purpose of this sacred symbol was to aid the incoming soul in the first three months of life physically, emotionally, mentally, and spiritually by surrounding them in Love as they adjust to the frequencies of this earthly dimension. Even later as we teach children language, research supports the use of singing, rather than just verbally reciting the alphabet, to provide greater retention.

Ama-Deus classes that Alberto taught were filled with music. Alberto predominantly played music from *The Mission* as the participants practiced as a group during class. When he performed individual healings, either in private or during a class demonstration, he usually used a classical piece. Gustav Mahler was one of his favorite composers.

In Alberto's workshops at the end of each class segment, he played a particular contemporary song that was related to universal love. He played the songs and encouraged people to sing. I can vividly remember how he threw his head back, closed his eyes, and in his beautiful, full rich voice sang, "People, people who need people, are the luckiest people in the world." He did not expound on the Guaraní way of song. He simply

147

incorporated song into the class, and his infectious enthusiasm caused everyone to join him in singing. People smiled and hugged. The whole group felt the unity and experienced the raising of their spirit.

> There is no doubt that "music is a potent social force for drawing people together, inspiring them, coordinating them, adding meaning to ritual, generating emotions, strengthening belief systems, changing group dynamics, and channeling communal energies. Music also has physiological effects, stemming from rhythms, sounds, and the created harmonic vibrations. The healing force it brings inevitably must come from the combination of these two elements: one stretching out into the community and surrounding environment, the other reaching into the body itself."[114]

Sound is a powerful medium that affects our finely vibrating electromagnetic field. Since the universe and all its parts, including the body of man, is built through the power of rhythmic vibration, it follows that a scientific application of musical rhythm can be advantageously utilized for both the restoration and the maintenance of a physical well-being.[115]

With this keener knowledge comes our understanding for the Guaraní's beautiful word souls that are sung to them in the dream state, an act that comes from the feeling heart. Singing with people brings a cohesive feeling within the group, but it also entrains us to the great pulsating heart of the Universe, to the Love of God.

Henry David Thoreau's words describe Alberto's love for the Guaraní and what he felt the world most needed: "All that a man has to say or do that can possibly concern mankind, is in some shape or other to tell the story of his love to sing, and, if he is fortunate and keeps alive, he will be forever in love."[116] Alberto most assuredly recognized the potential power of a healing tradition that utilized love as a necessary component in what lies ahead for humanity.

The Guaraní people as well as other indigenous peoples understand that heart-based singing and focused breathing with traditional ceremonies are key links to the Divine Presence. They have demonstrated that breathing in harmonic resonance and singing are some of the key elements for maintaining balance through fast-changing times. Many people today are recognizing these fundamental practices and are incorporating them into their daily lives. Heart-centered intelligence is imperative with these practices. The importance of the heart is unfolding globally and is crucial to mankind's evolutionary path.

Heart Intelligence Is Nothing but Love

Across all cultures, a common thread speaks of an *all-powerful* feeling called Love. Cross-cultural creation stories speak of the active creative force of Love. This Divine Love is a common thread through all creation. We see it in nature, we hear it in finely polished symphonies, and we recognize it in the eyes of each other.

Current recognized leaders in the field of medicine have emphasized the importance of love. Andrew Weil, MD, proposed, "Love is the one source of sustaining comfort in life and it is of such force that it has miraculous powers of healing in the physical, mental, and spiritual realms. We must try to cultivate that force and to experience it as habitually as possible."[117]

Bernie Siegel, MD, answered the question why love is so important in healing with, "It is the most significant thing in human life."[118]

Likewise in business, a recognized business author and leader, Stephen Covey, looks "upon love as the supreme activity of life. You need to draw upon the divine energy from God so that you have the power to manifest or express this kind of love."[119]

The spiritual leader, His Holiness, the Dalai Lama, reminds us, "The essence of all religions is love, compassion, and tolerance."[120]

Alberto had the privilege in his international travels to witness diverse healing techniques, but like the Guaraní, he observed and believed that the essential ingredient or common thread in all healing was love. During an Internet lecture in 2008, Gregg Braden addressed the scientific discoveries of the electrical and magnetic properties of the heart that had developed in the past twenty-four months. He supported these scientific findings with observations from all the indigenous people he had encountered. Similar to Alberto, Braden noticed consistently with each and every community he visited that one common action was the physical hand gesture or placement at the heart, some physical movement at the heart occurred before moving into ceremonies of healing.

In her book *Eat Pray Love*, author Elizabeth Gilbert shares how her teacher Katut answered her questions about enlightenment with a picture he sketched during a meditation. The image was of an androgynous figure without a head standing on four legs with clasped hands in prayer. The extra limbs were for purposes of grounding into the earth. In the place of the head was a gathering of wild foliage and ferns. A smile face was drawn over the heart and explained in this way:

> To find the balance you want . . . this is what you must become. You must keep your feet grounded so firmly on the earth that it's like you have four legs instead of two. That way you can stay in this world. But you must stop looking at the world through your head. You must look through your heart . . . that way you will know God.[121]

Understanding from experience that love is a powerful transpersonal occurrence, and then love is always the potential that *supports* transformation from what feels to be disconnection or fragmentation into realizing a state of wholeness. This is the power of love in the healing process.

The Guaraní, again and again, sing out for the love of God, the Ñandéva, to tap into the power or force that binds, connects, and unifies all people. The Guaraní understand that the power they felt was the power of God. They also know all people have access to this Source. However, without the intention and purity of Love, the Ñandéva there could be no healing.

The ancient ways carried to us from the oral and written traditions indicate the language for Love is found in *feeling* the sacred in the heart. In communal harmony, the Guaraní poured out their heart in a song that continued until all encountered a connected feeling. This communal connection indicates the moment to begin their ceremony. This ancient way must be all-powerful, as this practice has been sustained for thousands of years, not only by the Guaraní, but also by many indigenous and mystic peoples.

Love is a Sacred Way

I believe we are all created with a sole purpose to love and be loved. In thinking of love, my thoughts take me to the highest source of existence, what is understood to be the Source of All that Is. Then love becomes

Love. Love is in everything and is all things. From a transpersonal or soul perspective, Love keeps all that exists joined to the Source of All that Is. These experiences of feeling connected to a Higher Source or God are the same feelings experienced when seeing a magnificent sunset or any act of nature that demonstrates breathtaking splendor. This experience takes the senses to a reality that is beyond the physical, and carries all meaning into a transpersonal encounter.

Throughout my life, I never lost sight of my desire to understand Love, which was a lifelong quest, not unlike the goal of restless seekers of the meaning of life. My childhood was surrounded with events that repeatedly raised this question about life's meaning. My father, a Greek Orthodox (inheriting the name Cosmos), and my Irish Catholic mother were deeply in love. They encountered, as I did, the challenges of their mixed marriage from friends, family, community, and most certainly, the two religions. Because of this exposure, I understood early on that God was not in just one church. My father was a kind gentle soul, and my mother was full of life and laughter. Together, they moved through life as a beautiful team, and wherever they went, their joyful kindness infected others. Every morning, my father said to me, "Be kind to your neighbor." So their marriage spoke of love and beauty, not sin and discord, and no family, friend, or church could take that away from me.

Instead, my search for deeper meaning of this beauty that was our family environment was a constant. In college, my hangout on weekends was a spiritual bookstore close to campus or hunting in the campus bookstore for books on the meanings of Love and mysteries of life. Everyone else in college was having love-ins, and I was having love quests! This lifelong quest eventually brought me to Ama-Deus and to a new threshold of understanding. I still hear Alberto's words ring in my ears, *"You cannot heal until you first love. Love is in all healing no matter what technique you use, without the love, it is impossible to heal."* Imagining the cacique tapping him on the heart reminds me of the true significance of these words.

My first profound experience of love was holding my newly birthed children. Holding these incoming souls in the first moments of claiming their terrestrial breath was deeply moving and opened my heart to a rush of joy and adoration. Knowing this feeling was my closest understanding of unconditional love. Knowing that I would put my child ahead of my own life also created my longing to hold onto this significant feeling of unconditional love as I cared for them.

———

The experience of love invokes the desire to know the Source as a continual living experience. The need to connect with others, to love and be loved during our earthly experience, is a force that directs us back to the Source. History abounds with reference to love as a Supreme spiritual aspect. In Baird T. Spalding's book *Life and Teachings of the Masters of the Far East* an explanation given for love is:

> The Universe is the sum total of all things visible and invisible that fills infinite space. The Universe is the great whole, composed of all its parts. It might be said that the Universe is another name for God ... It is the sum of all life, all substance, all intelligence, all power ... It is all love for it is bound together in a single system and operates as a single unit. Love is the integrity principle or the binding principle, which maintains the universe as a unity and keeps all its operations moving in perfect harmony and regularity.[122]

The ancient Essenes taught that each person has a feeling body as well as a material body. "If we examine what is behind our actions, we shall see there is always a feeling. Powerful feelings and emotions bring about action at once and automatically. It is not our thoughts which are behind our actions so much as feelings."[123]

One of the eight Beatitudes of Jesus states, "Blessed are the pure in heart for they shall see God." The greatest law of man's feeling body is revealed. According to Essene traditions,

> The "pure in heart" are those with a pure feeling body—a body nourished by love and not hatred, by forgiveness and not revengefulness, by compassion and not cruelty. Such a feeling body will see God, for he who complies with the great law of pureness of heart is in the antechamber of the kingdom of heaven.[124]

This description reveals such resounding synchronicity to the Guaraní way of life. Certainly, history records that the Guaraní were "nourished by love and not hatred, by forgiveness and not vengefulness, by compassion and not cruelty."[125]

The Guaraní position the seat of the spiritual or celestial soul in the heart, and their nature of reality is language born from this heart-soul connection. For them, the animal soul is located in the head. Understanding and recognizing the heart carries true knowing, for herein lies the spiritual soul and connection to the Spirit. The animal soul in the head gives us personality as well as a mechanical view of life, which alone does not lead us to spiritual truth. The head united with the heart is the true position for living one's life.

Your Sacred Heart

Physically, the heart develops first in the fetus before the brain and gives direction to the unfolding of our "holy temple" to prepare for the incoming soul. The heart is autogenic, meaning it beats without the direction of the brain, independent of a signal from the brain. The human heart is many times more magnetized and electric than the brain. It has the strongest magnetic pulse of all the organs.

Stephen Buhner, in his book *The Secret Teachings of Plants*, explored how indigenous peoples in relationship with nature use heart intelligence or a heart-centered perception. He includes detailed information on the physical heart that supports this perception.

> Between 15 and 25 percent of the cells in the heart are neural cells. They are the same kind as those in the brain and they function in exactly the same way. In fact, certain crucial subcortical centers of the brain contain the same number of neurons as the heart. The heart possesses its own nervous system and, in essence *is* a specialized brain that processes specific types of information. Heart neurons, just like those in the brain, cluster in ganglia small neural groupings that are connected to the neural network of the body through axon-dendrites. Not only are these cells involved in the physiological functioning of the heart, but they also have *direct* connections to a number of areas in the brain, and produce an unmediated exchange of information with the brain. (*Unmediated* means that there are no interruptions in the circuit from the heart to the brain) . . . the heart also has its own memory. The more intense the emotional experience, the more likely it will be stored by the heart memory.[126]

How often are we consciously in our heart? It is simple to move your awareness from your head to your heart. First, feel for your heartbeat. Place your hands over your heart and feel the rhythm harmoniously beating in tempo with the Universe. The physical pulsing reminds us that our energetic heart is our resonating connection to all life.

This umbilical cord to the Divine Creator is our sense of belonging and longing from our heart, and it is also our sense of connection to each other. Is this the great web the elders speak of? If so, imagine if we were to live with our hearts guiding our heads? Seven billion people could ignite this planet with a simple change in awareness in our daily activities. The energy of love is so powerful that its radiance lights every dimension of consciousness eliminating any shadows.[127] We could individually be a light for the world helping to foster a new consciousness. This filling of our hearts with a loving reciprocal feeling to the Divine Creator is the language of love and is the language our Divine Creator will respond to as we are made in the image and likeness.

Imagine the most beautiful unconditional love that you have experienced. Fill your heart with this feeling, and then breathe this feeling in gratitude to the Divine Creator. As you feel your heart receive this inexhaustible flow, open up your heart as a flower opening to the sun and let this flood your entire body. Think not Love, rather *feel* Love.

The feeling side of us is directed from the heart, and the analytical side is directed from our brain. Interest, questions, and increased sensitivity toward the more subtle fields that surround the brain and heart are gathering strong momentum from not only the public, but also from the scientific sector. As the dominant culture of the present world seeks this knowledge, a common conceptual framework for language of the subtle or spiritual dimensions of Light and Love will evolve.

Presently, ours is a mechanistic conditioned mind through which we perceive the world. This understanding is helpful when embracing new spiritual tools. Rather than overshadowing the tools with our present beliefs, an open heart helps to shift the perception and allows our minds to expand in new awareness. As we embrace and settle into our hearts and perceive our world from a soul energy perspective, a spiritually attuned mind will evolve.

The main point in our evolution is to view and know life from a spiritual or energetic perspective. The indigenous people and the mystics understand this and safeguard it with their lives, and *now*, some scientists are building a language for the subtle fields. We are finely vibrating oscillating bodies of light interwoven with the electromagnetic bodies of others, of the earth, and of the Universe.

As we learn this language and perceive from the heart, the veil of separation will dissolve. There is no separation in the physical world and the spiritual world. Viewing life from an energetic perspective sees all life as *one*, whether from the subtler spiritual planes or the denser physical material planes. An energetic perspective simply gives a more complete picture, and this perspective follows that all life is sacred and intimately connected.

The living mystic Amritanadamayi (Amma), often called "the hugging saint," who brought such healing comfort to me after touching my heart, said, "Real love exists in the heart ...Our hearts are the shrines where God should be installed. Our good thoughts are the flowers with which He is worshiped."[128] Amma, like the Guaraní, also sings before she starts any of her spiritual work. This creates the sacred space for her to compassionately embrace those who seek her out. As she sings and moves into her blissful state, the thousands of people, who have come to be near her, sing and chant along with her. In observation of her during this time, it is easy to see the building of ecstatic states and the outpouring of Divine Love during her chanting.

The Guaraní, as well as all the indigenous peoples and mystics, accentuate the importance at this time in Earth history for all to reclaim living in the heart. What has been recently described as "new age" will hopefully move into the *heart* or *compassionate* age for "there is a wisdom of the ages that has been lost in time."[129] This wisdom states, "*The heart is the place we must daily face for there we find ourselves.*"[130] Love carefully, gently embraces the world, as her global children are listening and feeling the urge to open up to the intelligence of the heart.

In the wisdom of a contemporary song titled "The Tin Man," "Oz couldn't give nothin' to the Tin Man that he didn't . . . already have."[131] Find yourself in your sacred heart; this awareness of filling our hearts with love and sending out love is a feeling language. "What the world needs now is Love, sweet Love, that's the only thing there's just too little of. What the world needs now is Love, sweet Love, no not just for some, but for everyone."[132]

I once heard a Tibetan proverb—all knowledge is contained within, in a space as far as an ant walks the bridge of the nose. *Within* rests all the potential for creating a sacred space.

1. Breath is the Spirit of Life
2. Music is the Resonance in Life
3. Heart is the Unifier of Life

These three foundational elements cost nothing and require no permission of you to choose and find peace. To resurrect and integrate these pieces of wisdom into a current practice of how you approach the beginning of the day and the beginning of the night will indeed enhance daily living.

Love is the great attracter in the great web of Life. Each one of us is part of the web. If you did not have the potential to make a difference, you would not be here. As Gandhi proclaimed, "If we could change ourselves, the tendencies in the world would also change. As a man changes his own nature, so does the attitude of the world change towards him . . . We need not wait to see what others do." A desire to change is the only prerequisite we need to seek out the magnificent beings that we truly are.

CHAPTER 10

Love for Purposes of Healing

If you bring forth what is within you,
what you bring forth will save you.
If you do not bring forth what is in you,
what you do not bring forth will destroy you.
—Jesus

The desire to change comes to most of us through cataclysmic events. I had such an event as a young divorced mother; that is for sure. My drive to heal and learn ancient wisdom led me to Ama-Deus, which is a heart-based method to access love, a sacred method to align with invincible love for healing the self or others. Ama-Deus moves from the purity of the heart's intention and offers the realization that the need to love and be loved is the spiritual force that is directing us back to the Source.

Ama-Deus is a method of connecting into Source for soul healing. The method enhances our spiritual growth and awareness while supporting our physical and emotional healing. Ama-Deus is one method of energy healing which predates many wisdom teachings and healing methods now available to people.

With Ama-Deus, students tap directly into the energy flow of Love by learning a specific invocation. The invocation has intention to access a stream of consciousness, an originally Uncreated Energy, as the name implies *to Love God*, which is enhanced and expanded by all who have ever used it. After invoking the energy, the student is able to use this source of energy for self-healing, or to transmit to others through the hands, or via distance healing treatment. Ama-Deus primarily helps to smooth, stabilize, balance, and bring tranquility as a gentle subtle energy adapting to circumstances and offering what is needed. Ama-Deus has the purpose for and is used to support the healing process.[133]

To place attention on the breath, and then allow consciousness to settle, and then to feel the heart center are the preparations to using Ama-Deus healing method. Still, a deeper perception comes from establishing a relationship with the energy. The student/practitioner is not the healer, but rather a conduit or vessel for a fluid flow of energy to the client.

Alberto said many times, "Let go and let God. No healer chooses the way they heal; it comes through the way God wishes. Do not structure it to your needs. You are a channel, an instrument of peace and light: know the Source, be clear about the Source, and use it with integrity."[134] As a practitioner of energy healing, it is important to understand this and to acknowledge that the healing process occurs between the Universe and the soul of the one who receives the healing. The practitioner is simply holding sacred space.

And so it is important for a practitioner to uphold respect, integrity, and love when holding sacred space for another. Healing allows access to your inner-self the inner labyrinth. Ama-Deus aids and supports during your inner journey of healing. Alberto shares in a lecture that, "*Ama-Deus*, the Love of God . . . is done only through touch of the fingertips, it is a gentle way of doing healing. They [the Guaraní] have taught me incredible things . . . and [the Guaraní] say this treatment induces to dreams and to revelations that one can and meet one's interior self [sic]."[135] Alberto loved and had great respect for the wisdom uncovered in this healing method.

Each of us has the inherited capacity to tap into Love. Each of us is unique in channeling the energy into this dimension. These two points are important to realize as there is no right or wrong; there is only our experience. In the experience of receiving, and then sharing love for the healing purposes, the opportunity to know oneself grows. Ama-Deus is an act of offering freedom to all souls to be who they are and to flow with the Light and Love of the Creator.

Upholding Sacred Tradition

Time after time, Alberto demonstrated the importance of keeping the integrity in using such a sacred gift. In the beginning of every class, he made clear that the information and sacred symbols were not to be shared with others outside of the class. He asked if there was anyone who was not comfortable with keeping the integrity of this oral tradition and would give them the opportunity to leave. In this way, the sacred meaning and intention of the symbols were preserved. By maintaining an oral tradition *from the heart*, the information passed on does not become a mental theoretical exercise; rather it becomes a way of knowing that is internalized *through experience* in one's heart.

Alberto was forceful in upholding Ama-Deus in the traditional manner as the Guaraní have upheld it for thousands of years through an oral tradition. I heard on several occasions his raised voice answering students' questions. His response was always intense in the fact that this healing method must be kept sacred and the information was not to be shared. On one occasion, a student with thoughtful intentions made copies of the sacred symbols from a computer. When he arrived in class and shared his copies, Alberto reacted strongly, stopping the distribution of copies, indicating that this was not a correct action.

He said, "You must practice and use the system until you have no need to look at your notes. These sacred symbols should not be displayed like this." According to the Guaraní and upheld by Alberto, the sacred symbols were guarded and were to be used in respect, integrity, and love. The sacred symbols are ancient and simple, yet powerful. Ama-Deus comes to us from thousands of years of storage in the heart through oral tradition.

Oral tradition is the electronic data bank for indigenous peoples. They rely on a singing heart to preserve and imprint sacred words on the brain. Once given a song from God or the Great Creator, it is carefully nurtured and recognized as the highest form of wealth. Sacred wisdom is intended to continue in this format as to safeguard and maintain a heart-centered relationship by all who use it.

Oral tradition is a time-proven expertise that goes on preserving sacred knowledge despite invasions, advanced technology, and environmental changes. The Guaraní, as well as other indigenous peoples, have demonstrated through the centuries the highly functioning format of oral transmission.

The Western mind often misunderstands the beauty and importance for keeping alive this way of communicating. Today's world is highlighted with high-speed technology that physically separates people. To receive love notes, or loving phone calls, emails, or text messages are all uplifting;

however, could they ever replace a loving touch, the feeling and experience of being in the presence of another, to gaze into their eyes and see their soul? The part of being wholly human to reach our full potential is missed. Oral tradition is intended for the ear. Oral tradition is where the voice is paramount in delivering the message imbued with tones, rhythm, and pitch, sounding in resonating frequencies soul to soul. Technology could never be the vehicle to transmit love. *Human interaction is the vehicle for the conduction of Love in this dimension.* Traditional oral teachings are the means for soul-to-soul communication.

When you speak orally, the storyteller's soul moves from the heart, passing the breath through the larynx to give rich and varied frequencies to tones. Oral communication reaches others' fields of receptivity in the fullest potential—in a spiritual potential. The frequencies of tones in the voice bathe the human electromagnetic field in color and sound from the breath of life. The heart giving direction to the brain is far greater than any computer as compared in the physical world.

This story of the Guaraní is about a group of humans who intended to maintain a spiritual path, who intended to develop their souls' potential. To those humans who create from a predominant material world, the spiritual path is labeled an inner approach. This label of "inner" comes simply because a material approach has overlooked other faculties within the ability of the human vehicle. Thus, this limited use gives limited understanding. A soulful use of the human vehicle creates a *whole* potential and both the inner and outer perspective—a soul perspective is recognized.

With this understanding of oral tradition, I have purposefully left out the sacred contents of specific teachings of Ama-Deus, which are only delivered in person, heart-to-heart, to those who are drawn to this method. The stories will hopefully awaken the passion in your heart.

Thus, in the following descriptions regarding the practice of Ama-Deus, only a general narrative portrays this beautiful healing method. In this way, the integrity and respect for this sacred method will be adhered to according to Alberto's instructions—by upholding sacred wisdom in the context to the original form of oral tradition. The full measure is always openly shared in class.

Experiencing Ama-Deus

The class format constructed by Alberto has two parts or levels. The first level includes an initiation and the sharing of the nine sacred symbols. The initiation replicates Alberto's experience with the Guaraní and is reserved in detail for the participants of the class. The symbols are shared to focus intent toward healing at the essence of an individual—the soul level. These ancient geometric symbols carry purposeful attention to achieve a specific goal during energy healing. The use of symbols with assigned intention lessens the personal intention of the healer and frees the mind, allowing a student/practitioner to become a conduit for the healing energy.

Each of the sacred symbols in Ama-Deus works with specific life processes to support the soul during earthly experiences, such as birth, transition, and death. As we learned earlier about the Guaraní ways, all life is sacred and has its corresponding ceremonies with the healing rituals that petition the grace of God. The Guaraní way of life is from the soul perspective, so too, the healing method is positioned from this point of view.

For example, four of the nine sacred symbols in the first level course include:

- One that addresses the intention to enhance and expand the heart center. As shared earlier, the heart center is of prime importance.
- A sacred symbol to purify anything that is placed within the physical body, the holy temple.
- Another assists in the dying process to support the soul in peace.
- One sacred symbol supports the soul after the last breath and aids the soul to move to the Light in peaceful love.

In this first level, instructions are given on how to send energy to another person, referred to as distance healing, or in Alberto's words, "absent-healing."

If one feels in resonance with this method, there is an additional second level course. The division of levels allows participants to digest the level one information, and then choose to continue if this system calls to their heart. The second level has seventeen additional sacred symbols.

The second level addresses several options for getting at the core of personal issues, such as the repetition of unsettling behaviors and attitudes. Two of these symbols access the subconscious for information, one through the dream state, and the other moves into our past. Both serve to relieve and heal stressful situations.

Also, a symbol for addictions is shared, highlighting the *energetic* healing of an addictive behavior in the overall rehabilitation process. This energetic piece creates a holistic approach to healing addictions. Another sacred symbol is to aid world leaders for the good of all humanity.

The teachings are positioned from a soul perspective, and you will find yourself with a glimpse of how the Guaraní live habitually in the spiritual realm. The participant finds a natural progression of moving into a soul perspective and, thus, fulfills what Alberto alleged before initiation: "This [soul perspective] can bring you new views, new life, new perspective."

In my first class, Alberto shared how to assist the soul during transition or assist the soul to the Light in peace when the physical body has retired. I wondered when I would ever use those sacred symbols. Of course, those exact symbols became one of my first most profound experiences.

This occurrence started with a knock on my door by a pleasant-looking gentleman whose psychologist referred him to me. The man was looking for massage therapy to help him cope with physical discomfort related to AIDS. In a direct and respectful way, he asked if I was comfortable working with him. At that time, fear and uneasiness flourished in the general public about working with this disease. His question made clear that he intended to respect this line.

I welcomed him into my home, thanking him for being openly respectful. We started our first hour of massage that turned into a weekly routine for several months. Within that time frame, as we became better acquainted, we shared discussions around Alberto and learning Ama-Deus. Alberto would be returning soon to teach, and my massage client was excited to meet him and take the class. However, a sudden decline in my client's health occurred.

As he became weaker and could not drive, I went to his home for his biweekly massage. I noted his transition was near, and small frequent sessions to help his pain tolerance became our goal. One day, I entered his bedroom and, by reading his face and body language, took note that his pain was immense. While assessing how to best work with him, a sudden surge of energy flowed into my hands, while the image of the sacred symbol for transitioning appeared in my mind's eye. The prompting of the energy moved me to take the transition position until the energy subsided. Opening my eyes from this short encounter, I saw my client in a peaceful slumber; I gently moved to massage him. Returning in two days, he was alert and demanded to know what had happened to him the previous session.

"What did you do to me?" He asked.

Surprised at his strong tone, I wondered if I had done something to hurt him. Again, he asked in a stronger tone, "What did you do to me?"

Standing there somewhat paralyzed with my heart shrinking and feeling sad, I mumbled and slightly shrugged my shoulders, "I do not know."

He vigorously continued, "When you touched me, I felt so peaceful, I saw this wonderful light and all that I saw was so beautiful and there were flowers." I was shocked in listening to his description, as his portrayal happened to be almost the exact words I had used in an Ama-Deus class with Alberto!

During class, Alberto first described the meaning and how to use a specific sacred symbol. Then for some of the symbols, he demonstrated an actual healing by having me lie on a massage table. At the end of the demonstration, he asked me to describe the experience to the class. My description from Alberto's healing demonstration with the sacred symbol used for dying people was like descriptions of near death experiences. There was so much peace and light around me. Now, in stunned silence, I was hearing this man repeat my exact dialogue.

My heart shifted from being small with the fear of hurting someone to feeling large with the extraordinary beauty from this experience. God will teach us about God. We are not in control. My nervousness released, and happiness ensued from an experiential moment as to the importance and the blessedness of the Ama-Deus process.

The simplicity and subtlety of Ama-Deus may cause some to pass over it as unworthy of attention, especially if you are looking for something instantly deep, mysterious, or non-understandable. "Trust yourself. That is what makes the magic," Alberto would repeat in class. I trusted and moved with my feelings for the three years before Alberto passed, and time and again, an experience was offered, such as with this man, directly showing me the powerful potential with each of the sacred symbols.

I have been asked which sacred symbol is my favorite. I have no favorite; however, there is one symbol I used frequently to enhance, enlarge, and expand the heart center. Understanding that the heart center is our sacred connection moved me to intimately work with and experience this sacred symbol. After the first class, I set aside time in the afternoon, as my children napped, to work with this powerful sacred symbol to facilitate healing the heart center.

Personal experience is what brought me into direct relationship with the energy. I did not find myself thinking of the mysterious outcomes; an inborn trust had developed from my feelings and observations in the blessings and glory of the Divine in action. This relationship gave me inspiration and support to continue to heal myself, and the joy in knowing we are not alone.

Total trust brought many varied experiences. All sorts of people came for healing. The sessions averaged from twenty minutes to half hour. Infrequently, there would be one that lasted little more than five minutes and others that lasted an hour. This variance definitely kept me aware that something greater was in control.

One short session occurred with a woman who was in need of emotional healing. At the time, I was still living and working out of the old farmhouse, and my healing table was set up in the center of a small living room. After explaining to me what she was looking for, we proceeded with the session.

"Are you familiar with the energy centers in your body known as chakras?" I asked.

"Yes. I have had energy healing before and know about chakras."

"Good! Well, this is how I mostly work. I scan your body with my hands over the energy centers. When I feel the energy flow in a particular area, I rest my hands gently on you until the flow stops. There could be several areas that will be worked with in the course of the session."

"Okay."

"All you need to do is relax, close your eyes, and listen to the music. The more you relax, the more you are able to receive. I will let you know when the session is complete. Please lie down here on the table, and I will cover you with this light blanket. Let's put this small pillow under your knees to help your back."

"Thank you. That feels comfortable."

After she was settled and had closed her eyes, I turned on a piece of classical music by Mahler that Alberto used during his healing sessions. I prepared for the session as always—exactly as Alberto taught. During the sessions, people would become more relaxed and several would fall asleep. In this particular session, she tensed up and repositioned herself a few times. I adjusted to her and gently returned my hand position. This went on for about five minutes and brought me to finally ask, "Are you okay?"

"No, I am in so much pain!"

I immediately retracted my hands saying, "Are you sure energy healing is appropriate?"

"I have tried so many other healing methods. I am in so much pain. I was hoping this one would work. I do not think I can continue this session." She continued to share how she had tried several other methods of healing from different people and nothing seemed to work for her. I felt she was hoping for a quick fix of her emotional pain and suggested that the issues for her healing might be best addressed with professional therapy. Her response indicated that she was running from professional help, clearly carrying a deep fear.

She repeated more than once, "I don't know why this hurt."

I explained to her that during a healing session, if pain or an uncomfortable feeling becomes present, it is not that the energy is not working; rather it is a reaction of the individual. Healing energy will not mask a problem. We discussed other options for her.

She was regretful for not completing the session and wanted to pay me. Because of my own personal healing experiences, I empathized with her, but more importantly, I understood where my limits were as an energy practitioner. I politely refused payment with a strong recommendation to seek professional help.

I learned through my own healing process that in the healing state, an ego or part of the self that is deeply hurt would often accept Light before accepting Love. We are finely vibrating frequencies of light. Our being is oscillating electromagnetic fields of light, and there is nothing in you that need to be awakened in the receiving of Light.

Can you see how significant it is to discern that there are healing modalities that work with light and modalities that work with love?

Light can be given for healing purposes and easily accepted as nothing is required. However, when love is given, because of its glory, it will usually awaken a response to receiving the love. In the initial healing state, there is not always the ability or the capacity to respond. When one has moved through the healing phase and has accepted the light and has moved forward in healing, it becomes easier to accept and respond to love.[136]

I like to think of light and love being related to the description "We are made in the image and likeness of God." We are the image or "light" of the Uncreated Light and the likeness or "love" of the Indescribable Love. Though it is not comprehensible *how* light and love separate out from the One or Source, having this distinction for healing purposes is valuable.

Alberto expressed that he could not heal some people, and he would send them to other healers or to the medical community. Through Ama-Deus, one learns, as an energy practitioner, that healing sessions are between the soul and the Universe, and each person's path is unique. We must be respectful of the choices people make on their healing path and love them without judgment to their choice.

What Does Healing Have To Do with Freedom?

How often have you heard that healing is each person's birthright and that everyone has the capacity for healing? As you read previously, the Guaraní understood everyone has the ability to access energy for healing. The purpose is to maintain the sacred balance—to be a light in the Universe.

When one chooses the path to heal, an opportunity opens to reevaluate the meaning of life. To heal is to bring into sharper focus the situation that creates distress, not as a helpless victim, but rather as an empowered participant. Curing places awareness on the elimination of symptoms from the physical body, whereas healing focuses on spiritual awakening for the whole self.

The great teachers do not accept passivity from those who are seeking healing. "Healing is to recognize and change what needs to be changed in order to move in a self-directed way to a point of understanding."[137] The personal experiences encountered during the healing process open to a deeper understanding of our significance in the Universe. "True healing means self-examination and emotional release. To heal is to repair or correct a situation that causes distress and imperils well-being."[138]

Ama-Deus is one tool that gives support through the healing process. "When you discover the need for healing, you take the step that leads to the replacement of negative light-obscuring emotion with an emotion that enhances the light within you."[139] Healing is always possible. Healing is about becoming whole.

In the spirit of healing, there is always a giving and receiving, an invitation to transform consciousness on all levels. Personal growth requires discipline in spiritual practices and active listening. What is inherent to an individual soul will surface from the healing process. Through this process, natural gifts will surface and the proverb "Know yourself" will become clear. Insight and spiritual power are gifts, not to be pursued for spiritual or material gain, but rather graciously received.

The Universe chooses how energy healing is transmitted. Holy or spiritual people have great courage. In the Guaraní culture, this classification comes after much sacrifice, fasting, prayer, seeking vision, ceremonies, herbs, and of course, the number of beautiful word songs. They dedicate their lives to be in contact with both the physical and the spiritual dimensions to aid humankind for the highest good of all. The title of pajé or shaman is given and is reserved for those who demonstrate the worthiness of such a responsibility. Spiritual attainment is not acquired through a certificate or a textbook.

Energy healing methods do not focus on symptoms. Holger Kalweit, in her book *Shamans, Healers and Medicine Men,* observes that indigenous methods are not based on symptoms,

> rather [they revive] life and heal our relationship with the world—for is illness not the clogging of our spiritual pores, a blockage of a global perception of the world . . . our bureaucratized and materialistic medicine—this mechanical model with an active therapist and a passive patient . . . this kind of healing belongs to the mechanical age. Today, however we are already daring to make the transition to "organic" medicine, "spiritual healing" through personal transformation, through the transformation of consciousness on all levels . . . If we are seeking classical models for this kind of healing, they exist: the masters of basic health—shamans, primeval healers, primal physicians, wise men and women.[140]

Malidoma Somé, a wise man of the Dagara tribe, shares in his book *Of Water and the Spirit* a beautiful personal story depicting the role of healing from an indigenous perspective.[141] Somé claims that his elders are convinced that the West is as endangered as indigenous cultures:

> There is no doubt that, at this time in history, Western civilization is suffering from a great sickness of the soul. The West's

progressive turning away from functioning spiritual values, its total disregard for the environment and the protection of natural resources . . . In the face of all this global chaos, the only possible hope is self-transformation.[142]

Self-transformation is concerned with healing one's self to regain the sense of loss of interconnections and make you whole for your benefit and the good of the community. Presently, we are witnessing a reawakening and reconnecting of the self to feel and attune to the energetic world. Many are taking the path to healing. Healing takes a dedication and perseverance. As we choose to do our healing, love supports and gives strength for accomplishing our task. This support and strength is recognizable. For example, how often have you felt "in" love, causing us to let go irritating events or brush off negative situations? We instead take on an air of indifference or nonchalance. Why? Love not only lifts us up, but also carries us through the healing process.

During the four years after my great life-changing events, prior to receiving the knowledge of Ama-Deus, I chose to actively walk a path of personal healing. In the vow to God to raise myself out of a low despondent feeling also came the request for spiritual aid. From that moment of stating a vow and summoning spiritual help, my time has not been idle.

My children were and are my primary focus. So as to not disrupt my family with this personal choice, I created an agenda to foster change and followed it within my own community. I would not travel to a distant country to work with a guru or to a different part of the country to find a famous healer.

Ask and you shall receive! My first major healing phase came through my experience of an unconventional approach to psychology from the advice of a dear friend. This practice at the time was in its developmental stage by a practicing psychologist. My friend Katharine worked in the psychologist's office as a bookkeeper. Skeptically listening to her describe this approach in what would eventually be called *Soul Centered Healing*, my curiosity and interest built up to give it a try.

Entering a typical clinical office shared by a group of practicing psychologists, I was greeted by a warm and friendly middle-aged man who led me to his private office. Not ever being in therapy, I had no idea what to expect. This was a therapy or healing session that worked with a person's "higher self." The higher self was used in this instance to mean the communicative part of the soul, and trusting my friend's highly recommended referral, I ventured into the situation.

The psychologist asked me to sit in a chair and explained how he would conduct the session. "Please close your eyes with your hands resting gently on the arm of the chair." He continued to explain that two fingers from either hand were the communicative tools to bypass the conscious mind. At the beginning of the session, one finger was designated as a "yes" finger, the other was a "no" finger; and the whole hand in a horizontal movement indicated neither. Through this finger dialogue of asking questions, called ideo-motor signaling, a yes or no answer was how communication took place with the higher self.

The session began with counting from one to ten and repeating between counts that relaxation was beginning in my feet and moving though my entire body. After this counting step, my body settled into a pleasant relaxation response. He then asked to communicate with my higher self via the fingers as the conduit. At first, my mind wanted to laugh with this procedure, then amazement set in as my fingers moved in response. Closer to the end of the session, an awkward feeling crept in, and I chastised myself for having spent so much money.

In a hurry to leave when the session was complete, I was standing at the counter to write my check when Katharine approached, asking with bright eager eyes, "How did it go?"

I fumbled around with words, but also found myself unable to navigate writing the check. At this point, suddenly, the situation became apparent to me. I was in a much deeper state than just a relaxation session. I could only laugh and say, "Something happened, I am not sure what!"

"Do you think you will come back?"

I heard myself saying "yes" to her and wondered all the way to my car what had really happened. Another session was scheduled for a week later. I felt the need to give this method a chance because I trusted my friend's referral. The second session delivered a most profound experience of traveling back in time, a powerful session for me.

After I registered and attended a third session, my mother finally remarked, "What are you doing? You've changed!" Indeed, I had changed. In just three sessions, a major block in my personality was lifted, one that had been with me all my life. My self-esteem was so low my mother always worried she had done something to me, and so it would be natural for her to witness my different presence or demeanor. The fear in meeting people had lifted. I stood taller, walked more at ease, and could look people in the eye without feeling extreme discomfort. With these results, I did not care what it was called or how the fingers were functioning. I was elated with the outcome.

Certainly not wishing to alarm my mother in using an unconventional approach, I was silent about being in this therapy, especially one that I was not prepared to explain or understand. Yet the effectiveness was very telling when I joined my mother to attend a party. As we entered the lavish garden party, my mother moved to speak to the host and surrounding friends. I lingered for a moment in the entrance and slowly made my way through the crowd to where my mother was engaged in fun conversation. Approaching, I heard her comment in surprise, "That is Beth!" My mother's friends who were also my acquaintances had not recognized me from a distance. Mother turned to me with a questioning face, "Could you believe they thought I brought someone else?"

I was immediately bombarded with "You look so wonderful, how are the children?" I stood comfortably without feeling self-conscious and held easy eye contact throughout the lively chatter. This peaceful feeling in this gathering of friends, which at an earlier time was extremely awkward for me, was confirmation of my healing transformation.

The three therapy sessions and the strong experience of change in myself confirmed my decision to continue with this technique. The therapy sessions were not cheap, and my massage work out of the house simply kept food on the table and the rent paid. I took on added work to pay for the sessions. Coincidentally, a friend of the family needed a place to stay for a few months, and so an opportunity opened to work evenings stocking groceries while she stayed the night with my children.

Three years of weekly sessions brought not only healing, but also knowledge and understanding of my inner landscape—a soul landscape. This was not book knowledge; the experience of the sessions exponentially expanded my understanding to an energetic awareness. This expansive understanding was an answer to my prayer and support for the decision to heal; a pathway unfolded and a journey began.

As a result of this decision, here in my own backyard, a healing process created a framework to see life from an energy perspective and introduced me to the meaning of a soul perspective. I was grateful, but not without periods that I desired to quit and to move on, or feelings that this was all hogwash, and other times, ready to use a flat tire as an excuse not to attend. You see my normal resistances to change popped up here and there. In so many instances, this healing journey was work. Yet I made that commitment as progress was apparent. I persevered.

To have this rich experience that seemed tiresome and exhausting at times certainly laid the foundation and the crucial next steps on my path to Ama-Deus. Most importantly, I learned the value of self-healing, A person's choice of healing is well summarized in this timeless message said to be on an unnamed Anglican bishop's tomb in Westminster Abbey (AD 1100) however presently shows as anonymous:

> When I was young and free and my imagination had no limits, I dreamed of changing the world. As I grew older and wiser, I discovered the world would not change, so I shortened my sights somewhat and decided to change only my country. But it, too, seemed immoveable. As I grew into my twilight years, in one last desperate attempt, I settled for changing only my family those closest to me, but alas, they would have none of it. And now as I lay on my deathbed, I suddenly realized: if I had only changed myself first, then by example I would have changed my family. From their inspiration and encouragement, I would have been able to better my country and, who knows I may have even changed the world.

The healing perspective dominated my thinking, overflowing in all parts of my life. Besides the *Soul Centered Healing* therapy, I was developing a keen interest in physical health. In hearing the statement "you are what you eat," I investigated macrobiotic cooking and the benefits of foods. I was especially dedicated to learning about beneficial foods for my children. In this study of an interrelationship with plants and foods, I became fascinated with the idea of fasting. My first fast lasted for three weeks and was intense, especially for my first time, but I determinedly held on.

One morning, my son exclaimed, as I was toweling him from a bath, "Mom, your breath smells like roses."

"Really?"

"Uh huh."

Standing and sticking out my tongue in front of the bathroom mirror, a radiant pink color met my eyes. I also noticed there was not the usual morning taste before brushing my teeth. Hmm, this must be the end point to the fasting and all the necessary experience gained from this lesson! This occurred only a few weeks before signing up for the Ama-Deus workshop. This seemed, in hindsight, to be a most fitting preparation for the initiation to Ama-Deus.

There were other incidents strongly related to my forthcoming relationship with Ama-Deus. One such magnetizing experience was related to music.

Kathy, my good friend, had called asking, "Beth, would you like to drive an hour away to the city of Holland? There is a woman who would like me to help with her research."

"Sure!" I always said yes to anything Kathy suggested, never questioning, as I thought so highly of her.

"When?"

"I will call her and find a time in the evening, does that sound good?"

"Great!"

We chatted all the way over about our children, and I did not ask anything in the car ride over about the little adventure where we were headed. Upon arriving, a nice soft-spoken woman in a warm comfortable office greeted us. Then she asked, "And who would like to go first?"

Looking at Kathy, I could tell she was a little hesitant.

"What are we to do?" Kathy asked.

"Oh, you will not have to do anything, but lie on a table and listen to the music. Did you bring your music?" Kathy and I looked again at each other, and together, we said, "Music?"

"Yes, you were to bring some music that you like to listen to."

"No, we did not bring music."

"That's okay I have some here we can use. Okay, who will go first?" Kathy was still hesitating, so I bravely said, "I will."

I stepped into a clinical-sized room that was mostly occupied with a geodesic copper framework with a long slab in the center. In the corner opposite the entrance was a large computer.

"Welcome to the Genesis Machine," she said as I carefully eyed the floor to ceiling copper rigging that resembled a tetrahedron. This large structure looked like a copper jungle gym. "Go ahead and climb up on the padding." One had to carefully climb in through the copper piping onto a padded horizontal platform. I laid on the platform that was probably four or five feet off the ground and suspended in the center of copper framework.

"Now, is there any type of music you would like to listen to?"

"No, I like almost anything."

"Okay, I will just select something for you. All you need to do is relax, close your eyes, and listen to the music. I will stay in the room to monitor the computer."

Of course, there was no fear of this experience because I was with my good friend.

Starting with a classical piece, the volume was set loud in the small room, and the platform vibrated with the resonance of the music. Soon, I was soothed into a deep state of relaxation. After several pieces of music came through, one piece absolutely alerted all my senses. My skin was raised and bumpy; my heart seemed to enlarge. My eyelids fluttered. This was so crazy, and I wondered why I reacted as I did. Maybe it had to do with the research. Then the music changed, and all the emotional feelings and physical responses relaxed. Two more pieces came, and the session was done. Taking a nice long stretch before climbing down off the platform, I declared, "That was nice, thank you."

"Well, what was with *The Mission?*" she asked.

"The *what?*" I quizzically shot back.

"You had such a reaction to this one piece of music from *The Mission.*"

"I do not know this score you are speaking of, never heard of *The Mission.*"

"Well, you had such a reaction your ratings were off the scale on the computer."

"Really?"

"Yes, the specific piece I selected for you was the *Ave Maria* sung by Indians."

"That was Indians singing? From where?"

"South America."

"Gosh, I am not sure what I could tell you. The *Ave Maria* is my most favorite piece to sing in church, but I did not register that it was *Ave Maria*, only how my relaxation was interrupted!" The conversation was in combination with my climbing down and walking out into the room where Kathy was waiting. She scanned me, as I know her to do when she reads someone clairvoyantly.

"Next!"

While passing me, she quickly asked, "How was it?"

"Great. Relaxing!" I responded.

Later in the car driving home, I discovered that Kathy did not have any idea what we were in for and wanted me to go first, so she could observe. We had some good laughs over this.

The long and short of this story is that this took place *two* years before my initiation into Ama-Deus. The music Alberto used in class was so intoxicating that I had to purchase it right away. He mentioned in class the movie *The Mission*. I registered a familiarity with the title, but exactly from where, I could not recall. At home, when listening to the entire piece, I froze when hearing again the Indians sing the *Ave Maria*, and I instantly recalled in full detail my experience on that platform suspended between copper piping.

When Alberto talked about how important music was to the Guaraní, he emphasized how singing brings them closer to God. I realized, yet again, how important it is to not shrink from opportunities that life presents, as we are not aware of how it could enrich our lives. This incident brought forth the importance to embrace life for all it has to offer, even a little road trip with a friend for unknown reasons.

There were other healing practices that caught my interest and participation. In reflection, all of them played a significant part in understanding the role of healing *and* the awareness of soul perspective prior to being introduced to Alberto and Ama-Deus. After experiencing Ama-Deus, I reflected in complete wonder on all the experiences that prepared me for this stage in my life. I was and still am committed and focused on self-healing.

Preserving Sacred Wisdom

I was well acquainted with Alberto's passion to preserve this method of healing and knowing the reason for doing this was not about him, but for the world. The world *needed* love. In the weeks after Alberto passed, a friend, who had opened her house to Alberto when he was ill, called me and asked to visit. She drove several hours from the East Coast to my Michigan home. This was a welcome visit for both of us to share about the last days with Alberto. During her long weekend stay, one afternoon, she called me into the bedroom.

"Let me show you something," she said. I did not realize the extent of what was happening until she unpacked some items and laid them out on my son's bed. The first thing she said while handing me a small pouch was, "Here, open this."

I opened a small cloth bag with drawstrings carefully and respectfully, feeling somewhat uneasy. There in my hands were two stones small enough to fit in the palm of a hand.

"What do you feel?" she asked.

Without any explanation, I knew these were Alberto's stones. Closing my eyes and taking a few deep breaths, I looked in her in the eyes and responded, "I am not sensing or feeling any energy."

"Good! That is what I felt also. The energy is gone. Would you like to have these?"

In the moment, I was captivated that she offered them. "I had no idea you brought these."

"I knew the two of you had a strong connection. I needed to meet you first before I shared that they were in my possession." She graciously made the journey to our house to meet and share feelings of our mutual loss. I had no idea there would be a display of some of Alberto's personal things. Meeting her eyes and finally responding to her question of accepting Alberto's stones saying, "No, thank you."

"Yes, I agree with you the energy is gone." She quickly bundled them and moved on to the next item, which was his yellow topaz ring. "Here, look at this."

Looking at the ring without touching it, I replied, "Thank you, this is wonderful." This process of sharing was a kind act. However, it was apparent she was relieved that I did not accept the stones or ring.

Quickly moving these items back to the cloth bags, she then offered another large package: "Here, you can have all these files. Most of them are in Portuguese. And here, keep his sweater and this pair of pajamas." I smiled, not feeling any remorse in declining the ring or stones. My greatest treasure was the knowledge and the relationship with Ama-Deus. I could feel gentle peace in my heart for not accepting Alberto's personal items and in her joy in keeping them. The most valuable item that Alberto left for me was Ama-Deus, and this was planted into my heart. I was solidly content with this.

After she left to return home, I carefully placed the file folders of all his notes in a safe drawer. His pajamas went to a close friend who had taken his class, and eventually, the sweater was returned to his family. This visitation brought forth deep reminiscing of the three profound, concentrated years of learning and using Ama-Deus, how Alberto selected me to experience many of the sacred symbols during class. Three years intensely working with Ama-Deus in support of my own healing, as well as others' healings, gave me a rich tapestry of practice and knowledge.

Recalling Amma touching my heart and jolting my mind with "you are to carry this on," I relished the few months before Alberto passed. I realized how, in his last eight months, Alberto prepared me immensely for a new role. As I trained, he coached. I had all the necessary sacred symbols to initiate others and to conduct the classes. Now, I organized myself for a new journey to safeguard and carry forward the sacred teachings.

The revelation and loving support from Amma and the continued dreams with Alberto prodded me to move forward. I thought of all the synchronicities and the personal healing work that obviously were stepping-stones to my receiving Ama-Deus. All of these added up to my strong sense of accepting and applying this method of healing. In accepting this new journey of teaching, the wisdom would be safeguarded.

First, I meticulously went through the files that held all his personal notes on the classes. All his handwritten lectures were translated and the taped lectures transcribed. I sought out several people, whom I held in high esteem, and requested their notes from his class to check for the possibility of missing any information. In this manner, assurance was provided for holding the sacred teachings as Alberto taught.

Since 1993, I have taught this sacred healing system in the same spirit as passed on to me in respect, integrity, and love. Teaching became a natural extension from my heart and led to my next phase of growth. Sharing this sacred knowledge with others opened a whole new set of adventures. I soon learned how teaching is a powerful role. The power comes in the act of empowering others to claim their own self-healing ability and uniqueness to help themselves as well as others. The initiation ceremony, a symbolic giving and receiving to this day, stands as one of the most powerful actions in the teachings and reminds me constantly of the sacred wisdom being preserved. As a steady stream of classes in my community expanded, so too international travel evolved, taking me all over the world.

The exact teachings are to be delivered soul to soul in respect, integrity, and love. I have shared some of the intentions for the different sacred symbols, the importance in creating sacred space and preparing oneself for a ceremony of life, and the most central motive in employing this energy practice—the purpose of healing. Without question or doubt, life is a sacred journey if we open ourselves and allow our hearts to feel the Love all around us. Alberto was right when he said, "Life is in the Love and healing, the rest is just waiting."

In accepting the "just waiting," the love of my relationship with Ama-Deus not only expanded into teaching, but also led to a clinical setting to conduct research with cancer patients. I never dreamed of teaching or conducting research. However, such is the phenomenal loving journey when you hold your intention dearly in your heart.

PART IV
AMA-DEUS:
FROM THE CLASSROOM
TO A CLINICAL SETTING

Arapotiyu stood at the edge of the forest that surrounded the village. Unnoticed, he watched the aging pajé, his father, lying in his hammock giving the morning instructions to the forest people. Arapotiyu easily slipped into his past, recalling a similar scene from his youth. So much had occurred since that decisive day when the arrow pierced his grandfather's chest.

In vivid clarity, he relived being taken captive and encountering the great being who came to his aid in the image of a jaguar. She had guided him out of the coastal village and set him free in the forest to begin his solitary journey with the spirit world. This wonderful being had come to him at a point of great change in his early life, one that marked the beginning of his solitary apprenticeship in the forest.

In the three years that his father, Mbaracambri, relocated the forest people's village, Arapotiyu grew to be a powerful shaman. In nourishing his celestial soul, he ate only substance made from sunlight, he fasted, and danced long hours in order for his body to become lighter. He lived in a hollowed space at the base of a very large tree. He communed in the spiritual dimensions learning many songs, visiting many realms in the universe. He became a renowned karai, a prophet shaman to villages near and far.

After three years of living in solitude, he received a vision showing him to return to the coastal people's village and claim his mother. He acted on this vision. As he entered the coastal village, the people, at first, did not recognize him. He was tall and walked in great purpose. They did acknowledge him as a powerful karai, welcoming him with great respect. Only his mother recognized him. All along, he had communed with her through the dream state. When Arapotiyu requested to see the good healer Yyvkuaraua, there was no resistance from Tupanchichù, as all villages understood and respected the power of the karai. The coastal people and their chief stepped back to let Yyvkuaraua pass. As she stepped forward and spoke her son's name, he recalled seeing the trembling fear of the coastal people when they finally recognized him.

Arapotiyu led his mother, along with the surviving forest people, safely to the new village location. It had been many seasons ago that he had led his

181

mother and people back to the village. Now, standing on the edge of the forest, he is watching her sitting off to the side of his father, quietly working a reed basket.

After the joyful reunion of the village people, his father, Mbaracambri, had moved the village two more times. Eventually, settling where the two rivers meet in an uncorrupted space, just as his beautiful word souls shared, a place of no evil for the forest people to continue their way of life.

Even though he led a solitary life, Arapotiyu kept a particularly close watch of his birth village. The forest people could always count on a glimpse of him during their movement as if he were clearing a good path. During the final move, Mbaracambri spoke with his son on a short encounter in the forest. Sitting together, away from the many forest people, Mbaracambri broke the silence.

"This move is especially long. I sense this to be one of my last movements, my son. I had a strong vision showing a clear space, feeling the vibrating aliveness and presence of all life from the fertile living earth, to the pulsating celestial lights, and beyond."

"Yes, Father, I too see this sacred space for the people to gather the necessary strength for the coming great change. To live and breathe in the vibrations of the great Love and scintillating Light, through our word souls of gratitude that will help us all stay in alignment with the changing vibrations of Mother Earth."

"My son, you have grown to be a great pajé, all that our dreams told us. My heart is big when I recall the memory of the vision telling me of your coming birth. Never forget your songs to keep your heart strong." Saying this, he gently tapped Arapotiyu on his chest. "I agree with your images of strange times coming. I trust now that you comprehend how the journey will always be different but the same. Keep safe in your heart the wisdom you have gained, for there resides the true paradise."

"My dear father, I love your beautiful soul words and hear your beautiful message. I will pray hard to maintain this path." They met eye to eye, expressing their love of a spiritual relationship that helps to maintain peaceful mbiroy.

Coming out of his reflective state, he smiled at the good memories; yet watching his mother and father, he wondered what it would be like to have a partner of his own and to be a father. He had lived alone in the forest now for many seasons of the maize, renouncing the social ways of his people. Some described his life as solitude, but he smiled again remembering the feeling he had watching the butterfly land on the bush with edible berries. He gave a great sigh of breath and relaxed his mind at that moment, knowing full well he was not alone. The world was filled with celestial music, and he longed to listen. This was his way.

The morning Light brought him, as he did on other occasion, to share messages from the celestial world. He was never far from his forest people, even though he was called to serve other villages. His father was aging, and there was change in the air. His recent dream indicated a message of this change to be delivered this sunrise to the forest people.

Breaking the spell of remembrance, he stepped out of the forest into the opening. The elder pajé stilled in his hammock for a moment from his discourse with the small boy. Looking in the direction where his son stepped from the forest edge, his heart filled with great love as he proclaimed, "The good and blessed Karai Arapotiyu has arrived in our midst in the first gold light of morning!" All the village people stopped what they were doing. Some women ran to sweep the path clean for his approach. Such was the love and respect they had for their karai. Without spoken words, Arapotiyu moved gracefully as if he were drifting on air toward the elder pajé. He met his mother's eyes, sending great love to her while approaching and embracing his father.

Without speaking, Mbaracambri knew the reason for Arapotiyu's visit. In a recent vision, the sacred stones had spoken to him of changes to come. He also knew his son seldom made an appearance. He only came to help with serious illness or to deliver beautiful prophetic soul words.

Mbaracambri signaled the young boy to sing his newly received song for Arapotiyu. The forest people gathered around the pajés, listening to the sweet song that had just arrived in the dream state to this young apprentice. Arapotiyu moved into a sitting position next to his father and, with closed eyes, listened to the song. When the song was complete and the village stillness hung in the gold rays of light coming through thick green foliage, the Irapuru sang a song from the forest canopy. A feeling shivered through the forest people creating a connected feeling of love and for all the life that entrained their hearts. At the moment, this feeling rippled through the village. Arapotiyu recalled the beautiful words of his father, telling him the land without evil is within. He felt himself in his heart as he spoke to the forest people.

"There will come a time when the hearts of men will become cold, and the light within will seem as an ember from your fire. But the forest people, where the two rivers meet, will not lose the sacred knowledge. As the great circles turn the universes, there will be a great many moons, seasons, and generations of darkness. It will seem as if the earth people are sick in soul. Mbiroy will seem to have disappeared behind a cloud. People of the Forest stay strong, you must

pass down the sacred knowledge through your beautiful songs. Some will come to the village and try to change your word souls. Keep strong your songs and sacred ways, for there is no end to the soul and no end to the beautiful word souls. Death, as you know, is only a movement to the celestial world and will be used in Ñande Ru's great plan. If you hold on to this truth, you have nothing to worry."

"Aje racó, yes, indeed," rumbled through the forest people in response to the beautiful word souls.

"Through this darkness, your lifelines to Ñande Ru are your songs. Keep them alive in your hearts, in every breath. There will be those who come to your village who have no song in their heart. You will know them by their searching for beautiful words outside of their heart. Their hearts have only a spark of light. The darkness leads their minds. Their hearts have become very small with just a spark of light. And so they have no recognition of the great light that resides in their heart. Let your heart speak to their deaf and cold hearts, but do not share your songs. Listen to their ways, but keep silent the songs in your heart. Do not let the sacred knowledge leave your lips."

As he was speaking the message of his dream, he turned speaking directly to Mbaracambri. Gazing into his father's eyes, he continued, "Safeguard the true way of the forest people in your heart until the sacred stones are unearthed. My father, Mbaracambri, will pass knowledge of keeper of the stones to this young one who has received the song. He, in turn, will pass the knowledge. Countless seasons of the maize, our future ancestors, at the appropriate time, will unearth the sacred stones. This will indicate the ending of the great cycle of darkness. At the perfect time, the stone keeper, through his song, will know when to unearth and present them to one who will open a path for the entrance of a new great cycle. This is Ñande Ru's plan. Keep sacred ways and maintain harmony with the plan."

Again, the community of forest people responded in passionate voice, "Aje, racó, yes indeed!" and "Emaé, you see!"

"The gods showed a vision of my receiving the sacred stones, not at this gathering, but at the ending of this dark cycle. Once again, as of now, I will not be of one village, but from many villages, even those villages that seem strange to us with cold and lifeless hearts. This village of forest people, however, will always be closest to my heart." Arapotiyu gently rises to his feet and opens his arms to the village of forest people.

"My dear forest family, know the allotted role that Ñande Ru has asked of you. Walk the path given to us in this vision. At the unearthing of the sacred

stones, when the dark cycle begins to weaken, a new cycle of great light will penetrate the earth, and all life contained here will feel drawn to the brilliance. We are all one people with Ñande Ru—even those who seem to have no song in their heart—for they will come out of their deep sleep and remember whom they are.

"The opening and sharing of the forces and power of love within your heart will begin to fan the ember of light in the earth people. The release of the knowledge you hold will ignite the light, and a new awakening will prevail. This new life will come to us from the sacred direction of the rising light in great waves and dispel the land of evil. As once darkness spread easily, now the Love will spread like the vines in the forest circling the earth, assisting in her transformation. Do not feel doubt. Hold fast, as there are others like us positioned on the earth that have also been charged with protecting the sacred knowledge. They too have their ways of communing with the celestial beings and Ñande Ru. They too will open as the flower greets the golden light of day at the appointed time once again and share the sacred knowledge.

"Our word souls tell us that the land without evil is within you. As you safeguard the seeds of your maize for the next season of food, also keep strong your heart. Go within and seek your song to keep you strong in the luminous Light, in the ways of the forest people. As you keep the sacred ways, there will come a time when the land without evil is so strongly desired and projected from a great number of people, that Love will flow like the great rivers on this beautiful earth."

Arapotiyu begins singing a song: "A paradise awaits those who hear the song. The forest people are taking a journey into the cycle of darkness. But know that the Light and Love that will safely lead you is in your heart and in your songs. The forest people will take a journey, where the beginning and the end are different but the same." As Arapotiyu is singing these last words that his father and grandfather kept alive in their songs, he acknowledged by looking into the eyes of the aging pajé, the one who still held strong vision, and the village of forest people broke out in song.

Arapotiyu immediately felt a force in connection with his father's eyes. He drew in a deep breath and felt his physical body relax as he slipped into a deeper trance.

"I hear the singing of the village faintly. Now, I seem to be falling." A beautiful glow was approaching him, and his ears were straining to hear the faint sounds of a song. In recognition, Arapotiyu cries out, "Oh, this sweet song I have heard long ago! I have not seen your sweet presence for so long. My heart is so filled with joy."

185

"You have arrived Arapotiyu. You have been of great service to your people. You are being asked, however, to carry forth one more journey." He watched as the beautiful glow turned into the all too familiar image of the great cat. Then she danced around as if to be playful with him, but before he could respond, she laid back her ears and let out a piercing scream that blew out a great force of sound together with her breath. The force of her breath was cold against his heart, instantly shocking and knocking him to the ground.

As he opened his eyes, he found himself lying on the earth next to a large fire. He felt the warmth of the fire on his skin, and with his face on the ground, he inhaled an earthy smell. He clutched dirt in his hands to feel his surroundings, and then he pushed up with his arms to a sitting position. Looking at the dirt in his hands, and then circling his eyes around to gather his bearings, as he often did when moving between dimensions, he noticed the forest people were different but somehow the same. The elder pajé was the first to speak.

"Are you here with us again?" the elder pajé softly asked. Trying to find his voice, as he was still swimming between worlds, he closed his eyes and responded, "Have I been here long? It is cold now."

"Yes, you have sung and danced long into the night. Soon, it will be morning."

"I had this very moving vision. I seemed to be watching an earlier life with the village people. Then the great cat returned and said there was one more journey."

The elder pajé smiled and said, "This is good, my son. I have been waiting to hear this message." While he was still on the ground, he opened his eyes to watch the elder pajé place a small stone in each hand. "Take these sacred stones and share the Love, the Ñandéva, with the world. Our word songs, your coming to our forest people where two rivers meet, and this sacred vision mark the time to share with all villages." As the elder bent down to help him stand, they locked eyes again, and the elder continued, "We will work together with you as you begin your journey, for this too is in our songs. Always remember the Ñandéva when you leave this village and to always move from here." As the elder pajé says this, he taps Alberto on his chest in the same place the great cat had blown her forceful breath.

Alberto is moved to tears for all the kindness of the forest people, of their love for him and the unending sharing of their sacred ways. Now, as he looks into the all too familiar eyes of the pajé, he is caught up in the evocative clarity of his vision.

CHAPTER 11

Keeping the Knowledge Intact

Caretakers of sacred knowledge do not misuse.
We have to answer for everything we do.
—Bear Heart

How amazing! Twenty-four years after graduating, here I am teaching energy healing in my old high school. The high school building is located on several acres of beautiful woods within the city limits. The familiar feel of the spiritual background still resides within the walls and was a rich environment for a private school.

In 1970, I graduated high school from an all girls' academy run by the Dominican order of nuns. The buildings also served as the motherhouse for the order of Dominicans in the United States. In recent times, the decline of interest in private schools forced the school's closure. The administration residing over the building reorganized, reopened, and rented out meeting space for lectures and workshops—a wonderful setting to hold the spiritual Ama-Deus workshop I presented in 1994.

In the middle of my third class at the Dominican Center, I introduced myself to fifteen people when a nun, who was barely five feet tall, boldly walked from the back of the room.

"What are you teaching here?" She asked as she pointed her finger at me. Everyone quickly turned in their chairs to see from whom and where this voice came. As she walked down the center aisle toward the front, she continued to talk, "I read the sign out there, and do you know what Ama-Deus means?"

I smiled, a true Dominican always wishing to teach! Yet there was no time to answer as she quickly blurted out, "It is Latin meaning to love God!"

"Yes, Sister, this is exactly the meaning we are using and sharing."

"So tell me what you are doing?"

I could feel everyone grow tense and hold their breaths when they heard the nun's question. Energy healing in our city had not quite found a comfort zone. In fact, after learning Reiki several years prior to being introduced to Ama-Deus, other Reiki practitioners warned me to simply say it was a relaxation technique. Otherwise, I would be shut out by the community and severely criticized.

After taking the Ama-Deus class, however, the experience was so powerful that I chose not to hide. A strong desire rose within me to explain honestly when asked. In several conversations, I responded to others in confidence, "I have no fear in stating what this practice is about." Then I laughed and said, "If they wish to sue me, all I own is an old horse and a massage table!" People chuckled at my comments.

In total openness, I gave the nun a gentle brief explanation, and my voice was the only sound in the silent room. Sister Consuela stood, looked up into my face, and the seated students listened with baited breath. She responded directly, looking into my eyes, "I know all about this healing power of love through my ministry. I have served most of my time in New Mexico, and I am very familiar with the practice of the native Spanish and indigenous people. I would like to attend this session. May I?"

"Of course, Sister," I responded with surprised happiness. Everyone in the room relaxed, and bright smiles appeared on their faces.

No Need to Question Why, Just Be

In accepting the journey from a personal practitioner level to a teaching level, my ongoing lessons in the importance in the role of loving others and myself continued. The first Ama-Deus class I taught was for close friends, who had missed the opportunity to learn from Alberto. I thoughtfully prepared for this class in much the same manner that I had prepared for other presentations. My profound lesson after this first class was, again, that I am not in control. Thus, no preparation was needed. My role was to share the information and be present.

My role as the facilitator or teacher was to be open, loving, and present to meet and empower the people where they were at on their journey. My role after sharing the information was to listen, and then encourage people to embrace the teachings and develop their own relationship with the *Energy*. God teaches you about God. Their healing and trust with this heart-based method offered them experiences from which to draw their own conclusions. Each person is unique and requires a safe, loving environment to achieve awareness of the power of Love. After that first class, each and every class offered countless opportunities to share and receive love. I just needed to be present and open myself to the circumstances.

At the start of my teaching experiences, I found many people signed up for the class to see how this modality was different from other healing methods. Drawing on my own experiences with other healing methods, and then with Ama-Deus, it was natural to share that all healings are from the same Source. There are no differences at the core of each healing modality. What creates differences among the methods are the intentions, varied applications, and the cultural aspects.

After several years of teaching, I noticed a newer trend that dominated the attendance. This time, seasoned practitioners in other healing modalities signed up with interest in the expansion of their personal practices. Interestingly, these attendees immediately embraced the Ama-Deus method with great respect and renewed enthusiasm for energy healing. I sensed this was because of the perspective that Ama-Deus is delivered.

I witnessed a common occurrence from this new trend. First, when people learned the intent for each sacred symbol in Ama-Deus, they experienced strong realizations and awareness in healing at a soul level. The Guaraní see life from this soul perspective; thus, the symbols indicate the energetic soul perspective of their way. The students leave with a new awareness, seeing life situations in a different light.

Second, every class, without fail, prompted lengthy discussions around aspects of life associated with each sacred symbol, whether it was death, birth, purification for the physical body, healing from drugs, locating the core of an issue through past lives, or exploring earth-bound spirits. These discussions stimulated the learner's review of the intrinsic value of personal healing, as well as identifying how to work with difficult clients and family members. Most important, students reevaluated their beliefs about living from a material perspective compared to an energetic perspective.

My strength in this new role as a teacher came from the *Energy*. A week before a scheduled class, I felt my energy grow and expand, as if the Universe were setting the tone and vibration for the event.

The format for sharing the Ama-Deus spiritual healing technique continues in the exact format I received verbally from Alberto Aguas, inclusive of his personal notes. I listened intently during the many classes and conversation with Alberto, all of which were etched in my heart.

I never thought during my instruction time with Alberto to ask why topics were organized or formulated in his classes. At that time, I had no conscious intention of teaching Ama-Deus. My strong connection was the gift and focus, never attempting to define the *Love of God*. I simply had a great desire to open myself to experience this eternal presence of Love and Light.

In the teaching role, the resource to answer questions about Ama-Deus came from Alberto's stories, my direct experience with Alberto, and my healing process. The most important resource though is my continual relationship with the Energy. And so I often suggest to students to trust and seek answers from within, as they establish their personal relationship with the Source of this healing method, for we are each unique instruments, conductors, and transformers of this sacred energy for our earthly experiences.

All the classes have been truly memorable. Each time that I share Ama-Deus, I take pleasure in a deep connection in my heart with all life. To teach is to share the love in a Guaraní tradition that has been preserved for over six thousand years.

The Role of Teaching Strengthens

In the beginning, I taught classes in my own community because of my responsibilities for my two sons. As they grew older, I travelled and expanded the class schedules from requests in the northern hemisphere. Eventually, my schedule quickly filled, teaching in the Southern Hemisphere, as well as several European countries.

Teaching Ama-Deus expanded into new cities and settings, and I kept an open eye for people who had known Alberto. His friends made the first contact with me after they noticed scheduled classes in their cities. Most of Alberto's friends did not know he had unexpectedly passed. They just knew that, suddenly, he had not connected with them for some time. Our conversations were around closure and healing feelings from the loss of a dear friend.

In my initial efforts to write about Alberto's accomplishments, I connected with conferences where Alberto frequently presented, taught, and developed strong ties of friendship. *Life Spectrums* was one organization that provided opportunities for personal and spiritual growth in Pennsylvania, and another was the *International Institute of Integral Human Sciences* (IIIHS)—a nongovernmental organization affiliated with the United Nations in Montreal, Canada. Dr. Marilyn Rossner, who is a clairvoyant, medium, teacher, and expert in the field of parapsychology, founded IIIHS, and she travels globally to help demystify the spirit world and to share love. Alberto, who frequently lectured and taught at her conferences, was her good friend.

In a welcome gesture, Dr. Rossner invited me to lecture and teach Ama-Deus that turned into annual requests for training at her institute. During these trips, my endless desire was to ask for Alberto stories. In glad heart, Dr. Rossner always found endearing words to share:

> When Alberto was a keynote speaker at one of our international conferences, we all witnessed the fact that God is in the miracle working business! For many years Alberto and I shared time together at conferences. He always, and under all circumstances and in all places, wanted only the best for all. His presence is with us even more now as we witness the depth of his work occurring on Earth. Surely Alberto's light continues to shine from his Heavenly abode, and he continues to encourage all to keep on keeping on.

Dr. Rossner not only shared many stories, but she also opened her archives of taped lectures from past conferences to aid in my research on Alberto's life.

Attending *Life Spectrums* was another wonderful weeklong experience of meeting friends of Alberto. The program committee accepted an introductory lecture on Ama-Deus for a summer conference. My first inquiry of Alberto from the attendees seemed to carry an air of caution and protection in sharing any stories. However, after the introductory lecture, Brian Pierman, who monitored the class for excellence, left the room crying. He was moved by his memory of an old friend and of the deep wisdom of the teachings he left us. Brian's report must have been positive, as everyone eventually became more comfortable and at ease with my presence.

The second visit a year later as a fully endorsed lecturer at this conference found me sitting around a lunch table listening to the Paul family members, active in the Life Spectrums management, joyously share their thoughts and stories of a loving, talented Alberto Aguas. Later, when I requested written stories of Alberto, I sought out Lynn Paul, an active board member for Life Spectrums. She enthusiastically responded and her following description brilliantly captured Alberto's brightly colored personality and his awe-inspiring connection with the spirit realm.

In 1983, I attended my first Life Spectrums conference at Elizabethtown College in Elizabethtown, Pennsylvania. It was there and at subsequent one week July conferences that I experienced Alberto until his passing in 1992. Now, many years later, I can still recall his passion for life, his vibrant energy, and colorful personality. I felt fortunate to have been in his presence.

My first memory was watching him enter the evening lecture hall with a quick stride, wearing either colorful attire, or a white tailored shirt with tight pants and clogs. He exuded intensity, and a passion for the moment he was living. With a loud voice, laugh, and passionate hug he greeted warmly those he knew. He spoke quickly and moved on like a humming bird to his next of life's sweetness. He caught my eye; I felt his loving energy from afar. I thought to myself what a colorful person among the 600 plus attendees. Later I was to learn his name, Alberto Aguas. Everything about him seemed to be a bold statement, even his name. I heard he was Brazilian. I wondered if all Brazilians had such passion for life. When I inquired about him, I learned he was a healer from South America having learned from the Indians in the Amazon. He was passionate about the Rain forest and its protection.

I remember watching him during our healing service. A circle of healers would surround the room. An usher would cue the rows of participants to file forward and accept the next available seat with an open healer to do a laying on of hands for healing. I would observe as this process unfolded. My eyes would gaze upon Alberto. As he laid his hands upon a retreatant his head would tilt back. It appeared as if he was connecting to universal life force energy. He would smile and beams of joy and passion would exude from his space. For me, it was witnessing the divine being expressed here on earth. Alberto's ecstasy was clearly evident. I would marvel at his joy, his passion, his energy, his radiance in that moment. He was fully engaged in his craft. There was no shyness, it was as if all of God's glory was there for all to witness. When he laid his hands upon someone, you could feel electrical energy, vibration, and heat from his hands. All the Life Spectrums committee would wish to sit in Alberto's chair.

In short, Alberto was a man of passion who expressed his depth of heart and spirit with his warmth and unique style. I will always remember watching the Divine being expressed through him in his healings. As a Life Spectrums' community, we mourned him greatly and still remember him fondly. We feel he still joins us from spirit.

Meeting people, who intimately knew Alberto, fueled my passion to maintain integrity, respect, and love for sharing Ama-Deus. As I reached out into my community, and eventually moved out and traveled to different parts of the world, life was enriching to say the least. One of my most heart touching classes occurred in Brazil, which in good time ultimately led me to Alberto's family.

When the request came through the Ama-Deus website, I was so excited for this inquiry from Brazil that I did not stop to think who this person might be or what adventure lay ahead. All I felt was joy to visit Alberto's home country. I shared this Brazilian adventure on the phone with my son, who quickly brought me to my senses.

"Mom! You can't go to this country alone! You do not know who this person is that is hosting the class. You just met him on the Internet!" "Hmm, you have a good point." "The only way you can go is if I go with you."

This sounded like a great plan. So the trip and the Ama-Deus class were scheduled during his college spring break. Upon our arrival to

Brazil, we were instantly relaxed with our most gracious host, Christian. We learned he was a humble, loving, and a spiritually aware person. His attentiveness to every detail of our trip was beyond expectation. Christian organized a weekend class in a beautiful small town on the ocean south of Rio de Janeiro. We also developed a beautiful lasting friendship.

Christian had arranged for a Fulniô shaman to greet us upon arriving at the ocean hotel and classroom. In an outdoor setting, we watched her prepare numerous, delicious, traditional dishes of manioc over an open fire. The final dish was a dessert, manioc made with bananas. We slept peacefully with full tummies, being lulled by a gentle ocean breeze.

The next morning, we awoke to new sounds and ocean smells; the morning light glanced off a beautiful emerald-colored ocean. Everything seemed magical. The Brazilian people who attended the class were open, loving, and passionate about participating. This Ama-Deus class, as formatted by Alberto in partnership with the Guaraní, was the first workshop on Brazilian soil to my knowledge. This was enriching, enlightening, and not without expressed amazement from the Brazilian people that a white woman was bringing a piece of their heritage to them.

I returned the following year to Brazil to teach and also to investigate Alberto's background, filling in the information found in his lectures and notes, and searching for his family. After several failed attempts to locate them, one last phone call three days before my return flight brought success as we heard Alberto's brother speaking on the other end. I flew to meet Alberto's family the very next day for a planned meeting of two hours at their home. The Aguas family opened their hearts and shared their stories and family photographs of Alberto. The two-hour meeting turned into a full day of delightful conversation, a shared meal at Alberto's favorite restaurant, and a tour of their beautiful city. My gracious hosts had to quickly drive me to the airport so as to not miss my flight. I left them with joy in my heart and with plans to return the following year.

During this second visit with the family a year later, they announced their interest in learning Ama-Deus so we planned a return trip for a few months later with Christian as our translator. He took time from his work schedule to accompany me to their home and the family lovingly received Ama-Deus, which opened the way for personal discussions around Alberto and his relationship with his family.

One sweet story from Alberto's niece Angelica recounted a memory from her childhood at a party when she was two or three years old. She was living in Londrina, a city in the countryside of Parana attending a festivity with much picture taking. She remembered how her Uncle Alberto played with a burnt out flashbulb from a camera and how astonished everyone was with his act. Alberto came to her, holding something hidden in his hand. He would surprise her with light coming from his hand. She opened his hand and found the burnt out flashbulb. She took the bulb from his hand to try to make light but nothing happened. She recalled, "I was amazed that a flash lamp could work in someone's hand even when in a camera it did not work anymore. In my hand nothing happened. This is a story I will never forget. Besides this, we have a picture in my parent's house, with a light behind him. Uncle Alberto left a lot of "saudades", teachings of love for everybody, he was a fantastic human being who only did good."

I left their home with a more complete explanation and strong sense as to why Ama-Deus had not been taught in Brazil. Alberto was concerned with the protection of his family as well as the Guaraní. Part of Alberto's relationship with the Guaraní was in his concern to save their land, which brought him to disfavor with the Brazilian government. To expand Ama-Deus instruction to another continent safeguarded the involved parties in Brazil and raised awareness and money from another country to aid the Guaraní.

I never dreamed how valuable was this experience of teaching and safeguarding a sacred oral practice. The Guaraní are still living an unwavering life of reciprocity in love with their spiritual journey. I was also in love with sharing this sacred information and thrilled to watch how Ama-Deus has blossomed in response from people around the world as humanity is wakening to the power in this ancient wisdom.

CHAPTER 12

A New Journey in a Strange Land

Love is in all healings, no matter what technique you use.
—Alberto Aguas

Reflecting on my experiences with Ama-Deus, my personal healing created the steps to prepare me for the role of teacher. Then I lost my teacher, another step on my soul path. My journey to teach Ama-Deus was unfolding; I gained clarity about the purpose of healing and strengthened my relationship with the spiritual realms.

Teaching and conducting healing sessions eventually brought me the opportunity to practice Ama-Deus in a clinical setting, an unfamiliar territory with an amazing level of growth. First, I had to acclimate to the environment, and then engage with the staff and patients in new ways—all a great learning. In due course, the medical establishment laid the groundwork for conducting research and using Ama-Deus as the intervention. This was beyond my wildest dreams. Here is the story.

For four years, I was in private practice as an energy practitioner, instructor for Ama-Deus at the Dominican Center and massage therapist for postpartum clients of a local gynecologist. With hard work, I established a foothold in a local hospital, Spectrum Health and created an on-call service for this gynecologist, who offered the first holistic massage therapy service to patients in the hospital. Massage therapy was offered as a gift to new mothers and their babies. A year later, after the upstart of this service, the medical staff in the Pediatric Oncology Department requested this therapy for the hospitalized children. The steady increase in scheduled sessions at the hospital, along with a steady booking of weekend Ama-Deus classes and private healing sessions, kept me very busy.

Then the local Catholic hospital, Saint Mary's Health Care, presented a wonderful offer. The hospital CEO requested a meeting with me to discuss the development of a "mind-body-spirit" program. At the time, I was not interested in taking on another hospital program since I was well established in the one across town. At the persistence of a good friend and local philanthropist, I accepted a meeting at the Catholic hospital simply to be cordial. The meeting included the hospital's chief executive officer and vice president of operations and provided details of the program they envisioned to implement. My past experience with hospital administration demonstrated their broad skepticism toward any holistic program. These two institutional leaders however, wanted to create more patient-focused care; moreover, they understood the basic foundation of the term *holistic*. How refreshing! My usual preparation heading into such a meeting was to explain terms and to make a case for the advantages and benefits of hospital-based holistic services. My past experiences in these meetings were substantially in defense of the benefits of a cutting-edge holistic practice. There was not enough substantial information in view of clinical standards nor had any modality gone through the rigors of clinical trials.

This meeting, however, turned out to be pleasurable with stimulating conversation. Both administrators were knowledgeable and had thoroughly read about the potentials of hospital-based integrative therapies. There was no tone of condescension or awkwardness, only discussion around how to implement a holistic program.

Still, even in the midst of this wonderful conversation, I had no desire to switch hospitals. I loved the freedom of working for myself, balancing my private practice, conducting weekend workshops, and being on-call for the gynecologist, Dr. Fred Rohn. Dr. Rohn had paved the way for my initial step into the present clinical setting. He paid me to deliver massage to all his new postpartum moms. What a novelty that was! I did not wish to give up my loyalty to him nor the path that he and a few dedicated medical staff at that hospital forged already. Why didn't I just say no?

There, I sat in the expansive office of the senior leader of the Catholic hospital. I pulled out my last straw, a one-page description of the Ama-Deus class, thinking this would definitely turn them off from a partnership with me. Then I could leave in peace. I passed the flyer to the CEO saying, "Before we have further discussions, I wish for you to know all that I do. I practice and teach a method of energy healing. I am sure you have heard of the Reiki healing circle for cancer patients that was shut down at the other hospital."

"Yes, we have heard."

Without any more words, he reached for the paper from my hand. The CEO carefully read the promotional flyer. I lowered my eyes and concentrated on breathing, anticipating that I would hear parting words from this man. I took a cleansing breath feeling complete with honoring the string of appeals from their supporting philanthropist, and my new stepfather who was a past board member. In good conscience, I thought I could go on with my simple life, organized in time as to give my two sons the most attention they needed.

The CEO looked up, as did I, and paused for two seconds, leaned forward in his seat, and looked straight into my eyes, as he was passing the paper to his VP. He responded intently, "I hope you teach this here one day."

I was speechless. Did he really understand that this was energy healing? Many people in our town labeled energy healing as the work of the devil. Before I could open my mouth and respond, he requested a second meeting.

"I would like you to prepare a proposal for a program and, along with the proposal, give us a salary range."

"A proposal?"

He broke in before I could ask for more details. "Not too elaborate," he said, "just an outline of how you would implement a holistic program. Is two weeks enough time to develop the proposal?"

I robotically answered, "Yes, I will prepare the proposal and finalize all the terms in two weeks for the next meeting." What was coming out of my mouth? I had been away from such professional tasks for a long time—since the birth of my second son.

"Great." The CEO turned to his VP, "Would you set this up?" Then he turned back to me quickly stating, "I would ask you to leave the other places of employment before accepting our offer."

I quickly countered, "Please keep in mind the start date that you are considering will need to accommodate the obligations I have to other people."

"Absolutely," he said, while rising from his chair, indicating the meeting was complete.

We parted amidst our exchange of niceties. That was that. I walked to my car wondering what in the world had happened. Why was I was so willing to accept another meeting? Yet I felt lighter! I chuckled at how my teaching Ama-Deus, as presented by Amma, was unfolding. Wait until I share this one with close friends! Yet the idea of having a structured office day was appalling. I had not made the final commitment, which helped to settle my emotions toward this potential change.

In sharing the details of the meeting with my close family, all were very happy and supportive of the outcome and encouraged my acceptance of this move. My boys, in particular, were excited. Certainly, this hospital employment would be easier to explain to their friends rather than referring to their mother as an energy practitioner.

The two executive leaders were impressive in their sincere heartfelt determination to create a program. The CEO was no-nonsense and to the point. Clearly, his point was to create a program *now*. No one else was stepping out with such a bold action. Not in our town. What influenced my final decision were my sons; both boys were at an age of being self-responsible for a few hours after school on their own.

In the next meeting, I accepted the position at Saint Mary's. However, my drafted proposal for the meeting did not include a plan for energy healing. Hopefully, this would come later. Our community had too many fears around the practice of energy healing.

Along for the Ride

The true success of this holistic hospital-based program came from the senior administration's direction, a handful of physicians, inclusive of a family practice physician, Dr. Susan Radecky, who headed the residency program. She intrinsically understood and realized the beneficial value in holistic practices. This group of hospital staffers was meeting regularly before I was hired. Their sincerity to create a new environment of more patient-focused care that integrated holistic therapies was another sound reason for my taking the job.

From the first step in developing and implementing holistic practices, I never dreamed I would encounter such invaluable experiences. Everyone seemed to gain something beautiful: the patients with their story, the nurse or physician with compassionate care and openness, and the hospital administration, as well as me. The Universe worked loving miracles. Eventually, the hospital became a research site for my doctorate, and we practiced and taught Ama-Deus. Who would have ever thought this would occur? Not me, that is for sure! The Universe does not always deliver *my* expectations because life is a sacred journey of self-discovery. I quickly learned, as with the Ama-Deus, I was not in control. I was simply along for the ride and needed only to be present.

Loving Touch in a Clinical Setting

My first days on site were a total immersion in the hospital's structure and navigation of the clinical procedures. In addition, the task force directed by the vice president of operations required that I attend the weekly meeting. The intended goal of this task force was to create a structure for implementing a mind-body-spirit program. Their first launch was my hospital-based program followed later by an outpatient clinic.

We discussed different holistic services and which ones to integrate, such as massage therapy and music therapy. All sorts of fears from the administration and physicians were voiced. One feared meditation, while others renounced the idea of chiropractic care. Understanding their fears helped me to navigate this new terrain in my first days.

Eventually, a first round of modalities was agreed upon. Massage therapy was the first practice we introduced into the hospital with my employment. Music and acupuncture would be the next programs. As talk of energy healing came up, I quickly intervened and strongly suggested that this therapy be considered after these initial programs were well established and embraced. I strongly voiced my opinion to the group. "It would not be respectful or courteous to introduce this modality to the medical team at this time. It is a great stretch to bring in massage, which is the most tangible of the practices. My goal is to create, at the least, a neutral ground with the physicians. I do not expect them to embrace all of these practices. Moreover, I am looking for a common ground whereby we can create an adjunct to their care." No one objected to my suggested plan.

My first agenda was to successfully integrate massage therapy in the Women and Children's Department. I was familiar with this floor from the clinical experience at the previous department. The medical staff was polite but apprehensive. No one wanted to engage me in conversation or accept a free shoulder rub. Massage therapy in our city was not widely known and made some people uneasy when presented for discussion.

Finally, one day, the unit secretary spoke up, "I will take one!" What a relief that someone finally spoke with me. The unit secretary was not afraid of the word *massage*. She simply said, "Oh my, this is so wonderful. You can do this all day!" As I massaged her shoulders, she called out to the attending residents and the staff nurses seated in the break area, "You all are really missing something." I could see people's heads bent down over charts or food, as they pretended to be occupied, yet their eyes were trying to look. "Well," she continued to prod, "on second thought, I am happy that you don't want one 'cause now I get more!" I blessed her for her courage and friendship.

My first actual patient came unexpectedly. I was seated in the nurse's station with my new found friend, the secretary. I was hoping to start at least a postpartum massage sometime soon. However, I needed a physician's referral and a willing patient. I patiently waited for possible conversations as the doctors made their morning rounds. This particular morning, I noticed a doctor and nurse, who appeared to be in serious conversation, walk toward me.

"Would you like to work with a patient?" The doctor asked me in reserved seriousness.

I responded with possibly too much enthusiasm, "Yes!"

The physician explained in a quiet soft-spoken manner, "Well, we have a situation of twenty-eight-week fetal demise. The mother is anxious and grieving. Perhaps a massage might help her relax."

"Certainly, I would love to work with her." I was so pleased to finally be invited into a situation, but I was unsure of the full implications of a fetal demise. The medical team indicated the room number of the patient, and the nurse walked with me to the patient's room and quietly gave a quick notation of the meaning of fetal demise. I calculated the situation as I pushed open the door. This was the mother's first pregnancy, and she was still carrying the baby she just found out she lost. This was the seventh month of her pregnancy, and it was one week before Christmas.

Taking a deep breath to keep myself calm and centered, I found the patient standing in the far corner of the room. She turned and looked at me with very frightened enlarged eyes. My compassion took over in seeing this scared new young mom. She was so alone.

"Hi, I am Beth. Have you ever had massage?"

"No."

"Would you like to try?"

"Yes."

I had expected her to say no and was glad for her yes. "Okay, lets help you to be comfortable on your back here in bed."

"All right."

I helped her climb into bed, tucked the sheets around her in a nurturing fashion, and placed a pillow behind her knees to make her comfortable. I positioned myself at her feet, the farthest point from her face, hoping to make her feel more comfortable with the first touch. Pulling the sheets up, I massaged her feet while speaking in soothing tones, recommending she close her eyes and tune into her breathing rhythm. I sensed her immediate relaxation response from my touch, as she followed my suggestions for breathing.

Then feeling for acupuncture points near her ankles that support contractions; I closed my eyes and synchronized my breathing with hers. I opened myself to the flow of energy as I applied rhythmic pressure.

Shortly into this rhythmic pressure near her ankles, she responded, "I feel this movement coming up my leg, and it is passing through my uterus . . . oh, it is going back down this other leg!"

"Really?" Pleasantly surprised at this quick encounter, I replied, "Hmm, this is good. Stay relaxed and focus on your breathing."

Continuing to support her using my hands and voice, in the next few minutes, she exclaimed, "I feel contractions starting."

"Wonderful," I responded in silent joy and amazement.

The relaxation, the loving touch, and energy flow all contributed to giving her the space to allow emotional and mental clarity. Her eyes had softened, and calmness and determination took over in approaching her situation.

This single, first massage on the birthing floor opened a flood of responses from the medical team, and a wonderful relationship developed among this referring physician, the staff nurses, and me. We developed a specific routine for labor massage and a massage procedure for the postpartum phases that the nurses demanded to learn to better care for their patients. I introduced simple massage of the feet to the nurses for creating a relaxation response for their patients. For any unusual, difficult cases, my therapy strategies were now requested. More importantly, the staff on the birthing floor accepted me as part of the team. We were off to a grand start.

The buzz was spreading. Repeated scenarios, similar to the physician's request on the birthing floor, echoed throughout all the departments of the hospital. In short order, the nurses wanted instructions in how they could help their patients in such conditions as pre-op, post-op, pain control, nausea, anxiety, and for women in labor. The hospital staff now stopped me in the hall, chatted on the elevator, and sought me out in the lunchroom. What a marvelous turnaround in attitude from the first few weeks I started on the birthing floor!

One day after this explosion of new interest, a nurse stopped me in the hallway and introduced herself. She asked if I knew anything about energy healing. I came to full attention, raised my eyebrows, and answered yes.

She continued, "There are several nurses from the hospital that have been meeting for over a year now. We discuss holistic nursing practices, and we are very interested in energy healing. We would love for you to join us at our next meeting."

I enthusiastically answered, "Yes!"

These professional women, who sought information in holistic nursing, learned that over thirty thousand nurses across the country in the nineties were working with Therapeutic Touch™, an energetic healing program designed by a nurse for nurses in clinical settings. They were keen to learn and enthusiastically requested a class in Ama-Deus. I never dreamed this would happen so quickly; this new hospital journey was turning into a joy ride. I felt a kindred spirit with this nurses, who taught me that nurses are the greatest allies for integration of holistic therapies.

The most successful integrations in my first year at the hospital came unexpectedly with nurses in the neonatal unit. From the birthing floor, I progressed next in integrating the holistic therapies in the neonatal department. On the labor floor, some of the massage requests were to work with women on bed rest for preterm contractions. Massage was ordered to help relax their bodies and soothe their emotional and mental stress. With this patient population, I also coached them in the beneficial outcomes of using touch to bond with their newborns. Their deep personal experience with touch after weeks of bed rest provided an experiential understanding of how touch helps shape their baby's brain, social responses, and bonding.

Simultaneously, this buzz for holistic practices was catching on, as the CEO was ready to take the next administrative steps to integrate insurance reimbursement for these services. He set up a meeting with three insurance providers, who were clear that there was the need for clinical trials to substantiate reimbursement. As a result of the meeting, the CEO sent me to the *Touch Research Institute* (TRI) for training on how to conduct research in clinical settings using touch as the intervention. Capturing the positive benefits of touch in a clinical setting would support the request for reimbursement. The program at TRI provided lectures on clinical designs, as well as hands-on work, in the standard of care with a touch routine for neonates.

I returned after this training with renewed enthusiasm for setting up clinical outcomes but also to participate in the neonatal unit. This training opened the door to touch the neonates and share the added benefits with the parents. In addition, the nurses, who observed a positive response to the touch routine, were insistent on learning for themselves. Everyone benefitted from this process: the nurse, the parents, and most assuredly, the infant.

I loved working in the neonatal department with the fragile incoming souls. One day, I was looking over the newest arrivals and saw a particularly agitated infant. With an inquiring look to the assigned nurse, she said, "Cocaine baby." This baby was not at the feeder-grower's stage, which meant that he was at either a micro-preemie or preemie stage. The stages of micro-preemie and preemie levels were off limits to my practice. My training at TRI was only with the babies in the feeder-grower's stage.

Yet I had such a strong feeling to touch this anxious infant. I turned to the neonatologist and asked, "Doctor, may I work with this infant?" I was not sure how this doctor would respond. He had recently arrived to head up the department, and his first move was to request my "uninvolvement" in the department, as he claimed there was no research to document the benefits. He did, however, with my encouragement, review the TRI research documents on touch for neonates. Then he made a decision. I received a professional phone call from him saying he was not in total agreement with the research. However, he would let me return to his department and continue the work. He had politely acknowledged my presence and work in his department with no in-depth conversation up to this point. The request to help this particular infant was my natural reaction. His response, "Show me a baby in here that you cannot work with," was kind and without hesitation. At this positive juncture, I knew that he must have been keenly observing me and had listened to his medical team's report of my activities.

I scrubbed up and approached this infant with a strong desire to soothe his soul that was struggling in his first moments on earth. I adjusted my touch routine so as to not over stimulate or disturb the fragile infant's life support. Within the first minute of working with him, he became relaxed. The doctor walked over and in an observational stance interjected, "I don't want to know all that you are doing, just do it." This comment was puzzling. On numerous occasions, the energy would flow when touching and working with patients. Could it be that he understood subtle energy fields? At that moment, permission was given to work with this infant, and this was sufficient.

The occurrence of the energy flowing was a welcomed presence in the hospital setting. One of my first profound energy experiences with an infant was with a new mom at the previous hospital. Entering her hospital room to massage a new mom after delivery, I found a distressed mom in bed with a fitful crying infant. Before any introductions, she asked me to hold her baby.

Crossing the room to the mother in the hospital bed, I reverently embraced and lifted the crying newborn into my arms. Immediately, a flood of energy poured through me. I turned toward the bassinet, took a deep breath, and an image of the sacred symbol for newborns entered my mind's eye. For a brief moment, I saw and felt this soul's presence. Through this short process, the infant dramatically went limp in my hands before my astonished eyes.

With my back to the mother, I heard her say, "What did you just do to my baby?"

Not sure how to respond, a simple honest answer came forth as I turned to the mother and looked in her eyes. "Love. You have a beautiful baby." Unknown to me, this woman was sensitive and had the ability to energetically interpret the scene. Her natural abilities offered a wonderful conversation during our session together. All the while, her infant slept peacefully. At her request, I shared about Ama-Deus and explained the knowledge of working with newborns up to three months of age. Alberto taught that incoming souls for the first three months of life are transitioning from a higher frequency into the denser frequency of the earth. The importance of sending Love at this time aids the soul to adjust physically, mentally, emotionally, and spiritually in the new environment. The touch training coupled with energy training provided invaluable tools for the neonatal department. The combination of a trusting physician with sensitive nurses laid the foundation for a highly specialized technical department to integrate massage and other holistic services.

In a short time, the nurses enthusiastically embraced touch as one of their daily routines. Some nurses reached out for certification in infant massage and participated in learning Ama-Deus. Eventually, massage became a nursing protocol in this department, which drew a visit and, subsequently, a photo for an article in *National Geographic*. This department was the first in the hospital to completely integrate a holistic practice with practitioner, parent, patient, nurse, physician, and administration.

The news of expanding holistic practices in the birthing and neonatal departments fueled the spreading wild fire that was reaching each department. This dramatic unfolding felt to be an act of God, and I was simply along for the ride. Moreover, unplanned opportunities to use Ama-Deus continued. The next department that developed a comprehensive use of holistic practice was oncology, with which I was familiar from the previous hospital where I worked. When I answered the first phone call from this department, I heard a weak voice.

"Ah, we have a patient here who is requesting your services."

"Okay, I can be there this afternoon. Please request a referral from her physician."

"Well, I am not sure how to say this."

I could feel her uneasiness to talk and asked, "Is there a problem?"

"Yes, the patient's caregivers are asking for you, however, the attending nurse is afraid to request this service from the physician."

"Please, if she is nervous to approach her physician, I would be happy to make the call and answer any questions the physician may have."

"I am not sure this will work that easily. I will talk with the nurse and see if she will make the referral call. We will get back with you."

That afternoon, I took the initiative to visit the nurse's station to introduce myself to the staff. As soon as I announced myself, everyone became silent and dropped their heads pretending to be busy. This certainly was not a new response in the clinical setting.

"Do we have a referral from the physician?" I asked.

"Yes, but ONLY massage," responded a nurse as she reviewed her charts.

I figured that this response came from the attending nurse of the patient. So I opened the conversation. "Hi, thank you for getting the referral. Could you please share any contraindications for this patient?"

"Well, the patient is not able to speak. It is her caregivers who are requesting you. They were carrying on with the physician about how they knew you and were raving about your practice. They are from the Dominican Center.

"Really?" I wondered who this might be.

"You must also know that this physician is not particularly happy with this request. *And* this physician is working the floor right now." She went on to explain the full extent of what I could and could not do with this patient. All the while, I thought how fortunate to run into the patient's doctor, especially given it was the afternoon, as most do their rounds in the morning.

"Thank you so much. I will report back to you after I am finished."

I walked to the room without the least bit of worry. Instead, I reveled in the thoughts of such Divine intervention. How synchronistic! My first referral in the oncology department was from the compassionate sisters that I knew from the Dominican Center. I had heard about this physician, who was known in our community to shut down Reiki energy practices for cancer patients at another hospital. I did not register any fear, only amazement at the opportunity for great healing, and I visualized meeting this physician as a positive encounter.

Rounding the corner of the hallway at the same time, a Dominican nun came out of the patient's hospital room, saw me, and exclaimed, "Oh, I am so happy to see you. We just know you will be able to help sister be more comfortable." As she spoke in tones of deep gratitude, I quickly noted the nearby physician's body tightened up while standing at the charting kiosk located near the patient's door.

"Sister, I am very happy to be of service. I will be right in. Please let me check in with her physician first."

"Perfect, we were just going for a bite to eat."

"Then I will see you when you return." Next, I introduced myself, "Hello, Doctor, I am the massage therapist and here to answer the referral. Do you have any concerns that I should know for this patient?"

Without looking up from charting, the response came, "As long as you keep your hands on her and not raise them above her body, I don't have a problem."

"Certainly, I always work touching the patient. Thank you very much for this referral, and it was a pleasure to meet you."

This simple five-minute interaction opened the eyes of the nursing staff about the process of stepping through the fear of a physician's acceptance. Our future interactions with this physician lightened up considerably and a professional neutral zone established. To me, great strides of healing occurred at all angles.

As in the other departments, once the medical staff on the oncology floor witnessed this session, another flood of referrals occurred. Adding the oncology department seemed to define that I was working with birthing souls or transitioning souls. Each day, I answered referrals for massages, pondered how to accommodate the growing requests, and reach out to other departments. The opportunity to use Ama-Deus presented itself consistently, and my understanding of the power of Love expanded wondrously with each experience.

I contribute my ability and ease to work with different age groups to my mother. Being an only child, I was frequently surrounded with visiting aunties and uncles with thick Irish brogues or older Greek relatives, who conversed with me in Greek as if I understood. Babysitting as a first job provided experiences with the younger generation. I felt comfortable with any age group, and this was invaluable in the hospital setting. If I was not up on the birthing floor working with someone in labor, or in NICU with struggling infants, I was on the oncology floor working with fears from all stages and ages in the dying process.

A twenty-five-year-old mother, admitted for a three-week pretreatment for a bone marrow transplant at the University of Michigan, was added to my rounds when the oncology department requested help in managing her pain and emotional state. We bonded easily as she opened to her first experience of massage. She talked of her five-year-old daughter and husband, who were with her during the day and spent nights with her in the hospital.

One morning, before entering her room, the nurses alerted me that she was having a difficult time adjusting to the drug treatment. Opening her door, I found the room in total darkness, hearing her softly sobbing in bed. She was laying in a fetal position with her hands over her face. I gently called her name.

She heard me and cried out in such anguish, "I cannot see!"

I came to sit on the edge of her bed, which is not the protocol, however, she was rocking herself, and I felt inclined to hold her. Then I asked, "May I place my hands on your eyes?"

"Yes," she responded in a shaky voice.

I closed my eyes and felt the energy flow while gently placing my hands on her face. Soon, a calming peace descended over both of us. She breathed easier, and the tension in her body relaxed. In the most soothing voice I could find, I asked her to simply watch her breath and stay relaxed as long as possible. When I left, she was almost asleep.

Entering her room the next day, I found the shades were up and sunlight filled the room.

"Hi," she lilted. "I can *see!*"

"Oh, how wonderful!"

"After you left the room yesterday, I peeked open my eyes, and I could see a little. I was not so scared anymore, and so I relaxed and went to sleep. You know, they said my vision would return, but I was so scared." She paused for a moment and said, "Your hands got so warm on my face."

"Hmm, that is nice to hear. I can show you how to do this for yourself, if you like. You will have this for your trip to the university."

"I would like for you to come and do this energy healing, please."

I followed this patient along with several others to the university for their bone marrow transplant on my days off. Some of these people learned Ama-Deus to give themselves support during the stressful hospital days and the anxious moments at home. Others preferred to just receive the treatment. The university hospital staff recognized my presence and was particularly taken aback when they learned of our hospital's holistic program. Physicians, as well as nurses, were full of curious questions about the details of our integrated holistic program. The good news is that they were not annoyed by the discussion of energy healing. How refreshing! I made a mental note to have a discussion with our team, thinking that after six years, perhaps it was time to define and introduce the education of energy healing in our hospital.

Certainly, touch was a bridge in the clinical setting to demonstrate how holistic therapies affect the healing process and to start the discussion of how healing is different than curing. No patient or medical professional was immune to the power of loving touch. This building block of touch was a stepping-stone of opportunity for the use and acceptance of energy healing in the clinical environment as indicated in the following scenario.

One summer day, a nineteen-year-old man entered the hospital's emergency department with flulike symptoms. These symptoms turned out not to be flu, but rather an aggressive form of cancer. Three months later, this courageous young man made his transition. During this short time, the attending physician requested therapy for pain control, and a close relationship developed with him and his family, particularly the mother. When the time came for a decision to continue life support, she openly shared her feelings with me. While sitting one evening outside the main entrance to the hospital, she was fearful for many reasons, especially in not knowing how shutting of the life support happened or what would follow. She asked for my presence. Without hesitation, I honored her request.

The next day, as the elevator doors opened on the floor, I entered a hall filled with the patient's family and friends waiting in somber quiet. His mother spotted me and beckoned me forward into the room. I had no idea what to expect or what she expected of me. I simply followed her request and came into the room. Family and close friends were gathered around his bed close to his head. They shared stories and shed tears. The medical team had no indicator of how long he would live an hour, a day, or a week after the removal of the life support. This moment pulsed with anxiety, fears, and uncertainty. I stood near the foot of the bed next to the attending nurse and closed my eyes to say a prayer.

In this sacred space, I suddenly felt a strong sense to work with the specific Ama-Deus symbol that assists souls in transition. I opened my eyes to see what the nurse was doing. She did not seem to be attuned to my presence. Instead, she was watching over the monitors and the family's needs. This was only the second time that I had occasion to be physically present during a transition. Normally, in a situation as this, one does energy healing from a distance or what Alberto called absent healing. I took a deep cleansing breath and removed any thoughts of being self-conscious for my actions.

The energy moved through me. I was immersed in the glory of the feeling. No more than ten minutes had passed when the physical sensations stopped. This indicated the end of the healing session. I opened my eyes slowly, saw the backs of the grieving people, and then glanced at the monitor displaying the patient's vital signs. At that exact moment, I witnessed the rhythmic heart pulse change to a flat line. The family members were still talking and holding him and were not aware of this transition. I turned to the nurse, fairly certain of the outcome, but asked, "Has he passed?"

"Yes," she responded, without taking her eyes from the monitor. She then gently stepped forward to speak with the family.

I left the room. The family members were alone for the final moments that came so quickly. I moved silently through the people in the hall, bypassed the elevators, and headed toward the stairwell to make a less obvious exit. Immersed within, I had mixed feelings, thinking how suddenly this whole episode came to this family, and in a next instant, feeling praise and gratitude to the Divine presence during this peaceful, loving transition.

Someone opened the stairwell door with great gusto. "Where are you going?" I jolted out of my reverie to turn from the middle of the stairway and looked up at his wide-eyed mother. I did not have time to respond. She quickly demanded, "I want you to come back with me, *please.*"

I nodded and affirmed, "Okay," without much thought as to what her appeal might entail. She led me in silence through all the people. As she entered her son's room, she brusquely asked everyone to leave and stated she wanted to be alone with her son. Her husband, mother, and I were left in the room. She opened her arms and collapsed, sobbing and embracing her son around his neck. Her mother and husband moved silently to the opposite side of the bed. Before I could even think of what might be expected of me, the grandmother gave a motion of her hand and said, "Please do what you do for him."

Here was my cue. I knew without any apprehension to begin the healing session for aiding this soul. This was my first experience of being in the presence of a person using Ama-Deus and the specific sacred symbol to assist the soul after the physical body expired. Once again, a strong movement of energy came through my body, as I gently rested my hands on him. Next, profound peace came over me and expanded around me with every breath I took. When I felt the energy subside, I slowly removed my hands and opened my eyes.

At that moment, the mother instantly stopped crying. While still embracing her son, she turned on her elbows, as her arms nestled his head. She looked directly at me, lingering in a locked gaze, and said, "You are going to think I am really strange." She paused, then exclaimed, "But I ... I feel so peaceful."

I gently said, "I don't think you are strange at all. You feel peaceful because he is at peace." This was not a premeditated response nor learned in a book. My response came from trusting and experiencing the relationship with the Energy intended for healing.

My drive home in the late night hours was in amazement of this beautiful encounter. The glorious feeling of peace stayed with me for days. In my understanding of the death process, the soul, once released from the physical body, has the choice either to move to the Light or not. I often hear in stories of the great presence of Light in near-death experiences and usually loved ones, who encourage us to move toward the Light, are present.

Alberto said that this particular sacred symbol's purpose was "assists the soul to move in *peace* to the Light." Working with this young man was a gift to me of sharing intimate moments with the family. Also, the direct encounter of Love's power showed true interdependence with each other to the Source of all healing. I experienced the same peaceful, glorious feelings during the birthing of a soul as during the transition of a soul. Time and time again in the hospital, God taught me about God through the practice of Ama-Deus. I had moments of resisting the desire to work in this sterile clinical environment. Yet I reached far more people, who would never ask, yet sought energy healing in the hospital where staff suggested its benefits. At these momentary miracles of awareness, I could hear Alberto singing to me, "What the world needs is *Love*."

When I reviewed the overall progress of the hospital's plan for holistic therapies, I pronounced it a notable success. I hardly walked down the hospital corridors without medical staff, doctors, or nurses asking questions about holistic therapies or referring patients for specific help. The introduction of holistic modalities ignited their desire to not only help their patients, but also sparked the idea of healing themselves. Some professionals even grasped and accepted the concept of subtle energy fields, which eventually led to requests for more training in energy healing. All the different applications resulted in the staff's understanding of how they could integrate the therapies, which became a vehicle to extend loving care to their patients. Love is the greatest support during the healing process.

My ease in working with the staff continued to increase over time. I felt their growing caring and kindness toward my presence. Not everyone was on board, nor did they agree with the practices, but a respectful neutral ground was definitely established. Calls came in now with ease rather than hesitation, such as one from post-op saying, "Beth, this woman is asking for something that we just cannot understand, but we are sure you will know what she is requesting." Teasingly, she added, "You know, it is one of those healing things."

Laughing at her comment, I said I would be right there. The patient was coming out of anesthesia, and the nurses were not sure of her words. Using energy healing, as the woman requested in her semiconscious state, relaxed the nurses and the patient.

These stories within a clinical setting were profound experiences of how touch eventually led to energy healing. Touch was the medium and hands were extensions from the heart. I learned about the *power* of touch. No one was immune to touch. Touch brought me into closer relationship with the medical staff and patients and closer to educating about healing versus curing. The use of energy facilitates healing.

Energy healing is about working with the subtle energy fields that surround and penetrate the physical body. If these subtle fields are harmonized and balanced, the physical body being the densest of all fields will adjust accordingly. These subtle energy fields are tangible. One can be taught to feel and assess these fields. If these fields are truly palpable, then there would be a way to qualitatively quantify the presence. Research is the means and guidance of the Western mind to understand the physical world. Some nurses had already pioneered a path of research in the field of holistic therapies to attain measureable outcomes and validate the efficacy in a clinical setting. I did not foresee the upcoming phase of research using Ama-Deus. I simply accepted the next step of my journey in this strange new territory.

CHAPTER 13

Ama-Deus and the Scientific Connection

Everyone who is seriously involved in the pursuit of science
becomes convinced that a spirit is manifest in the laws of the
universe—a spirit vastly superior to that of men.
—Albert Einstein

After seven years of watching the expansion and acceptance of holistic care within the hospital, there still was not an integrated financial reimbursement plan. Insurance required the validation of how the holistic interventions were a cost-saving factor. Research was the forum to provide proof to medical personnel and the action necessary for insurance carriers to accept new procedures. My training with Touch Research Institute (TRI) and the neonate study needed replication of statistical data, according to the insurance providers. I needed further academic training because of the growing acceptance of the outpatient Mind, Body, Spirit Department of over twenty employees and excellent services.

The patients' satisfaction in the hospital grew positively at the availability of the holistic therapies at no additional cost to them. The modalities of massage therapy, acupuncture, music therapy, pet therapy, and art therapy were integrated into the care plan at no cost to the patient. The anecdotal observations from the staff motivated them to learn more about the modalities. Eventually, the energy healing method of Ama-Deus was introduced and made available as a therapy to the hospital patients. The hospital's former CEO's hope for Ama-Deus to be taught was becoming a reality. Even though the classes were not taught on the hospital premise, physicians, administrators, nurses, and other hospital personnel sought out the knowledge in weekend workshops.

What I shared and felt was the most valued attributes of holistic therapies was bringing awareness and permission to the medical staff to live and work from the heart in a highly technical, statistical, business environment.

Learning how other medical practitioners worked from the heart came through interesting conversations. For example, during a lunch meeting with a transplant physician, curiosity got the better of me to ask how he felt taking an organ out of one body and placing it in another. He explained how he reverently prayed every time he transplanted an organ to another human being. I realized that we resonated with the same intention *to pass love into the world.* This physician practiced heart-centered regard in his love and respect for another's body in his care.

Meantime, my next project for the hospital was to determine how to validate the holistic therapies. In 2002, I attended the International Society for the Study of Subtle Energies and Energy Medicine (ISSSEEM) conference. This group was predominantly comprised of and operated by PhDs and MDs. The academic papers and scholarly presentations from scientific minds around the globe interested in energy consciousness were impressive.

At this conference, I inquired about the graduate programs for the study of holistic practices. This inquiry led to my conversation with Bob Nunley, the dean of admission for Holos University Graduate Program (HOLOS) and board member of ISSSEEM. In the course of this initial inquiry with the dean, I did make a verbal commitment to enroll in a doctorate program with Holos. Adding education from a credentialed doctorate program that specialized in holistic therapies seemed the ticket to advancing our department in the hospital. This step would bridge the gap and integrate reimbursement.

I wondered if I could make such a commitment of my time and focus with my sons at home. What would it be like to step into the academic rigor? How would I pay for this? Yes, my mind had questions about the practical side of this endeavor. However, never would I doubt that my heart me pulled forward on the spiritual journey, especially when it involved my Ama-Deus mission.

First, I announced my thoughts to my family. My oldest son was attending college, and my younger son was in his senior year of high school. Both were fairly independent and allowed a loosening of parental obligation. My supervisor was notified of my intent. Then a miracle happened. A gift from a local philanthropist funded the academic costs, and this financial support was the driving decision for going ahead with this plan. This meant keeping a full forty-hour work week, traveling on weekends to teach Ama-Deus, and carrying a full load of postgraduate work. There were late nights and frantic moments; however, the value of such an opportunity that seemed to arrive effortlessly in my path drove me forward.

During orientation at Holos University, my first task, besides adjusting through immersion to the academic language, was choosing which healing modality or intervention I would use in research for my doctoral dissertation. As the faculty, in that first three-day orientation class, moved us to finalize our thesis statements, I did not know which therapy to use for the intervention. I tossed out ideas of researching massage or acupuncture knowing there was already much attention to these areas in clinical trials. My thoughts were leaning toward energy healing, as this was the least understood at our hospital. I confidently spoke up as my turn came to declare my intervention, "Energy healing and cancer."

"Too broad," came the abrupt answer from a panel of faculty. "You need to narrow this down." With a puzzled look on my face, it was apparent I was not sure where to go.

Norm Shealy, MD, the founder and director of the school, looked at me and said, "Beth, why not work specifically with Ama-Deus, and then choose a specific diagnosis in cancer. In fact, I would like to see you work specifically with this healing tradition that you practice and teach." In hearing his words, pure joy and utter relief brought tears to my eyes.

Of course! Why not? My whole being exploded with enthusiasm. There was research already with Therapeutic Touch and Reiki, and so now Ama-Deus! Investigating Ama-Deus would certainly meet with Alberto's approval.

This overwhelming emotional experience from Dr. Shealy's suggestion reminded me that that I was on a journey, and the only requirement was for me to be present and stay open to all possibilities. Go figure that I, who was so interested in archeology and ancient cultures, would now conduct energy healing research in a clinical setting! How strange and wonderful this world is! I was on my way into the academic domain to tell the story of how the Guaraní's gift to the world, this ancient form of healing, is still valid today. Moreover, people need Love and the connection it brings.

Science Validating Subtle Fields

Energy healing, an ancient art of laying of hands, is as old as massage and acupuncture and has no religious associations. There are cultural specifications to the technique, the same as massage and acupuncture. Massage and acupuncture are different in the Amazon and different again in Tibet. So too, energy healing varies in its application in different parts of the world. However, the intention to access energy to help relieve distress, create balance, and bestow harmony remains the same. Eastern traditions have mapped out the surface layers of energy meridians. Indians have demonstrated that energy vortices called chakras are gateways to our personal biofield for energy interactions. We are not disconnected from the Universe as we swirl through space. Our spines act as antennas, and the incoming information is received through these meridians and vortices or portals.

When Alberto described how Ama-Deus was used in the Guaraní community, he specifically observed that the pajé or shaman would not begin healing until he or she sensed or felt a certain vibration created by a group of people. This suggests a scientifically observable phenomenon. Such a phenomenon explains how energy healing works and lies in the realm of quantum physics—a possibility that sparks thought and fuel for further studies.

Lynne McTaggart's book *The Field: The Quest for the Secret Force of the Universe* brilliantly described a scientific perspective on energy that indigenous societies and spiritual masters have understood for several thousand years. In her chapter "Beings of Light," one encouraging example that aligns with Alberto's experience of feeling a tangible vibration was in the work of Herbert Frohlich, a physicist and the recipient of the annual Max Planck Medal for his outstanding career as a physicist. McTaggert reports that Frohlich was:

> One of the first to introduce the idea that some sort of collective vibration was responsible for getting proteins to cooperate with each other and carry out instructions of DNA and cellular proteins. Frohlich even predicted that certain frequencies [now termed "Frohlich frequencies"] just beneath the membranes of the cell could be generated by vibrations in these proteins . . . Frohlich had shown that once energy

reaches a certain threshold, molecules vibrate in unison, until they reach a high level of coherence. The moment molecules reach this state of coherence, they take on certain qualities of Quantum mechanics, including non-locality. They get to the point where they can operate in tandem.[143]

With quantum physics knocking on everyone's door, herein seems a plausible description of how what may "seem"intangible is really tangible.

Cultures that practice healing methods claim that energy healing recruits forces beyond belief and expectation.[144] Ama-Deus involves the direction or channeling of a "biofield," or healing energy, through an individual toward an acquiescent recipient or directed toward self with the goal of improved health outcomes. Sara Warber gives the definition of "energetic biofield" from the National Institutes of Health Office of Alternative Medicine as "a massless field,not necessarily electromagnetic, that surrounds and permeates living bodies and is postulated to affect the body."[145]

A book published in 2005 titled *The Scientific Basis of Integrative Medicine* by Leonard Wisneski and Lucy Anderson, includes a comprehensive listing of and references to research in energy healing.[146] Of particular interest is the discussion of Dr. William Tiller and Russel Targ's work. Tiller, a scientist, researched the structure of matter in the Department of Material Science and Engineering at Stanford University. He demonstrated a very specific exchange of electrical current that occurs as healers perform their work.[147] Targ, a physicist from Stanford Research Institute, conducted investigations funded by the Central Intelligence Agency (CIA), providing a theoretical basis for the transfer of energy from person to person. Targ's work confirmed how information is acquired psychically, or what he termed remote viewing. He maintains that spiritual healers are in touch with their interconnected and nonlocal minds in facilitating healing.[148]

Those who consciously use energy for healing, purport that it is not based on religious views—there is no dogma. "If there is more to energy healing than belief, then such effects should be able to be isolated by appropriate methods."[149] Explorations such as Winkelman's and Frohlich's contribute to and expand the knowledge of energy healing by bridging indigenous traditions and science.

The growing use of energy therapy has piqued the interest of science enough to engage in research to understand the benefits. This movement was in perfect timing at my stage of involvement with the hospital. These clinical trials in energy consciousness were the support to open the door for research within our community.

Ama-Deus as the Intervention in Research in a Clinical Setting

My research with cancer patients for the Ama-Deus study required a sizeable patient population for participation to assure statistical significance for the study. I chose breast cancer patients because there was a large patient population at the hospital. I sent a personal letter to the chief physician in the oncology department requesting permission to work with his patients, and he granted permission.

Shortly thereafter, a newly hired gynecologic oncologist requested a meeting with me. He heard of my proposed study, and he indicated his strong interest to consider his patient population for my research study. He was knowledgeable in holistic practices and did not even hesitate when I explained that the study intervention would be the Ama-Deus energy healing method. He was passionate about his ovarian cancer patients for the study. How could I turn down a physician that actually desired energy healing for his patients? I agreed to work with him and his patients, and he assigned his nurse as the secondary investigator. Both the doctor and the nurse became my key supports in this study.

This change called for a new literature review for ovarian cancer—one that opened my eyes to the complexity and severity of this diagnosis. There were no known energy healing studies with this population in the literature review. I learned that most women are diagnosed in stage III or IV, indicating unnerved and sick participants. Taking on the challenge included changing the study's hypothesis from breast cancer to ovarian cancer as follows: Does Ama-Deus energy healing (treatment) have a greater positive effect on anxiety and depression in women with stage III and IV ovarian cancer, as compared to a general relaxation (control)?

This hypothesis was tested in a simple crossover design, which is a research strategy where the participants receive both treatments, as opposed to the better-known design studies where participants are randomized into either the treatment or the control group. The fragility of the women was my reason for choosing this design. The significant level of psychological and physical stressors this patient population faced was tremendous. With a crossover design a participant would not be randomized to receive only one intervention. Each participant would experience both, only at different times according to the particular grouping. They would be their own control and engage in both treatments.

This crossover design consisted of a seven-week protocol for intervention. The sessions started with three weeks of treatment or control, a one-week waiting period, followed by another three weeks of treatment or control. Each person was randomized into group A or B. Group A started with twenty minutes of Ama-Deus healing twice a week for three weeks, rested for a week, and then twenty minutes of relaxation sessions two times a week for three weeks. Group B had the same schedule, however, started with relaxation sessions first, rested for the following week, and then received Ama-Deus healing for the following three weeks. The relaxation sessions consisted of a scripted guided meditation.

After two years of recruitment, we had fourteen participants that completed the study. My faculty permitted me to conclude the study with this small sample size. Anecdotally, the attending physician, nurse, and recruited energy practitioners observed positive change, as well as reported positive handwritten notes from practitioners. However, we were joyously enthused when the statistical outcomes of the study demonstrated statistical significance. The statistical significance, even though from a small sample size, indicated in Group B, anxiety was reduced with the relaxation session. Greater statistical significance was achieved after the Ama-Deus sessions, suggesting that the addition of Ama-Deus energy healing helped to decrease trait anxiety. This statistical significance indicated how well Ama-Deus energy healing works for making good health care better. Based on the review of the literature and the findings in this research, which examined stress and quality of life, a conclusion that stress was decreased and the quality of life increased for the research participants was achieved. The women in the study experienced the reduction in anxiety and depression, which accounted for most of the variance in their quality of life.

The small contribution of this study to validate Ama-Deus energy healing as a non-pharmacological support for patients in their healing process is promising for use in a clinical setting. More importantly, it demonstrated how we could aid in the empowerment of patients in what often is seen as a hopeless journey.

In seeing the significance of the final results, I remembered the magic moment of my profound feelings when Dr. Shealy suggested that I consider Ama-Deus as the intervention. This academic journey was a long road, but how thrilled Alberto would be, for he too desired to scientifically validate the tangible outcome with energy healing.

In review the entire hospital journey, from the first meeting with the CEO in October of 1996 to the completion of the significant Ama-Deus research in 2008, created a movement that is still gathering momentum. I learned to drop my fears, as it was clear to me God or the Universe was in charge. The strange new clinical setting was filled with people, who had the same needs, but just spoke a different language. If I had not accepted this part of my soul's journey, I would have missed innumerable opportunities to share Ama-Deus with so many others. In opening myself to the clinical world, I was gifted with extraordinary experiences, all of which expanded my understanding of *Love*.

Bringing Love and Healing into the Community

Teaching and sharing Ama-Deus with others has been a highlight in my life. The lessons and experiences generated from working with these sacred teachings provided a spiritual foundation that has lovingly guided my path.

The hospital offered valuable lessons and experiences for bringing heart-centered care into my community. Personally, I learned to be open and not fearful of being myself while working in an environment that resonated with a different point of view. Certainly, this work offered challenging personal growth, yet favorable conditions brought the Ama-Deus healing method to the forefront in research and applications.

The hospital setting brought together, in large, the suffering of humanity, and the medical team, who were extremely dedicated people caring for the suffering. The medical team was a strong coalition of like-minded people, and they held strong to their fraternity. Some of the health professionals were open to a new idea, especially if there were any possibility to help patients. Still others held steadfastly to only their ways of seeing life, and this also happens in spiritually aligned groups. I have observed this rigidity in viewpoints and behaviors in many conferences, meetings, and lectures while teaching Ama-Deus. If the subject of the medical community is brought up, there are those who violently oppose medical procedures. Also, some spiritually minded people are happy working with the scientific or medical worlds. People are people, no matter their grouping or their mindsets.

My task, while experiencing any group of people, was to bring the heart to the forefront to enhance the situation and bring Love into the equation. How do we carry forward our true selves into *any* setting regardless of its alignment with our personal perspective? Being in the foreign, medical, or scientific environment indicated how truly imbedded was my spiritual foundation. My opening to work in a clinical setting created the space to bring into expression the spiritual world that I yearned to comprehend and to reside in more consciously and to spiritually see and interact with all people.

Medical anthropologist Alberto Villoldo said, "Reality at the level of the body is 99% matter and 1% consciousness. At the level of spirit, reality is 99% consciousness and 1% matter."[150] My challenges were there for certain, but the outcomes brought me closer to nudge the percentage of my consciousness toward the spirit world.

My hospital experiences came to a timely close in 2008. The research, funded through grant monies, continued for three additional years. Meantime, my teaching journey continues to expand and grow globally.

What Will the Journey Look like Now?

After leaving the hospital and before reorienting into expanding my travels and teaching Ama-Deus, I felt the strong need to weave together the life of Alberto Aguas, the man who courageously and in total dedication opened to the world this heart-based healing practice called Ama-Deus. Now was the time to account for his work, to write a book, something unforeseen and unfamiliar—a new journey.

I wrote with a self-imposed responsibility to give homage to Alberto and the Guaraní for their selfless act in preserving an ancient wisdom, as well as to bring attention to my teacher's story and his quest to make obvious that to Love is the sole purpose for living. In beginning the journey of writing, for certain, a new territory, a second purpose, to the book unfolded. The sharing of personal stories of Alberto, the Guaraní, and me demonstrates significant hope that the Love in our hearts is the beginning and ending of all journeys.

Throughout his life, Alberto Aguas had no fear to speak the truth, to share his amazing ability to heal with the world. Destiny called, and

Alberto fervently responded. If he could see how Ama-Deus has spread around the world, which I believe he can, how pleased he would be. He cared greatly for Ama-Deus, this heart-based healing method. He cared greatly for all to know themselves as part of this Love. I hear so often Alberto's words echo in my mind, "Life is in the Love and healing. Everything else is just waiting."

Like the Guaraní who did not lose heart during the long years of historical dominance and invasion, neither should we give in to the energy of fear. Pick up your rattle, find the song in your heart so that "we will measure our wealth not by how much we accumulate, but by how much we give,"[151] from the heart. As in the riddle from the aging pajé, *it will be different but the same.*

There is a reason why there are seven billion people on the earth. Imagine the level of harmony we could attain if just half of the global population moved from their heart intelligence. The flow of unity would raise the vibrations of all fields to a point that would certainly herald the prophesied new golden age. Let us dance to lighten our bodies, let us sing to lighten our souls to unveil the land without evil within us!

Indeed, we all have moments where we feel the world is on a path of destruction, and we turn a blind eye to global events as we go about our daily tasks. Individuals rise each morning looking to do their best, yet persistent feelings of helplessness to global situations continue to nag us. If it is true that the Guaraní's Land without Evil is not somewhere else, then it is within, right where we stand in the here and now. Then we must embrace it in order to comprehend how to make conscious the choice of changing our world. This conscious choice is the responsible action to our community and us as an act of reciprocity.

Instead of looking at your life as a historical recording, piece together *your* journey of love. It's there. Bring your story forward. Just thinking gratitude for the wonderful events in your life will start the Love flowing in your heart. This change in heart is the first step in creating a more harmonious world.

The chaotic global events will fold into themselves and emerge from the strength inherent in the goodness of all people, birthing a new journey, a new cycle. Journeys or cycles end and begin; we need only to awaken the love in our hearts and follow that path. *Love is the Act that Brings Hearts to the Truth.*[152] Recognizing this and bringing attention to this new source, to *re-Source,* is to find our true essence in our sacred heart.

This is not about taking on drastic changes in lifestyle, but it is a simple repositioning of awareness to your feeling heart that oversees the thinking mind in all that you do—simply a choice to live in your heart, to move, breathe, and listen from the heart. In time, this will lead you to heart-based practices that will expand, enhance, and enlarge the heart center, the sacred space that pulsates with the rhythm of the Universe, to bring you alive in the image and likeness of the Uncreated Light and Love. It costs nothing to do, yet the result of doing this action would change the world. This action dispels fear, and the absence of fear is only peace.

The Guaraní withstood centuries with this approach. Different scenarios in their history played out, but in the end, they are the same loving generations of forest people. I hope this story moves you to experience Ama-Deus or any practice based on Love so that your personal journey will turn on your heart light for all the world to see. The Guaraní are still on this journey. Their sharing with the world their gift of Love—Ama-Deus—is our opportunity to awaken the Love in our heart and join in creating mbiroy, unity, and harmony for all.

EPILOGUE

What you do for yourself dies with you;
what you do for others and the world remains and is immortal.
—Albert Pine

The seated elder pajé stared into the jungle with fixed, hazy eyes. A long time elapsed since he spoke his last words in the predawn shadows. The sun was beginning to shed the first rays of golden light through the forest canopy. He finally broke the silence, "Alberto, look up in the tallest branches where the gold morning light is coming through ... you will see the sacred Irapuru." I sat upright in anticipation and followed his eyes to a high point in the trees. I could not discern anything through the green foliage. I strained my eyes in hopes of a glimpse of this magical bird; I had heard so many wonderful stories.

"Relax your eyes and use your feeling to find the Irapuru." In the moment, I shifted to relax my eyes, I caught a movement in flight through the striations of morning light high in the canopy. I gasped in wonderment at this sighting.

"The presence of the Irapuru is a very good sign that comes this new morning after your vision. Two seasons of harvest have past since you have first approached our village. Our dreams and our songs told us you would be coming. When you first came with all your clothes and canned foods, we laughed to ourselves and waited. Now, as you visit us, you arrive with only a small bag. You eat our food with us. You pray with us in the Opy. Now, you finally have this dream vision with word souls. We have been waiting for you and this message from your dream." Pausing slightly and returning his gaze to the forest canopy, as if caught in his own thoughts, he continued, "With this dream, you are free to move to the Opy as you need. I will share with the village that, now, you will work along side me in the Opy, and together, we will connect and share the Ñandéva, the Love that binds us all as one. When the sun rests today, we will prepare for your initiation in the sacred way. The children will sing a song that imitates the Irapuru for you. Drink a lot of water, eat very

227

little, and have no meat." The elder paused again, this time looking into my eyes. Gently, I took in a deep breath and reverently responded.

"I am so honored, dear elder. I am so moved by the love and the giving of the entire village and by the wisdom you carry deep in your hearts. I am ready to listen and learn with you."

"It is not this elder pajé you listen to, my son. It is Ñande Ru that you ready yourself to have open ears, to hear in your heart. Ñande Ru, through me, touched you after your dream proclaiming, 'Ñandéva.' Your dream vision has given you great responsibility. The imbalance we feel in our Mother Earth is not natural. It comes from people, and the people must change their ways."

Again, he seemed to drift into thought, while looking down at his hands. Then he spoke again, "These sacred stones you are holding in your hands are a sign that now is the time to openly share once again with the world. We have kept strong within us the sacred wisdom for many generations, many journeys. You have followed your heart, which led you here. Your dream vision and word souls from the great cat made clear to you that there is another journey. This dream vision of a journey is the same as ours, to share with all villages the Ñandéva. Keep them close to you to help remember the word souls in your dream, the Ñandéva; the true path of healing that comes from the same place within each of us. It comes from the heart. It comes from the power of Love. Go now. Prepare yourself for this evening. Your training is just beginning ... Ñande Ru will have new experiences and new life for you."

◊   ◊   ◊   ◊   ◊

In the late 1980s, Alberto Aguas emerged from the Amazon jungles with a treasure. The elder pajé said to him, "Take these sacred stones and share the Love, the Ñandéva, with the world." He cared greatly for all to know themselves as part of this Love, for all to have access to this ancient wisdom. In his last years of teaching, he never lost sight of his dream to share Love with the world and empower all to be catalysts in the awakening of the heart center. This journey of hope and trust is truly a story of Love.

I still look and listen for the cardinal in the morning, holding on to feelings of missing my dear friend. My heart smiles at knowing there are no goodbyes. I took an incredible journey investigating Alberto's background, visiting with the Guaraní, teaching on three different continents, and practicing energy healing in a hospital. These experiences brought me a deeper understanding of Alberto's drive to pass Love into this world. Also, I have found my passion, like that of my teacher, to share this wonderful heart-based healing method.

Cataclysmic life events brought me to my knees and opened my eyes to a journey of healing, and I find myself reflecting on how rich my life has been since that day in the old farmhouse, that not-so-long-ago day that I committed to seek a peace-filled life.

Ama-Deus supported my healing process and allowed me the opportunity to experience Love. These experiences transformed my belief and faith about Love into the knowing that Love *is*. This knowing has shaped my heart and, consequently, my view of the world. It was different than what I had first imagined, but in the end, it was the same. We are *all one ancient tribe* seeking reunification.

As each of you continue your journey of healing, think of the sacred heart. Energy follows thought, and in that instant of thought, you are there. Breathe into the heart area; follow your breath into your sacred space. You are there. Now, listen for the beautiful word souls in your heart, not the cacophonic chatter in your mind, and you will find peace.

Besides the Uncreated Light and Love, the *only* constant in life is the soul. The purpose in healing is to be a Light in the Universe. The purpose in life is to *Love*. Love is the greatest of gifts from the Source of All That Is. It is the great unifier and harmonizer, the Ñandéva.

Ama-Deus taps into the stream of consciousness that is Love and is an exploration of Spirit and the Universe that enables life to heal and be healed. It invites the mind to breathe deeply from the heart and touch the soul. *It is a story that was sung in prehistory and is still singing today.*

I love you and wish you abounding Love on your journey. It will be different than mine, but the same *Love* that you forever are.

◊   ◊   ◊   ◊   ◊

Love is the force that holds the Universe together,
Love is the act that brings hearts to the Truth,
Love is the act of offering freedom to all souls to be what they are.[153]

NOTES

Kindness in words creates confidence,
Kindness in thinking creates profoundness,
Kindness in giving creates love.
—Lao-Tzu

The quotes throughout the text used repeatedly by Alberto may or may not be original as he was often fond of quoting others. He also shared that he spoke seven languages, and in his notes, it is apparent with all the clippings from newspapers, pages torn from books, and stacks of typewritten index cards that he was continually seeking how to best present in the English language. All who knew him and had the privilege to hear him speak would agree that he always had the best of intentions in giving due recognition when using specific references to reach his audience.

Also, in his taped lectures and personal handwritten notes, he used the Guaraní words *Ñande Ru* for *God* and *Ñandéva* for *Love*. This is the way he used the words. There has been some question to the use of Ñandéva as this commonly means "our people" or the "real Guaraní person." In knowing of his great spiritual abilities and given the fact that he worked along side the pajé, I am trusting of his intentions in the use of Ñandéva. To me, there lingers the idea of translation and Alberto seeing through to a deeper meaning of *our people.* If we understand that Love is the great unifier, perhaps *Love* is a true translation.

The intention of the author for further research is open. The most frequently expressed interest by participants in workshops around the world is the sacred symbol to aid in the healing of addictions. Addictions plague all cultures, and after concluding with the ovarian cancer research, the author intends to pursue a study that would help to draw attention to the need for energy healing in the process of addiction rehabilitation.

Of course, the brightest vision is sharing these sacred oral teachings, which has led to the development of the *International Association of Ama-Deus®*. This community is growing strongly, as indicated with the global presence of practitioners and instructors, who, in using and teaching Ama-Deus, are cocreating and maintaining the intention of Love in this dimension. *www.ama-deus-international.com*

Some have chosen to take these teachings to the electronic and printed path. This choice imposes a challenge on preserving a sacred oral tradition. Electronic communications and printed manuals from the Internet have already been proven to stray from Alberto's original teachings, and the treatment of some of the sacred symbols has morphed into a different meaning and use. These electronic means of passing sacred wisdom have not only strayed from his original teachings but also have been disloyal to the Guaraní and Alberto's intentions to pass this information from heart-to-heart through spoken words. To honor their wishes, our fervent responsibility is to maintain the format of teaching through the spoken word to safeguard this information for future generations.

The name *International Association of Ama-Deus® LLC* is distinguished with a trademark and has been set to represent the original teachings of Ama-Deus, as intended by Alberto Aguas, and to adhere to and maintain the sacred symbols intact. There is sound reason and great wisdom in maintaining these teachings through oral tradition, as indicated in the book.

And lastly, with open arms, I welcome any additional stories of Alberto's life and travels, or simply communication as a fellow friend. I am sure that this book will reach friends of Alberto that I have not found. I will be sure to add these to the website for all to read.

REFERENCES

Chapter One

[1]   Eliot, T. S., *Four Quartets*, Harcourt Inc., Orlando, Florida, 1943, p. 49.

Chapter Two

[2]   St. Clair, David, *Psychic Healers*, Bantam Books, New York, 1979, p. 276.

[3]   St. Clair, David, *Drum and Candle*, Macdonald & Co. Ltd., London, 1971, p. 279.

[4]   Ibid., 279.

[5]   Ibid., *Psychic Healers*, p. 284.

[6]   Ibid., p. 282.

[7]   Ibid., p. 281.

[8]   Ibid., p. 282.

[9]   Ibid., p. 283.

[10]   *Psychic News*, September 2, 1978.

[11]   Ibid., St. Clair, *Psychic Healers*, p. 273.

[12]   *Psychic News*, October 14, 1978, p. 3.

[13]   Ibid., p. 3.

[14]   Ibid., *Psychic News*, July 21, 1979.

[15]   Ibid., St. Clair, *Psychic Healers*, p. 285-286.

[16]   Ibid., St. Clair, p. 290.

Chapter Three

[17]   Cosmos, Elizabeth, *Ama-Deus Teaching Manual*, Grand Rapids, Michigan, 2004, p. 16.

[18]   Aguas, Alberto, personal handwritten lectures.

[19]   Ibid., Aguas.

20   Vianna, Christian Martynes Barreto, and Krys, Hannah, *Seminário Sobre a Técnica Energética Ama Deus*, January 2005, pg.36, registered with Ministério da Educação e Cultura, Brazil.

21   Ibid., Aguas.

22   Ibid., Aguas.

23   Aguas, Alberto. Disc 3, p. 2 of transcription, 1987.

Chapter Five

24   Monteiro, J., ed., *The Crises and Transformations of Invaded Societies; Coastal Brazil in the Sixteenth Century The Cambridge History of the Native Peoples of the Americas*, Cambridge, Cambridge University Press. 1999, p. 977.

25   Cushner, N. P., *Why Have You Come Here?* Oxford, Oxford University Press, 2006, p. 105.

26   Ibid., Monteiro, J., ed., p. 984.

27   Ibid., Monteiro, J., ed., p. 985.

28   Clastres, H., *The Land-Without-Evil: Tupi-Guranani Prophetism.* Chicago, University of Illinois Press, 1995, p.14.

29   Nimuendaju, U., *As Lendas Da Criation e destruição do mundo como fundamentos da religião dos Apapocuva-Guaraní.* São Paulo, Universidade de São Paulo, 1987, p. 156.

30   Ibid., De Léry, p. 99.

31   Hill, J. D., ed., *Rethinking History and Myth Indigenous South American Perspective on the Past*, Chicago, University of Illinois Press, 1988, p. 335.

32   Meliá, B., ed., *The Guaraní: Religious Experience: The Indian Face of God in Latin America*, New York, Orbis Books, 1996, p. 169.

33   Metraux, A., ed., *The Guaraní. The Tropical Forests: Handbook of South American Indians.* Washington DC, Smithsonian Institute, 1948, p. 90.

34   Ibid., Clastres, p. 4.

35   Ibid., Reed, p. 27.

36   Ibid., Metraux, p. 80.

37   MacCormack, S., ed., *Ethnology in South America: The First Two Hundred Years. The Cambridge History of the Native Peoples of the Americas*, Cambridge, Cambridge University Press, 1999, p. 104.

38   Garavaglia, J. C., ed., *The Crises and Transformation of Invaded Societies: The La Plata Basin (1535–1650), The Cambridge History of the Native Peoples of the Americas*, Cambridge, Cambridge University Press, 1999, p. 4.

39 Ibid., Metraux, p. 81.
40 Ibid., Keeney, p. 38.
41 Ibid., Reed, p. 109.
42 Ibid., Metraux, p. 89.
43 Ibid., Reed. p. 109.
44 Ibid., Metraux, p. 91, Nimuendaju, pp. 346–347.
45 Ibid., Schaden, p. 222.
46 Ibid., Nimuendaju, p. 302.
47 Schaden, E., *Fundamental aspects of Guaraní culture*, trans. L. P. Lewinsõhn. New Haven: Human Relations Area Files, Inc., 1969, p. 145.
48 Keeney, Bradford, *Guaraní Shamans of the Forest*, Pennsylvania, Ringing Rock Press, 2000, p. 88.
49 Nimuendaju, Curt (Unkel), "*Die Sagen von der Erschaffung und Vernichtung der Welt als Grundlagen der Religion der Apapokúva-Guaraní.*" Zeitschrift für Ethnologie, vol. XLVI: 284–403, p. 308.
50 Ibid., Nimuendaju, p. 370.
51 Ibid., Nimuendaju, p. 305.
52 Ibid., Nimuendaju, p. 307.

Chapter Six

53 Viveiros de Castro, Eduardo, *From the Enemy's Point of View: Humanity and Divinity in an Amazonian Society*, Translated by Catherine V. Howard, The University of Chicago Press, Chicago, Illinois,1992, p. 264.
54 Ibid., Nimuendaju, p. 304.
55 Ibid., Viveiros de Castro, p. 264.
56 Ibid., Nimuendaju, p. 305.
57 Ibid., Keeney, p. 75.
58 Ibid., Keeney, p. 80.

Chapter Seven

59 Ibid., Nimuendaju, pp. 336–337.
60 Ibid., Metraux, pp.91–92.
61 Ibid., Keeney, p. 56.
62 Ibid., Keeney, p.77.
63 Ibid., Viveiros de Castro, p. 13.

[64] Ibid., Keeney, p. 61.

[65] Ibid., Keeney, p. 10.

[66] Ibid., Nimuendaju, p. 306.

[67] Ibid., Metraux, p. 91.

[68] Ibid., Reed, p. 87.

[69] Ibid., Reed, p. 88.

[70] Ibid., Schaden, p. 163.

[71] Ibid., Schaden, pp. 80–81.

[72] Ibid.,Schaden, p. 103.

[73] Ibid., Schaden, p. 78.

[74] Ibid., Schaden, pp. 248–249.

[75] Ibid., De Léry, p. 144.

[76] Ibid., Meliá, p. 187.

[77] Ibid., Meliá, p. 193.

[78] Ibid., Meliá, p. 208.

[79] Ibid., Meliá, p. 208.

[80] Ibid., Meliá, p. 181.

[81] Ibid., Melia, p. 202.

Chapter Eight

[82] Ibid., Reed, p. 84.

[83] Ibid., Schaden, p. 50.

[84] Ibid., Meliá, p. 210.

[85] Ibid., Meliá, p. 215.

[86] Ibid., pp. 316–317.

[87] Ibid, Reed, p. 107.

[88] Ibid., Keeney, p. 40.

[89] Ibid., Keeney, p. 43.

[90] Ibid., Keeney, p. 42.

[91] Ibid., Keeney, p. 84.

Chapter Nine

[92] Aguas, Alberto (1986), Taped Lecture in Montreal Disc 2 track 3 transcript p. 3.

93 Ramacharaka, Yogi, "*Science of Breath*," The Yogi Publication Society, Chicago, 1904, p. 18.
94 Ibid., p. 17.
95 Ibid., p. 26.
96 Aguas, Alberto (1986), Disc 3 track 1 transcript p. 1.
97 Aguas, Alberto (1986), Taped Lecture in Montreal Disc 3 track 2 Transcript p. 2.
98 Ibid., Nimuendaju, p. 351.
99 Capinegro, Andy, "*The Miracle of the Breath*," New World Library, Novato, California, 2005.
100 Ibid, p. 5.
101 Gioia, Ted, *Healing songs*, Duke University Press, Durham and London, 2006, p. 24.
102 Storr, Anthony, "*Music and the Mind*," Ballantine Books, New York, 1992, p. 1.
103 Nakazono, Mikoto Masahilo, *The Source of the Present Civilization*, Kototama Books, 1990, p. 5.
104 Ibid. p. 242.
105 Maman, Fabien, *Healing with Sound Color and Movement*, Tama-Do Press, p. 61.
106 Paul, Russill, *The Yoga of Sound*, New World Library, Novato, California, 2004, p. 67.
107 Maman, Fabien, *The Role of Music in the Twenty-First Century*, Tama-Do Press, 1997, p. 81.
108 Minson, Ron, and O'Brien Minson, Kate, *Integrated Listening Systems Practitioner Course Manual*, Integrated Listening Systems, Inc., 2007, p. 7.
109 Ibid., p. 7.
110 Ibid., Buhner, p. 84.
111 Buhner, Stephen Harrod, p. 85.
112 Heline, Corinne, *Healing and Regeneration through Color/Music*, DeVorss Publications, 1995, p. 11.
113 Ibid., Corinne p. 12.
114 Ibid., Gioia, p. 42.
115 Ibid., Heline, p. 15.
116 Ibid., Buhner, p. 88.

117 Weil,Andrew, "A Loving Prescription" in *Handbook for the Heart: Original Writings on Love*, ed. Richard Carlson and Benjamin Shield (New York: Back Bay Books, 1998), p. 112.

118 Siegel, Bernie, "Love, the Healer" in *Healers on Healing*, ed. Richard Carlson and Benjamin Shield (Los Angeles: Jeremy P. Tarcher, Inc., 1989), p. 5.

119 Covey, Stephen, "A Loving Prescription" in *Handbook for the Heart: Original Writings on Love*, ed. Richard Carlson and Benjamin Shield, New York: Back Bay Books, 1998, p. 112.

120 The Dalai Lama "Love, Compassion, and Tolerance" in *For the Love of God: A Handbook for the Spirit*, ed. Richard Carlson and Benjamin Shield (Novato, California: New World Library, 1999), p. 3.

121 Gilbert, Elizabeth, *Eat Pray Love*, New York, Viking Penguin, 2006, p. 27.

122 Spalding, Baird T., *Life and Teaching of the Masters of the Far East*, California, DeVorss Publications, 1948, vol. 4, p. 140.

123 Szekely, Edmond Bordeaux, *The Essene Jesus: a revaluation from the Dead Sea Scrolls* International Biogenic Society, 1977, p. 19.

124 Ibid., Szekely, p. 19.

125 Ibid., p. 19.

126 Buhner, Stephen Harrod, *The Secret Teachings of Plants*, Bear and Company, Rochester Vermont 2004, p. 82.

127 *Lyricus Teaching Order for the Expansion of Consciousness*, http://www.lyricus.org/links/downloads/energeticheart_epaper.pdf

128 Amma booklet, p. 31, no. 2 footnote.

129 Ibid., Lyricus.

130 Ibid., Lyricus.

131 America (folk rock band) "The Tin Man" from *Holiday* album released by Warner Bros. June1974, http://en.wikipedia.org/wiki/Holiday_(America_album)

132 David, Hal, lyrics and Bacharach, Bert, composer, "What the World Needs Now is Love," first recorded and made popular by Jackie DeShannon, released on April 15, 1965.http://en.wikipedia.org/wiki/What_the_World_Needs_Now_Is_Love

Chapter Ten

133 Ibid., Cosmos, p. 20.

134 Ibid., p. 26.

135 Ibid., Aguas, Alberto (1986) Disc 3 p. 1.

136 Mackey, Katherine, *Gerod*, from a lecture.
137 Ibid., Mackey, lecture notes.
138 Mackey, Katherine, *Soul Awareness: A Guide's Message*, 2012, p. 25.
139 Ibid., Mackey, p. 25.
140 Kalweit, p. 2.
141 Somé Malidoma Patrice, *Of Water and the Spirit: Ritual, Magic, and Initiation in the Life of an African Shaman* New York: Putnam, 1994, p. 1.
142 Ibid., p. 1.

Chapter Thirteen

143 McTaggart, Lynne, *The Field: The Quest for the Secret Force of the Universe*, New York: HarperCollins, 2002, p. 226.
144 Crawford, C. C., Sparber, A. G., and Jonas, W. B., "A Systemic Review of the Quality of Research on Hands-on and Distance Healing: Clinical and Laboratory Studies," in "Definitions and Standards in Healing Research," eds. Jonas, Wayne B., and Ronald Chez, *Alternative Therapies in Health and Medicine* 9, no. 3 supplement (2003): A96–A104.
145 Warber, Sara, "Standards for Conducting Clinical Biofield Energy Healing Research," in "Definitions and Standards in Healing Research," eds. Jonas, Wayne B., and Ronald Chez, Alter*native Therapies in Health and Medicine* 9, no. 3 supplement (2003): A54–A64.
146 Wisneski, Leonard and Anderson, Lucy, *The Scientific Basis of Integrative Medicine* (New York: CRC Press, 2005), p. 251.
147 Ibid., Wisneski and Anderson, p. 251.
148 Targ, Russell and Katra, Jane, "The Scientific and Spiritual Implications of Psychic Abilities," *Alternative Therapies in Health and Medicine* 7, no.3 (2001) pp. 143–149.
149 Ibid., Crawford, CC. , Sparber, A.G., and Jonas, W.B., p. A96
150 Villoldo, Alberto, DVD for Munay-Ki rites.
151 Schaefer, Carol, *Grandmothers Counsel the World: Women Elders Offer Their Vision for Our Planet*, Trumpeter Books, Boston, Massachusetts, 2006, pp. 166–167.
152 Ibid., Mackey, p. 73.

Epilogue

153 Ibid., Mackey, p. 73.

ABOUT THE AUTHOR

Elizabeth Cosmos, Th.D., Ph.D., has practiced integrative therapies for more than thirty years. She was responsible for the development of a comprehensive, hospital-based integrated medicine program for alternative therapies at Saint Mary's Hospital in Grand Rapids, Michigan, and she is also the founder of the International Association of Ama-Deus, LLC. Her work has been featured in such international publications as *National Geographic*.

Beth is an ordained Minister in the Science of Mind Church for Spiritual Healing. Her formal education includes a PhD and ThD from Holos University Graduate Seminary and a B.S. from Michigan State University. Beth still resides in Grand Rapids, Michigan and travels internationally teaching the *Ama-Deus®* healing method.